INTERSECTING WORLDS

INTERSECTING WORLDS

Colonial Liminality in US Southern and Icelandic Literatures

Jenna Grace Sciuto

University Press of Mississippi / Jackson

The University Press of Mississippi is the scholarly publishing agency of the Mississippi Institutions of Higher Learning: Alcorn State University, Delta State University, Jackson State University, Mississippi State University, Mississippi University for Women, Mississippi Valley State University, University of Mississippi, and University of Southern Mississippi.

www.upress.state.ms.us

The University Press of Mississippi is a member of the Association of University Presses.

Any discriminatory or derogatory language or hate speech regarding race, ethnicity, religion, sex, gender, class, national origin, age, or disability that has been retained or appears in elided form is in no way an endorsement of the use of such language outside a scholarly context.

Copyright © 2025 by University Press of Mississippi
All rights reserved
Manufactured in the United States of America
∞

Library of Congress Cataloging-in-Publication Data

Names: Sciuto, Jenna Grace, author.
Title: Intersecting worlds : colonial liminality in US Southern and Icelandic literatures / Jenna Grace Sciuto.
Description: Jackson : University Press of Mississippi, 2025. | Includes bibliographical references and index.
Identifiers: LCCN 2024041104 (print) | LCCN 2024041105 (ebook) | ISBN 9781496855497 (hardback) | ISBN 9781496855503 (trade paperback) | ISBN 9781496855510 (epub) | ISBN 9781496855527 (epub) | ISBN 9781496855534 (pdf) | ISBN 9781496855541 (pdf)
Subjects: LCSH: American literature—Southern States—History and criticism. | Icelandic literature—History and criticism. | Stereotypes (Social psychology) in literature. | Colonies in literature. | Racism in literature. | Postcolonialism in literature. | World politics in literature. | LCGFT: Literary criticism.
Classification: LCC PS261 .S344 2025 (print) | LCC PS261 (ebook) | DDC 810.9/975—dc23/eng/20240906
LC record available at https://lccn.loc.gov/2024041104
LC ebook record available at https://lccn.loc.gov/2024041105

British Library Cataloging-in-Publication Data available

This one is for the travelers, the wanderers,
all those who welcomed me on my journeys north and south,
and those I've yet to meet on my journeys still to come.

CONTENTS

Acknowledgments ix

A Note on Working in Translation xiii

Introduction: Liminal Colonial Worlds 3

Chapter 1: Delimiting Difference:
Language, Stereotypes, and Repetition in Halldór Laxness,
William Faulkner, and Svava Jakobsdóttir 23

Chapter 2: Aesthetic Radicals:
White Violence as Exclusion in Guðbergur Bergsson,
William Faulkner, and Jean Toomer 50

Chapter 3: "I'm Sick of Being a Girl!":
Nonconformity and Intersecting Hierarchies of Identity in
Halldór Laxness and Carson McCullers 80

Chapter 4: "A Woman's Wildness":
Power, Magic, and Intergenerational Ties in Tiphanie Yanique
and Fríða Áslaug Sigurðardóttir 113

Coda: Processing the Present, Looking to a Decolonial Future 148

Notes 159

Works Cited 183

Index 201

ACKNOWLEDGMENTS

I began conceptualizing this book in the midst of the recent global pandemic. While it represents a spatial shift in my work, in some ways, I consider it an extension. *Intersecting Worlds* continues to interrogate the inheritances from colonialism as manifest in personal dynamics and relationships represented in literature and examined in my first book through incorporating the Far North as a disruption to the neat formulations of the Global North and the Global South. In the deeply uncertain days of March 2020, I was drawn to reading about Iceland, a country I had already visited twice, and to learning more about its culture, literature, and history. I'll admit that finding a way to transform this comfort reading into a valid, viable research project was at its heart a method for quelling pandemic-based anxieties. I hold gratitude that falling into a research hole is one of my escapes when I want to tune out the world, and I recognize the privilege involved—not everyone's life situation afforded the time to read and think in the spring of 2020. Don't get me wrong: my early thoughts were hazy during the blur that was that spring, but as I read, the project began to crystallize, and I found a way to connect the Icelandic literature I was reading for pleasure to my research interests and frameworks.

I am grateful for those who were the first to hear about this idea and didn't just dismiss it as a stretch but instead considered it something worth pursuing. Jack Matthews, who not only encouraged me but put me in touch with Martyn Bone at the University of Copenhagen, has been an essential resource for this project, as has Ineke Jolink, whose interest in Halldór Laxness and William Faulkner was an important catalyst in the early stages. Martyn, thank you for all the guidance, encouragement, and day trips, as well as for putting me in touch with Ann-Sofie N. Gremaud, whose work has been essential to the development of my own. Haukur Ingvarsson, your support at the various stages, contagious enthusiasm, and generosity have been invaluable to this project, and I am honored to call you my friend and collaborator. Thank you for introducing me to the inspiring work of Icelandic scholars like Halldór Guðmundsson, Jón Karl Helgason, and Ásta Kristín Benediktsdóttir.

Kristín Loftsdóttir, your work is so essential to this project, and I am thrilled to now consider you a friend.

Institutional support also aided the development of this project. Thanks to a generous fellowship from the American-Scandinavian Foundation, along with a summer travel grant from the Northeast Modern Language Association and a year-long sabbatical from the Massachusetts College of Liberal Arts, I was able to join the English departments at the University of Iceland and the University of Copenhagen as a visiting researcher. Gratitude to Guðrún Björk Guðsteinsdóttir, Gregory Alan Phipps, Beth Cortese, and Haukur Ingvarsson for welcoming me to Reykjavík, and to Martyn Bone, Christa Holm Vogelius, and Dave Struthers for introducing me to Copenhagen; these cities share my heart.

Warmest appreciation to Sarah Gale and Archipelago Books for the advance copy of the new English translation of Laxness's *Salka Valka* by Philip Roughton. Special thanks to the University of Virginia for the Lillian Gary Taylor Visiting Fellowship in American Literature, which allowed me to work with the William Faulkner Collection a second time in the summer of 2022, expressly investigating Faulkner's time with the State Department (and a shoutout to my housemates in Charlottesville, Erich Nunn and Amy King!). An additional thank you to the Albert and Shirley Small Special Collections Library at UVA and all of the helpful and knowledgeable librarians there, as well as to the National Museum of Denmark, the National and University Library of Iceland, and Gljúfrasteinn-Laxness Museum for access to materials and permission to publish the images in this book. Many thanks to Victoria Papa and the Mind's Eye for the support through the 2022 Works-in-Progress Colloquium.

Eternal gratitude to the friends and colleagues who have read and commented on my chapters: Martyn Bone, Sarah Gleeson-White, Taylor Hagood, David Liao, Rebecca Nisetich, Kári Páll Óskarsson, Victoria Papa, Laura Wilson, and Xinyu Zhang, as well as Peter Lurie, Ahmed Honeini, and the anonymous peer reviewers working for the *Faulkner Journal* and the University Press of Mississippi; Liz Hartung for help with that footnote; and Amber Engelson and Tom Whalen for the sabbatical hikes. Additional thanks to my special issue coeditor, Ryan Charlton, for his extensive help—especially in the final stretch. Zack Finch, thank you for being game to read my work, even at its rawest. And Egypt Benjamin, much appreciation for your help with the Nordic Faulkner Studies Network!

Thank you to my many guides along the way: Nicole Aljoe, Kimberly Juanita Brown, Elizabeth Dillon, Jack Matthews, and Richard Lawrence, among so many others. Gratitude to my networks, from my Northeastern cohort to my friends, colleagues, and students (present and former) at MCLA (and those that have moved away, Dayne Wahl!) to Judge Mike Mills and the Mississippi June Bugs. A special thanks also to Mary Heath, Valerie Jones, and the team at the University Press of Mississippi. I'm grateful to be one of your authors!

And, of course, my love and gratitude to my family: Frank, Joanne, Kimi, and Brent (and writing companions Maggie and Zooey). To my nieces Brenna and Emmeline, I can't wait to introduce you to the magical world of books. My beloved forebearers—Grace, Pete, Ed, and Joan, whom I thank for my intellectual drive—you inspire me every day.

Portions of chapter 2 appeared in the *Faulkner Journal* and are reprinted here with permission.

A NOTE ON WORKING IN TRANSLATION

It is an understatement to assert that reading literature from other countries and cultures in translation has a fraught history inflected with colonial dynamics and unequal power relations. Indeed, following Zrinka Stahuljak, I recognize that in today's globalized world, "capitalist book and translation markets erase the heterogeneity of world forms of knowledge and knowledge-systems by conditioning the regimes of writing (themes, styles, genres) and their translation (into English)" (317). This is true, and at the same time, working in translation allows readers to interact with texts we might not otherwise be able to access. As Lee Haring inquires, "Without translation, how shall the art or philosophy of alien societies be made comprehensible to others?" (148). I contend that there remains a value to working with literature in translation when attention is paid to the specific cultural and historical nuances of texts and when they are not taken to be representatives of their countries or out of context as part of a generalized world literature.

I acknowledge that this book differs in form and purpose from one that I might write in ten years, working exclusively with novels and stories in Icelandic. I work in translation here in part due to my still developing Icelandic language skills and also to make this book and the literature it analyzes accessible to a broad audience. My imagined academic readers include those in US southern studies, postcolonial studies, world literary studies, and others beyond Nordic and Scandinavian literary studies (though hopefully the book will be of interest to those within this latter field as well). Additionally, I hope this book might introduce non-Icelandic readers to a wide range of Icelandic literature in translation.

INTERSECTING WORLDS

Introduction

LIMINAL COLONIAL WORLDS

On October 12, 1955, iconic southern writer William Faulkner arrived in Iceland for a five-day program as part of a State Department effort to broadcast US cultural achievements internationally (Blotner 612; Nuechterlein 73–74). The visit occurred against the backdrop of widespread discontent regarding the US military base at Keflavík. Faulkner was known for his distrust of the government, and his "deep anxiety over the inexorable growth of military industrial capitalism" is apparent in his fiction (Matthews 4–5).[1] Nevertheless, when asked about the US Army's presence in Iceland, Faulkner responded that "neither of our nations is responsible for the circumstances that cause American forces to be here," reminding people that the troops were not there under the auspices of the US but of NATO and that "the American soldiers are young men far from their own country, who do not like being so far from their families" (qtd. in Gibson 4). Faulkner asked the Icelanders, "Is it not better to have American forces here in the name of freedom, than a Russian one in the name of aggression and violence, as in the Baltic states?" (qtd. in Gibson 4).[2] While his work for the government positioned him on the side of the US military in this instance, the anticolonial undercurrent running through many of his novels has a different effect. If this trip serves as a central link—or, alternatively, a "weak tie"—between Faulkner (the ambassador) and Iceland (the Nordic nation resisting its neocolonial associations), then what other multilayered ties exist between Faulkner (the modernist writing out of defeat) and Icelandic novelists (writers reflecting on and responding to their own unique colonial situations)?[3] *Intersecting Worlds* demonstrates that we must read these norths and souths in comparison to one another or risk leaving localized stereotypes, fantasies, and conceptualizations of Whiteness uninterrogated. This book intends to recalibrate readings of US

3

southern and American writers by resituating them on a global scale through exploring comparable depictions of race, colonialism, Whiteness, gender, and sexuality in Icelandic literature.

While this project originated with a consideration of Faulkner's writing alongside Icelandic novels, more voices are required for an accurately expansive view of the US South comparable to Icelandic writers' intricate portrayals of their culture and society.[4] Faulkner's complex work grapples with themes, such as White violence as exclusion, also interrogated by Icelandic writer Guðbergur Bergsson; however, this comparison may be seen as displacing the perspectives and experiences of women and Black Americans. Only after incorporating writing by Jean Toomer into the discussion do we gain a fuller understanding of the impact of this racialized violence not only on the White perpetrators centered in Faulkner and Bergsson, but also on the Black and biracial characters. Thus, writing by twentieth-century Icelandic novelists Halldór Laxness (1902–1998), Svava Jakobsdóttir (1930–2004), Guðbergur Bergsson (1932–2023), and Fríða Áslaug Sigurðardóttir (1940–2010) is considered alongside the work of Faulkner (1897–1962), Jean Toomer (1894–1967), Carson McCullers (1917–1967), and Gayl Jones (1949–), with a consideration of the expanded US southern horizons after the transfer of the Danish West Indies explored in work by Caribbean American writer Tiphanie Yanique (1978–). Examining comparable themes and aesthetics in writing by Frederick Douglass (1818–1895), Richard Wright (1908–1960), and Toni Morrison (1931–2019), as well as Icelandic authors Indriði Þorsteinsson (1926–2000), Einar Már Guðmundsson (1954–), Auður Ava Ólafsdóttir (1958–), and Sjón (1962–), adds further layers to this comparative work. *Intersecting Worlds* explores the ways in which societal expectations and colonial hierarchies of identity are imposed on individuals and relationships, as well as resistance to those impositions, with a focus on characters who subvert societal norms, especially in the final two chapters.

More specifically, I argue that a focus on the colonial liminality that connects the US South to Iceland, and US southern and Caribbean American writers to Icelandic ones, reveals much about each region's history and the complexity of colonial dynamics. If liminality "refers to a threshold area, a spatial notion of inbetweenness" (Eidsvik 24), then colonial liminality refers to the space between the polarized positions of colonizer and colonized. I refer to these regions as *peripheralized* to engage with the complex power dynamics embedded within spaces. As opposed to reifying the core-periphery binary foundational to traditional postcolonial theory, I invoke Hosam Aboul-Ela's use of the term in his conceptualization of the "poetics of peripheralization," based in a "materialist vision that views global culture

Figure 0.1 This copy of *Brennunjáls Saga*, published by Halldór Laxness, was given to William Faulkner during his visit to Iceland in 1955. Laxness, Halldór, ed. *Brennunjáls Saga*. Helgafell, 1945. Library of William Faulkner, Albert and Shirley Small Special Collections Library, University of Virginia.

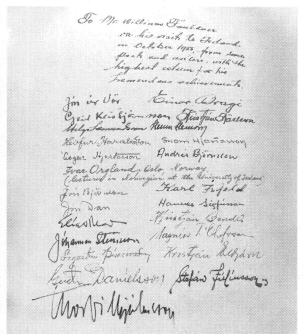

Figure 0.2 The book was inscribed to Faulkner and signed by Icelandic writers. Laxness, Halldór, ed. *Brennunjáls Saga*. Helgafell, 1945. Library of William Faulkner, Albert and Shirley Small Special Collections Library, University of Virginia.

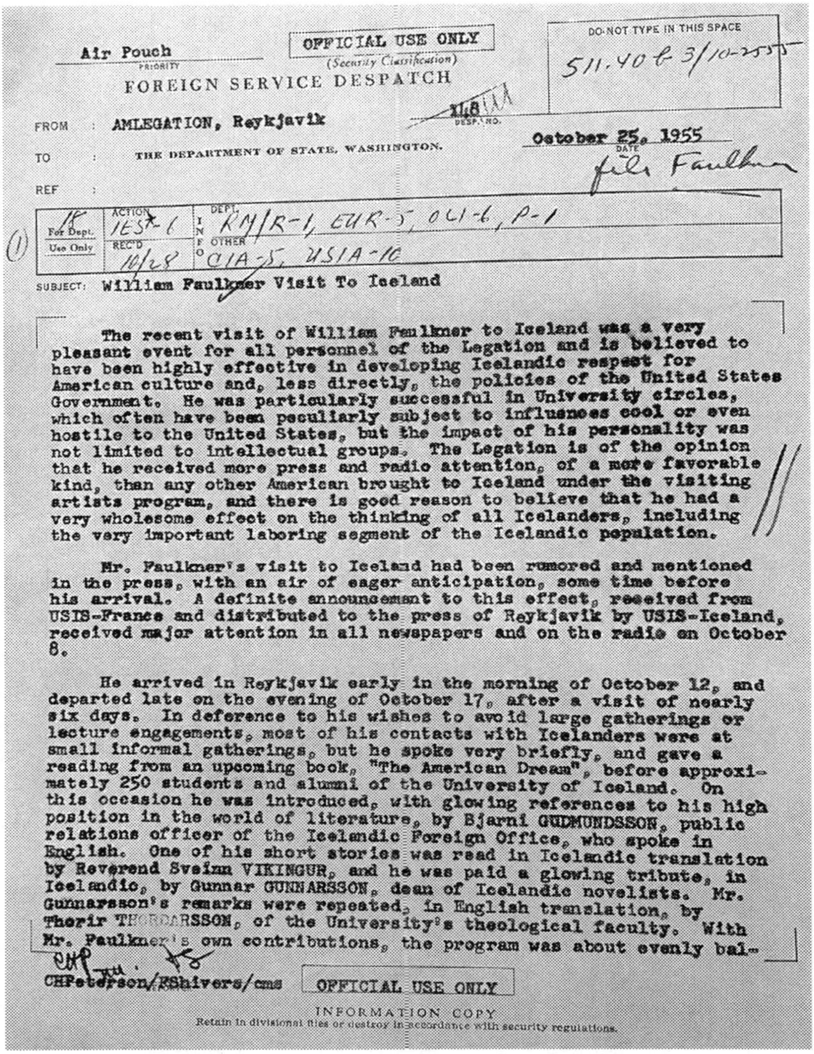

Air Pouch
PRIORITY

OFFICIAL USE ONLY
(Security Classification)

FOREIGN SERVICE DESPATCH

DO NOT TYPE IN THIS SPACE

FROM : AMLEGATION, Reykjavik

DESP. NO. 118

TO : THE DEPARTMENT OF STATE, WASHINGTON.

October 25, 1955
DATE

REF :

For Dept. Use Only | ACTION | DEPT. | OTHER | REC'D

SUBJECT: William Faulkner Visit To Iceland

The recent visit of William Faulkner to Iceland was a very pleasant event for all personnel of the Legation and is believed to have been highly effective in developing Icelandic respect for American culture and, less directly, the policies of the United States Government. He was particularly successful in University circles, which often have been peculiarly subject to influences cool or even hostile to the United States, but the impact of his personality was not limited to intellectual groups. The Legation is of the opinion that he received more press and radio attention, of a more favorable kind, than any other American brought to Iceland under the visiting artists program, and there is good reason to believe that he had a very wholesome effect on the thinking of all Icelanders, including the very important laboring segment of the Icelandic population.

Mr. Faulkner's visit to Iceland had been rumored and mentioned in the press, with an air of eager anticipation, some time before his arrival. A definite announcement to this effect, received from USIS-France and distributed to the press of Reykjavik by USIS-Iceland, received major attention in all newspapers and on the radio on October 8.

He arrived in Reykjavik early in the morning of October 12, and departed late on the evening of October 17, after a visit of nearly six days. In deference to his wishes to avoid large gatherings or lecture engagements, most of his contacts with Icelanders were at small informal gatherings, but he spoke very briefly, and gave a reading from an upcoming book, "The American Dream", before approximately 250 students and alumni of the University of Iceland. On this occasion he was introduced, with glowing references to his high position in the world of literature, by Bjarni GUDMUNDSSON, public relations officer of the Icelandic Foreign Office, who spoke in English. One of his short stories was read in Icelandic translation by Reverend Sveinn VIKINGUR, and he was paid a glowing tribute, in Icelandic, by Gunnar GUNNARSSON, dean of Icelandic novelists. Mr. Gunnarsson's remarks were repeated, in English translation, by Thorir THORDARSSON, of the University's theological faculty. With Mr. Faulkner's own contributions, the program was about evenly bal-

CHPeterson/EShivers/cms

OFFICIAL USE ONLY

INFORMATION COPY
Retain in divisional files or destroy in accordance with security regulations.

Figure 0.3 The first page of a foreign services despatch regarding Faulkner's State Department visit to Iceland in 1955. Gibson, William. "Foreign Services Despatch Amlegation, Reykjavik, Oct. 25, 1955," Hal Howland-William Faulkner Papers, Albert and Shirley Small Special Collections Library, University of Virginia.

and history in terms of spatial inequalities" (*Other South* 12). This vision, developed by dependency theorists like José Carlos Mariátegui, Samir Amin, and Néstor García Canclini, privileges unequal development in comparisons between nation-states and cultural traditions in the Global South (*Other South* 13), which I extend to the Far North, defined as the countries to the

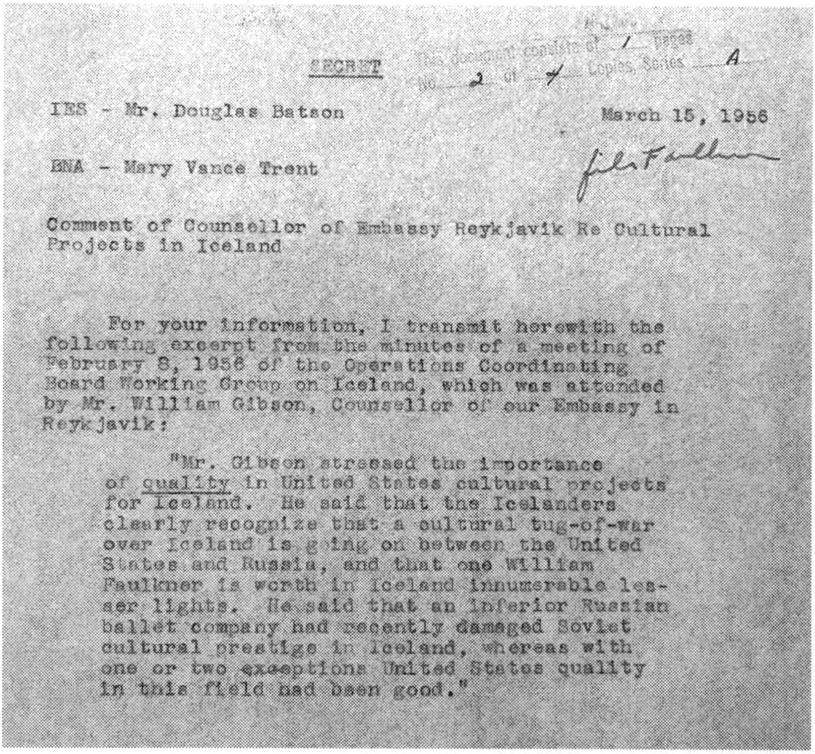

SECRET

This document consists of 1 pages
No. 2 of 4 Copies, Series A

IES - Mr. Douglas Batson March 15, 1956

BNA - Mary Vance Trent

Comment of Counsellor of Embassy Reykjavik Re Cultural Projects in Iceland

For your information, I transmit herewith the following excerpt from the minutes of a meeting of February 8, 1956 of the Operations Coordinating Board Working Group on Iceland, which was attended by Mr. William Gibson, Counsellor of our Embassy in Reykjavik:

"Mr. Gibson stressed the importance of quality in United States cultural projects for Iceland. He said that the Icelanders clearly recognize that a cultural tug-of-war over Iceland is going on between the United States and Russia, and that one William Faulkner is worth in Iceland innumerable lesser lights. He said that an inferior Russian ballet company had recently damaged Soviet cultural prestige in Iceland, whereas with one or two exceptions United States quality in this field had been good."

Figure 0.4 This secret memo describes the Icelanders' knowledge of their role in the cultural struggle between the US and Russia and notes that "one William Faulkner is worth in Iceland innumerable lesser lights." Trent, Mary Vance. "Secret," Hal Howland-William Faulkner Papers, Albert and Shirley Small Special Collections Library, University of Virginia.

north of Scandinavia (Ísleifsson 11). Peripheries are not singular but shift in specificity as a result of the local conditions on which they depend—with peripheral spaces of development located within regions and nations yet also cities and towns (Sciuto, "Introduction" 4). I intend to undo the core-periphery dialectic while still upholding its underlying commitment to interrogating structural inequalities and legacies within colonialism's hemispheric framework. Emphasizing not only development but multiplicity and local specificity, this framework is conducive to the exploration of the ambiguous colonial situations common to Iceland and the US South.

The stereotypes and fantasies associated with each region may obscure the resemblances between them, as explored in chapter 1. However, by highlighting connections between spaces generally considered distinctly, I hope to dismantle the commitment to ideas of Nordic and US southern exceptionalism, or assumptions that these spaces are fundamentally unique, as well as to advance the recent shifts toward unearthing and exploring coloniality in Nordic literatures and cultures. At the same time, I emphasize the parallels between them, such as the layers of Whiteness centered in both national and transnational contexts, as well as their dualistic experiences of colonialism and its complex impacts, as demonstrated through literature. Incorporating these norths and souths in particular into my analysis, as opposed to other colonial peripheries, emphasizes the challenge to dominant global spatial configurations. If spaces considered to be in opposite regions have such commonalities, perhaps we need to reevaluate how we think about the global impacts of colonization.

Indeed, *Intersecting Worlds* is the first critical account of the US South in conversation with the North Atlantic, reading US southern and Caribbean American authors alongside Icelandic writers. This work is interdisciplinary in nature, drawing on anthropology, history, postcolonial theory, critical race studies, gender studies, and queer theory to interrogate the intricacies of both regions' histories and experiences through the focal point of the individual.[5] I intend my analyses to be simultaneously panoramic through the sheer number of texts, authors, and intersections of identity considered and hyperlocalized through an emphasis on historical and local contexts, alongside the specific yet interconnected cultural genealogies of both spaces. Reorienting the focus to the north, this comparative analysis builds beyond the boundaries of conventional regionalism and the nation-state frame to avoid both essentializing the borders between regions and limiting our discussions of these histories to more expected comparisons.

BEYOND BINARIES:
THE GLOBAL NORTH AND THE GLOBAL SOUTH

The world is a "divided space" that is maintained by asymmetrical power relations (Hoerning 114). In terms of spatial mappings of the globe, the configuration of the Global South elucidates "the underdevelopment of countries at a peripheral remove from the core of metropolitan economic power," such that "various southern economies and cultures share comparable experiences of marginalization and unequal access to the resources of globalization" (Saldívar and Goldberg 187). The configuration of the Global North versus the Global South illuminates important socioeconomic and political power differences and relationships between regions; however, examining the coloniality of Nordic countries, like Iceland, alongside nations of the Global South adds important complexity to this world framing.[6] Comparisons between a case study from a place commonly associated with the Global North—Iceland—and the Global South—the US South—challenge the geographic coherence of a concept like the Global South, supporting Johanna Hoerning's claim that spatial binaries are not oppositional but are related intrinsically (132).[7] Ultimately, this comparative work demonstrates the reductive nature of these binary modes of interpreting the world that disregard the multiplicity within each region, as well as the expansive reach and detrimental effects of colonialism. This book explores how conversations about colonialism shift when we include a Far North location like Iceland, disrupting conventional understandings of space and complicating the geographic inflections of power.

While it is important to note that the history of Iceland and its geopolitical positioning differ from other nations' colonial experiences "where brutal violence, various dehumanizing practices and exterminations constituted a part of people's everyday lives" (Loftsdóttir, "Belonging" 58), the Nordic nation's "collective experiences of oppression and humiliation under Danish rule" invite complex comparisons to other formerly colonized spaces (Volquardsen and Körber 11). As Alaric Hall asserts, discussing a 2008 International Monetary Fund loan, it can be productive to put "Icelandic politics into a dialectic with the politics of the Global South" (191).[8] Further, Ann-Sofie N. Gremaud's application of Michael Herzfeld's theory of crypto-colonial spaces to Iceland, which she describes as "an open category with a focus on local complexity and internal paradoxes of European models of dominance," demonstrates the intricate, incongruous dynamics within and between regions ("Iceland-Denmark"). Gavin Lucas and Angelos Parigoris define crypto-colonialism more broadly as "the effect of colonialism on those regions or countries which were never directly annexed through the colonial project, and thus being neither coloniser nor colonised, fall between the cracks of western discourse" (91), which I agree applies to Iceland and to the US South. I am particularly interested in the liminality, ambiguity, and general unease that result when postcolonial theories are applied to both Iceland and the US South; therefore, I investigate the parallels and also the limitations to such comparisons. The labels and binaries created to represent colonial dynamics do not fit the liminal, in-between positionings of Iceland and the US South, and ignoring this complexity flattens the relationships within and between these formerly colonized and colonizing spaces.

COLONIAL LIMINALITY IN THE FAR NORTH
AND THE US SOUTH

Icelandic anthropologist Kristín Loftsdóttir has demonstrated that while Iceland was ruled by Norway and was later a dependency of Denmark, Icelanders also employed racist stereotypes of colonized people to differentiate themselves from other colonies and claim Whiteness ("Belonging" 57).[9] A focus on Whiteness thus illuminates Iceland's ambivalent coloniality. The country was invaded by the British military in 1940 and the US military in 1941, with the presence of the latter normalized until 2006 (Hall 22). Indeed, while Iceland became a separate state in a personal union with Denmark in 1918 and gained full independence in 1944 (Loftsdóttir, *Crisis and Coloniality* 7), the relationship between Iceland and the US can be productively considered in neocolonial or crypto-colonial terms, as supported through Icelandic literary depictions. Existing on the peripheral edge as one of the poorest parts of Europe for much of its history (Loftsdóttir, *Crisis and Coloniality* 4), Iceland shares a linguistic, ethnic, and cultural heritage with Denmark. The Icelandic sagas, for instance, are considered foundational texts for Denmark and Scandinavia more broadly and included "in the imperial canon as early and primary examples of Scandinavian literature" (Thisted and Gremaud 46–47). Iceland's positioning connects to the colonial ambiguity of the US South, a region depicted in literature as *colonized* by the US federal government during Reconstruction and the *site of the colonization* of the Black population through the slave system and its later iterations. Building on the notion of Iceland's colonial duality, I explore the ways in which Iceland both benefited from colonialism and racism and was negatively affected by its relationships to Denmark and later the US, in addition to the central role notions of Whiteness, "civilization," and Nordic identity play in this liminality.

For a time, discussions of colonialism were believed to have little to do with the Far North, with Nordic countries holding fast to "a self-image in which they were homogenous [*sic*], untainted by colonial ambition, and *exceptional*" (Höglund 240, emphasis mine). Nordic exceptionalism describes the "refusal to acknowledge Nordic involvement in colonialism [which] constitutes part of larger discourses that position Nordic countries as more peaceful and gentle" (Loftsdóttir, *Crisis and Coloniality* 5), despite evidence to the contrary. Nordic exceptionalism runs deep, and only in recent years has scholarship begun to reflect the centrality of coloniality, racism, and Whiteness to the histories and formations of Nordic nations (Loftsdóttir, "Dualistic Colonial Experiences" 35). Nordic Whiteness is marked as "a fluid and contested but also an enduring and powerful phenomenon, one that continues to shape global politics, culture, and social relations" (Lundström and Teitelbaum 151).[10] For example, historically Icelanders have drawn on associations of Whiteness with "civilization" to position themselves as European, closer to the metropole than the globally southern margins. Accentuating their Whiteness, Icelanders worked to explicitly differentiate themselves from inhabitants of other colonized spaces, such as Denmark's colonies in Africa, Asia, and the Caribbean, which I explore in chapter 4; the "Icelandic subject thus [became] 'always, already' a White subject" (Loftsdóttir and Mörtudóttir 215). In this way, "Iceland has both been a victim of imperialisms old and new, but also a participant in them, and indeed a beneficiary" (Hall 133), with Icelanders occupying a liminal colonial position as elucidated by postcolonial thought.

Along similar lines, a substantial body of scholarship explores the application of postcolonial concepts to the US South—for instance, the contention that the southern United States may be viewed figuratively as a colony of the North or essentially "the first colony of U.S. imperial expansion" (Handley 20).[11] This separation connects to southern exceptionalism, the belief that "regional distinctiveness moves the South outside the major historical currents in U.S. history" (Edwards 533). I have argued elsewhere that to "characterize the South merely as the periphery to the core of the North would be simplistic, given that the South technically exists within the boundaries of a First World nation," incorporating aspects associated with both the Global North and Global South (*Policing Intimacy* 177). Moreover, Jennifer Rae Greeson asserts that as both colonizer and colonized, the South "diverges from the nation writ large on the basis of its *exploitativeness*—as the location of the internal colonization of Africans and African Americans in the United States—and on the basis of its *exploitation*—as the location of systemic underdevelopment, military defeat, and occupation" (1).[12] Greeson notes that these factors may differentiate the South from the rest of the US, yet serve to align it with "formerly colonial, underdeveloped peripheries around the globe" (3).[13] However, not only "oppressed by an imperial North," the US South has traits making it "clearly part of the hegemonic United States, an oppressor of those further south" (Smith and Cohn 9). In this way, comparable to Iceland's complex coloniality, the US South is a liminal space in relation to postcolonial theory, challenging clean designations, such as core and periphery, colonial and neocolonial, colonizer and colonized.

Recent work in Nordic literary studies, including the scholarship cited throughout this introduction, has acutely addressed the region's colonial legacies, positioning in Whiteness studies, and Nordic exceptionalism. I acknowledge that as a US-based scholar, I explore Icelandic literature in translation from an outsider perspective.[14] As a reader positioned externally, it is likely that some cultural nuances, connections, and references will be lost on me. To help attend to these gaps, I rely heavily on the work of Icelandic academics, including Kristín Loftsdóttir, Ástráður Eysteinsson, and Ásta Kristín Benediktsdóttir, as well as others specializing in Icelandic culture, such as Alaric Hall, Daisy L. Neijmann, and Ann-Sofie Nielsen Gremaud. At the same time, I believe comparative work between Icelandic and US southern literatures also brings to light aspects of Icelandic literature lingering just beneath the surface, only visible to an unfamiliar eye.

I emphasize the reciprocal nature of this work and that canonical US southern novels can be conceptualized differently through connections to the writing of Icelandic authors, and vice versa. What might we learn about US southern literature in particular by positioning it alongside Icelandic? This comparative work challenges southern exceptionalism by underscoring that the region's history did not occur in a vacuum, unconnected to broader colonial histories and global patterns, and by making otherwise overlooked aspects of southern literature more legible. As in US culture where White people can see their race as "transparent, something of a non-issue" (Haney López 166), the Whiteness of certain US southern novels and its significance could be ignored. However, through comparison with other "Whiter" spaces—in terms of demographics or in the broader global imaginary—readers are forced to confront these aspects more directly. Scholarship by Icelandic anthropologists like Loftsdóttir emphasizes the importance of naming and examining Whiteness, a concept both impacted by distinct histories and cultures, as well as "global discourses of difference and power" (*Crisis and Coloniality* 6), in discussions of race and colonialism.[15] This cross-cultural comparison brings the specific depictions and effects of Whiteness in both bodies of literature to the surface—including the way that language can be used to reify Whiteness as a default category as well as how the violent protection of Whiteness results in racial exclusion, as I explore in chapters 1 and 2.

In addition to unmasking the detrimental effects of the overvaluation of Whiteness across texts, in chapters 3 and 4, this comparative work brings into sharper focus other patterns, centering associations of queerness with peripheral spaces and examining nonnormativity as resistance to familial and societal expectations, in chapters 3 and 4. For example, while the queerness and gender nonconformity of McCullers's young protagonists are a focus of previous scholarship, connecting her novels to Laxness's *Salka Valka* causes us to read these forms of liminality back through a colonial liminality. José Esteban Muñoz's concept of disidentification or a third mode of managing dominant ideologies in between assimilation or rejection might resonate with Homi Bhabha's concept of a Third Space or "the *inbetween* space" of a culture's hybridity (56). Thus, the various forms of liminality depicted in the novels converge with gender and sexuality read through the books' broader postcolonial frames, expanding the implications for McCullers's Deep South setting. In this way, the comparisons to Icelandic literature highlight particular aspects of the southern texts, in turn, causing us to read them differently.

More specifically, read together, the US southern and Icelandic novels examined here depict how language is used to hierarchize bodies, reifying distinctions of race, class, and gender and protecting the positioning of White, upper-class men; portray racial violence and exclusion, with forms of self-annihilating Whiteness centered and the pain of Black and biracial characters erased; explore gender nonconformity as a form of resistance to cisheteropatriarchy and the societal limitations imposed on femininity; and analyze family dynamics between multiple generations of women who subvert social norms through their own forms of power. I also hope to bring these Icelandic novels in English translation—such as Jakobsdóttir's *The Lodger and Other Stories* (2000; *Leigjandinn*, 1969) and Sigurðardóttir's *Night Watch* (1995; *Meðan nóttin líður*, 1990), which are both out of print in English—to a wider US audience, creating more space for cross-cultural comparative work.

CONFRONTING EXCEPTIONALISM IN US SOUTHERN AND ICELANDIC LITERATURES

Lingering a bit longer on the concept of exceptionalism and how it infiltrates the different spaces examined here, I define US exceptionalism as the ways in which the nation considers itself to be an exception to the rules and exempts itself from having to subscribe to the same norms that it promotes. US southern exceptionalism considers the South to be regionally distinct and primarily existing apart from the nation's history, including the ways in which the nation's "wholeness" has been "constructed through the abjected regional Other, 'The South'" (Baker and Nelson 236). In this sense, "the South" is "first and foremost, an ideological concept rather than a place" (Greeson 10), understood as "a symbol, an expression of collective identity, an *idea*" (Lassiter and Crespino 11). While the nation was associated with "democracy and change," the South was linked with "racism and tradition," with the national discourse recognizing the variance between "southern conservatism and national democracy" in ways "that localize this conflict—a 'backward South' and a modern or 'enlightened nation'" (Duck 3). As Leigh Anne Duck asserts, this tendency does not acknowledge the South's contemporaneity with the nation or the presence of apartheid in other regions (3), nor does it recognize the existence of multiple Souths. Jessica Adams emphasizes the heterogeneity of the South that "blurs not only into other parts of the United States but into the larger plantation region of the Americas" (17). In this way, as Matthew D. Lassiter and Joseph Crespino argue, "the region is inseparable from the nation" (7)—and, I'd add, from other hemispheric souths. They continue that "the South is not the antithesis of a progressive America but, rather, has operated as a mirror that reveals its fundamental values and practices" (7), with aspects associated with the southern region—namely, racism, conservatism, and underdevelopment—in reality spanning the nation.

As southern exceptionalism attempts to exempt the nation from its violent foundational legacies, including slavery and the expulsion of Indigenous people, Nordic exceptionalism likewise promotes the view that Nordic countries are progressive and hence did not have a major role in colonialism. This view ignores the colonies across the globe held by Denmark and Sweden, as well as the multitude of other less direct ways in which northern nations benefit from and help sustain colonial hierarchies. According to Loftsdóttir and Lars Jensen, Nordic exceptionalism is "an idea about the Nordic countries' peripheral status in relation to the broader European colonialism and to the more contemporary processes of globalization" ("Introduction" 2).[16] However, Nordic nations uphold colonial ideologies in varied ways, given their different histories, including "the white, hegemonic majority [denial of] minority experiences of racial and other discrimination" (Hervik 28), resulting from color-blind approaches to race, as well as the "asymmetrical, even oppressive, relations between the Nordic nation states and indigenous peoples in the region" (Körber 368). Indeed, "coloniality and thus racism are intrinsic parts of the history and nation-making of the Nordic countries" (Loftsdóttir, "Dualistic Colonial Experiences" 35), although the ways that this manifests in each nation are singular—from Denmark's history as a colonial power heavily involved in the slave trade to Greenland's status as an autonomous territory that remains in the Danish realm.

More specifically, alongside other nations in Western Europe, "Nordic nation-states have embraced color blindness in an effort to achieve a postracial society" where race is not discussed directly (Lundström and Teitelbaum

153). This leads to a failure to understand the impacts of systemic racism and to hear and value the experiences of people of color. Mathias Danbolt and Lene Myong assert that "the long tradition for silencing and disavowing the Nordic countries' colonial involvements and 'colonial complicities' (Vuorela, 2009), as well as the countries' investment in eugenic social projects far beyond World War II, has been central to the naturalization of a historical, imaginary Nordic region as an area of notable racial homogeneity" (43).[17] However, these are regional myths, and as Anne Heith writes, "The Nordic countries have always been multi-ethnic and multilingual, and the borders which demarcate the Nordic nation states have changed through history" (160). Danbolt and Myong add that Nordic countries' racial exceptionalism "has been central to the branding of region's unprecedented commitment to equality, tolerance, solidarity" (43), including the ways these nations exhibit themselves to the rest of the globe. Yet, as Kirsten Thisted describes, the treatment of Indigenous people is a direct challenge to the concept of Nordic exceptionalism that remains of central importance during the present period, disputing the idea that "the Nordic countries put inequality and injustice behind them long ago" (331).

While it is important to consider these patterns in the Nordic region more broadly, I am interested in investigating how these dynamics manifest specifically in an Icelandic context. As is also the case with the US South, it is difficult to speak to the colonial history of the Nordic region as a monolith, given the multiplicity found within. I follow Lill-Ann Körber et al., who assert in the introduction to *Environmental Modernities: From the Age of Polar Exploration to the Era of the Anthropocene* that they avoid "totalizing Scandinavia as a homogeneous region" and foreground "discrete political and cultural formations with contrasting histories" (3). In line with this level of local specificity, I focus on Iceland's complex coloniality, which results from its liminal positioning and historic relationships with Denmark and the US, as well as the "insistence on the country's inno-cence from racism and colonialism of the past" (Loftsdóttir and Jensen, *Exceptionalism* 82). Additionally, I draw connections between the posi-tioning of the US South and Iceland as these manifest in literature, an artform grounded in the singular, the experiential. Because literature can particularize and personalize the narratives found in more formal histori-cal accounts, it offers an important lens through which to consider these histories, which in turn are essential to understanding the complexity of relationships in the present moment. In the coda, I briefly consider some of these, including Iceland's relationship to the European Union and the position of immigrants in Icelandic society.[18]

ENGAGING WITH THE POETICS OF PERIPHERALIZATION

Connections between Faulkner and Bergsson, including their experimental aesthetics and representations of anti-Blackness and violence sanctioned by their societies, provided the initial impetus for this study. As I've explored elsewhere, building on the groundbreaking work of Aboul-Ela and others operating at the intersection of Faulkner and world literature, the Mississippian and his works have resonated deeply with writers in other localities spanning the globe, including Colombian Gabriel García Márquez, Guinean Tierno Monénembo, Palestinian Ghassan Kanafani, Japanese Kenji Nakagami, and Guadeloupean Maryse Condé.[19] The critical connection between Faulkner and world writers can be explained in part by the overlapping use of modernist aesthetics, such as fragmentation, stream-of-consciousness, and polyvocality. Additionally, thematic and historiographic factors relate Faulkner's South to other global—and, in particular, globally southern—spaces: corresponding experiences of defeat, the inequity of plantation cultures, the processes of uneven development as a mode of rehabilitation, and the residual effects of history. A global lens reveals transregional patterns while leaving space for the specific intricacies of each locality's colonial histories and experiences. In this way, Faulkner's link to world writers results from his experimental aesthetics, alongside his attention to locally specific impacts of colonial histories that resonate with writers from various regions that have also experienced colonization.

Further, according to Aboul-Ela, Faulkner's aesthetics are directly related to the sociohistorical concerns of the texts through what he terms "the poetics of peripheralization" or the relationship between "novelistic structure (poetics) and multivocal, anti-Eurocentric histories of coloniality (historiography of the periphery)" (*Other South* 136). For example, Aboul-Ela cites nonlinear narrative structure common to Faulkner's novels like *Absalom, Absalom!* (1936), told recursively by multiple narrative voices, and those of other Global South writers—for example, García Márquez in *One Hundred Years of Solitude* (1967)—as an "ideology of form reject[ing] the notion of history as progress" (*Other South* 134). In other words, style as relates to both technique and "the geopolitics of the literary" is "mobilized within an important strain of writing within the postcolonial South" (Aboul-Ela, "William Faulkner" 6). These poetics connect to the other US southern writers with a primary role in this project, including Toomer's challenge to the centering of Whiteness through structural aspects of "Blood-Burning Moon" (1923), McCullers's and Caribbean American Yanique's multiperspectival focus on characters that subvert societal norms in *The Heart Is a Lonely Hunter* (1940) and *Land of*

Love and Drowning (2014), respectively, and Jones's blurring of linear time and individuals' experiences and voices in *Corregidora* (1975). Importantly, the experimental aesthetics of each writer perform important sociohistorical work in the novels—such as Toomer's disruption of the emphasis on Whiteness in literary representations of lynching or Jones's interrogation of the complexities accompanying the familial inheritance of intergenerational trauma, exemplifying Aboul-Ela's poetics of peripheralization.

Additionally, Bergur Rønne Moberg's view of "non-Western and non-metropolitan modernisms" as "marked by culture, history and geography to an extraordinary extent, compared with classical Euro-American modernism" is in line with Aboul-Ela's conceptualization ("The Faroese Rest" 166). However, for Moberg, this dynamic is not exclusive to the Global South; rather, he asserts that there is "a North Atlantic geography of modernism that is comparatively linked to non-European modernisms in Asia, Africa, India, the Caribbean, and Latin America" ("Place and Translation" 205). This conceptualization relates also to Susan Stanford Friedman's framing of "interconnected but distinctive transcontinental modernisms" that center "unexpected lines of affiliation across post/colonial difference" in *Planetary Modernisms* (12, 13). In scholarship more particular to Iceland, Henk van der Liet notes a comparable Icelandic literary response to the country as a "postcolonial landscape" that is "characterized by a high degree of descriptive stylisation, aestheticism, and a prominent role of visual forms of representation," such as Iceland's countryside featuring prominently (469, 468). This is a local specificity grounded in an Icelandic context, exemplified, for instance, by Sigurðardóttir's portrayal of the beautiful but treacherous landscape of northwestern Iceland in *Night Watch*. Even the importance of landscape in Icelandic literature can help to elucidate cross-regional literary connections because land is a weighted symbol in other postcolonial contexts. For example, Palestinian writer Ghassan Kanafani positions the desert as a sentient character with a narrative voice, highlighting the dispossession and displacement of his characters in *All That's Left to You* (1966), a novella with many aesthetic and thematic links to Faulkner's *The Sound and the Fury* (1929).[20]

Thus, as a result of aesthetics and thematic connections, Icelandic writers can be productively placed in conversation with Aboul-Ela's poetics of peripheralization, alongside the US southern and Caribbean American authors considered. This concept can be usefully applied to the stylistics of a number of Icelandic modernists, such as Bergsson's surreal vignette satirizing history, to underscore this link between poetics and politics. Moreover, the entwinement of these two textual aspects is overtly demonstrated by Jakobsdóttir's novella "The Lodger," which is told from the perspective of a woman whose home is infiltrated by a foreigner who begins to physically merge with her husband. Jakobsdóttir's critique of foreign influences on Iceland exists not only on the thematic level, but also symbolically through the aesthetics of the prose. I analyze the significance of such moments within the sociopolitical context of Icelandic history, in addition to the layers added through the focus on colonial liminality and the resulting connections to other, more southern spaces.

INTERROGATING WHITENESS, GENDERED EXPECTATIONS, AND HETERONORMATIVITY IN THE NORTH AND SOUTH

Through my cross-cultural approach and emphasis on colonial liminality, White violence as exclusion, and the intimate impacts of large-scale power structures on families and individual relationships, *Intersecting Worlds* advances conversations presently occurring in the fields of US southern studies, Faulkner studies, Whiteness and critical race studies, postcolonial studies, world literature, and Nordic and Scandinavian literary studies. More specifically, I intervene in these conversations through a comparative focus on two liminal spaces, Iceland and the US South, with added complexity granted through a consideration of the US Virgin Islands and its colonial and neocolonial relationships with Denmark and the US.

Often in this literature and beyond, the privileges granted to Whiteness, masculinity, and heterosexuality are linked, mutually reinforcing each other, and as Caroline Levine observes, consolidating "power and agency in the hands of white, male subjects" (83). In addition to an examination of Whiteness in both contexts, I'm also interested in its alignment with the related hierarchies of gender and sexuality, a thread running throughout but strengthened in the second half of the book. I explore the intersections of identity, racial dynamics, gender diversity, and queerness across the novels I discuss, with a focus on the negative impacts of colonialism, including hierarchical relationships and cisheteronormative expectations as well as resistance to these societal impositions.

In chapter 1, I examine two Nobel Prize–winning authors, Laxness and Faulkner, and their use of language and repetition to delimit Whiteness and dehumanize those who are different in their novels. However, I end with an example that complicates and contests White, masculine self-assertions of what constitutes difference and sameness, using a gendered lens to read another Icelandic writer, Jakobsdóttir. After exploring historic stereotypes of both regions, I analyze scenes from Laxness's *The Atom Station* (1961; *Atómstöðin*, 1948), a novel critiquing US interference in Iceland, alongside Faulkner's *Absalom, Absalom!*, a text attuned to the interrelation of the past and present and the webs of hierarchical relationships in the US South. One Icelandic family's use of African nicknames, or "barbarian names" (Laxness, *Atom Station* 1), for each other is complex: nicknames, intended to be continually repeated, enmesh the word or sounds with the identity of the named individual. Though used in jest, I argue that the family intends the names to ironically emphasize their own Whiteness, as well as elevated positioning in relation to the entwined hierarchies of class and space (urban south versus rural north) in Icelandic society. Relatedly, I investigate the repetitive use of terms such as "monkey n***" to reify distinctions of race and class in Faulkner's Tidewater, Virginia, as young Thomas Sutpen is interpellated into social relations (186). Examining these examples together elucidates the patterns by which Whiteness protects its privileged position, as well as how language is used to hierarchize bodies. Complicating my analysis is Jakobsdóttir's "The Lodger," in which an unnamed wife narrates the physical merging of her Icelandic husband, Peter, with an uninvited, foreign houseguest that she refers to as "the lodger." While the husband and the lodger would likely define themselves in opposition, by the end of the story the wife literally cannot distinguish between them, emphasizing the contradictions of identity or the discrepancies between self-perception and external perception.

My analysis in chapter 2 deepens the exploration of the privileges granted to Whiteness in both US southern and Icelandic societies, in addition to sanctioned forms of anti-Blackness and violence. The narrator of Bergsson's *Tómas Jónsson, Bestseller* (2017; *Tómas Jónsson, metsölubók*, 1966), Tómas Jónsson, fabricates a surreal episode during the US occupation of Iceland in World War II, extending from the historical agreement that no Black soldiers would be stationed there to the government-sanctioned murder of a mixed-race baby. I relate this vignette to the racial codes governing the "protection" of White women's sexuality in the US South and read anew the scenes of lynching of *Light in August*'s Joe Christmas and *Absalom, Absalom!*'s Charles Bon and the corresponding forms of toxic Whiteness and racial fanaticism. Failing to align with the historical stereotype known as the myth of the Black rapist, both Christmas and Bon unmask Whiteness in all its grotesqueness, ranging from the methodical vigilantism of Percy Grimm to Henry Sutpen's ultimate disavowal of Bon. These scenes of violence find a parallel in Toomer's "Blood-Burning Moon," which concludes the first section of *Cane* (1923) and centers an ill-fated interracial love triangle, elucidating the racial and gender codes of the US South. In each text, White violence consumes the story: Black futures are extinguished in Bergsson's Iceland and Faulkner's South, as is the potential for Black love in Toomer's South. Black, male lineage is intentionally thwarted, leaving only White male exploitation imagined as rape. The various forms of exclusion represented in each episode of violence reveal what is valued in each society and their specific colonial and racial histories, including the erasure of Blackness for a fictional "racial harmony" in Iceland and the endemic exploitation of Black women (and the resulting White wealth) in the plantation South.

In chapter 3, I investigate what the experiences of three gender nonconforming girls in novels by Laxness and McCullers reveal about Icelandic and US southern societies in terms not only of the strict social roles allocated for women but also the hierarchical expectations for relationships spanning class, gender, sexuality, and race. Salka Valka, beloved title character of Laxness's 1931 novel (first translated into English from Danish in 1936 and into English from Icelandic in 2022), is frequently read as a peculiar heterosexual young woman abandoned by her more worldly lover; however, I focus on her female masculinity in conversation with literary tomboyism—a reading that also leaves space for sexual fluidity. Like Salka, McCullers's gender nonconforming young heroines, Mick Kelly in *The Heart Is a Lonely Hunter* and Frankie Addams in *The Member of the Wedding* (1946), disidentify from traditional understandings of what it means to be a girl in their respective societies. All three carve out their own space within the confines of gender roles. For instance, Mick and Frankie prefer shorts to skirts and dresses, and Salka infamously wears pants, which she continues into adulthood, subverting the expectation that tomboys will outgrow their masculinity in adolescence. In this way, Salka, Mick, and Frankie demonstrate a queer resistance to cisheteropatriarchy and the societal limitations imposed on femininity that, read through the spaces' colonial histories, emphasizes the interconnection of multiple forms of liminality in the novels. Considering them together deepens our understanding of each, illuminating the interactions between tomboyism and other markers of identity. Race is approached more directly in McCullers's novels, appearing primarily in a coded way in Laxness's text through representations of Salka's pseudo-stepfather Steinþór, who in turn is related to the novels' varying ways of reckoning with sexual violence toward young girls. The depictions of gender, queerness, race, and sexual violence manifest distinctly in literature from each space, remote northern Iceland and the deep US South, elucidating the patterns that result from their various histories and lingering colonial dynamics.

The family dynamics between multiple generations of women are central to my exploration in chapter 4 of novels by Yanique and Sigurðardóttir set in nations formerly controlled by Denmark, with links to Jones's US southern geographies. Colonialism linked parts of the globe that had not previously been connected (Loftsdóttir and Pálsson 38), such as St. Thomas of the former Danish West Indies and Iceland, former Danish dependency. While the histories of Danish colonialism and US neocolonialism are present to varying extents in Yanique's *Land of Love and Drowning* and Sigurðardóttir's *Night Watch*, both are primarily interested in large-scale power dynamics by way of their impacts on women and their relationships. The complexities of motherhood and what is passed down between the generations are elucidated through comparisons to Jones's novel *Corregidora* and Ursa Corregidora's visceral connection to slavery's legacies of sexual violence. Like Ursa's subversion of familial expectations, the women of the Bradshaw family in Yanique's novel, particularly sisters Anette and Eeona, challenge societal expectations for their lives in their embrace of a sexuality not always linked to marriage and motherhood, as well as a beauty not tied to attracting a husband. Similarly, Sigurðardóttir's Nina keeps vigil over her mother Thordis's deathbed by frenetically recording the stories of her female predecessors, yet she has resisted her connection to them, viewing herself as modern—not "shackle[d]" by their collective domestic responsibilities of motherhood and marriage (122). In addition to their beauty, women in both families share a wildness that is coupled with mobility and borders on the dangerous. Various things are passed down between the entangled generations, from names, memories, and stories to material objects and physical or even magical characteristics for the Bradshaw women. Each novel centers the stories that are typically displaced in broader historical accounts to consider how we are remembered and what survives us for future generations.

As I explore in chapter 4, *Land of Love and Drowning* and its narrators have much wisdom to impart about the complications accompanying attempts to capture histories, revealed both through the aesthetics of the novel and direct statements by the characters. First, singular accounts of history are never definitive, as Anette, self-proclaimed family historian of the Bradshaws, proclaims: "This ain true history. I just saying that given what we know about the place and about the time, my version seem to have a truth somewhere" (33). Anette voices the truth that all accounts of history are someone's version grounded in their necessarily partial knowledge about the place and time. Further, stories and their referents can also change over time and may bear only a resemblance to historical truths. Yanique's novel thus highlights two considerations that are key to this project as a whole: the inaccessible nature of shifting histories and the multiplicity inherent within singular perspectives of events.

If accounts of history are never definitive, are susceptible to change over time, and contain multitudes, it is essential to leave space for their shifting and contradictory layers. Thus, in examining literature from Iceland and the US South, we must open to the liminality common to these spaces. Exploring the complexity of these regions' histories and experiences through their literature ensures the rejection of pithy stereotypes and fantasies, such as Iceland as an exotic but White space removed from colonial histories or the US South as distinct from the nation as a result of its retrogressive racism, which—like violence itself—is, to quote civil rights activist Jamil Al-Amin, formerly H. Rap Brown, "as American as cherry pie" (Nelson 155). As Audrey Horning inquires, "Why does colonialism matter, and why in particular does Scandinavian colonialism matter? Simply put, because its legacies remain unresolved" (298). The literature reveals that these histories are still with us, and their negative effects are still felt. This is another point of connection between the situations of Iceland and the US South: the impacts of these regions' diverse colonial experiences remain present, visible in the race for the Arctic's resources and the treatment of immigrants, women, and LGBTQIA+ communities, which I explore further in the coda. I agree with Andrew Stuhl that scholars of history "turn to the past not to discover what happened, but to make sense out of the world in which we now live" (*Unfreezing the Arctic* 13). And indeed, the stakes for this work are high. Understanding the complexities of the past is necessary for even a partial understanding of regional and global dynamics in the present, as well as any expectations for the future.

Chapter 1

DELIMITING DIFFERENCE

Language, Stereotypes, and Repetition in Halldór Laxness, William Faulkner, and Svava Jakobsdóttir

Copenhagen, 1904: A group of Icelandic students, including Gísli Sveinsson, is demonstrating against the Danish colonial exhibition showcasing Denmark's colonies. Sveinsson, who would go on to be Speaker of Alþingi, the Icelandic Parliament (Hálfdanarson, "Severing the Ties" 237), and the other protesters insist that Iceland, although a dependency of Denmark, does not belong alongside the other colonies: "We are being categorized along with uncivilized savage people . . . and being disgraced in the eyes of the educated world" (qtd. in Loftsdóttir, "Belonging" 57).[1] As the scholarship of Icelandic anthropologist Kristín Loftsdóttir demonstrates, the Icelandic students attempted to solidify their connections to Whiteness and Europe by emphasizing their distinctions from inhabitants of other colonized spaces. As a result, they perpetrated and enforced "stereotypes of colonized people in other parts of the world, positioning themselves very carefully as belonging with the civilized Europeans, instead of the uncivilized 'others'" (Loftsdóttir, "Belonging" 57), such as the people inhabiting Denmark's colonies in Africa, Asia, and the Caribbean. Viewed from the perspective of the West, Iceland embodies aspects of both the center and the margins in relation to the power dynamics of the Global North and the Global South. It is a nation on the periphery of Europe with its own distinct cultural heritage through its connection to the Old Norse language and saga culture. Iceland was positioned by more southern European nations as a wild yet White space against which they could define themselves. In reaction to their country's dependent status, the Icelandic student protesters attempt to claim Whiteness by defining themselves in opposition: we are European because we are not African, or we are White because we are not Black—which plays out on multiple levels, including that of language. Both Icelandic writer Halldór Laxness and US southern writer and fellow Nobel Prize winner William Faulkner—White, male writers of a certain class—employ repetition to highlight this impulse, emphasizing the ways in which language is used to delimit Whiteness and dehumanize those who are different.[2] However, reading their work in conversation with an example from Icelandic writer Svava Jakobsdóttir, emphasizing a gendered lens, complicates and even challenges such self-assertions of difference.

Iceland, a fully independent nation since 1944, has a complex colonial history. As a former dependency of Denmark that endured a US military presence from 1941–2006, Iceland's global positioning invites postcolonial understandings of its geopolitical relations. At the same time, there were important differences between Iceland's experience of dependency and those of other colonized spaces; it would be erroneous to equate the positioning of Iceland under Denmark with the brutality and dehumanization that accompanied European colonialism in Africa (Loftsdóttir, "Dualistic Colonial Experiences" 36). Relatedly, the US South underwent a brief occupation by the US military, comparable to the experiences of many other global spaces; however, this case was singular, with the South being a region of the United States itself. By examining literary examples across two very different cultures and histories—Icelandic and US southern—I hope to elucidate the patterns to how Whiteness protects its privileged position and how language is used to hierarchize bodies and draw lines of difference or, in Caroline Levine's terms, "the forms that organize texts, bodies, and institutions" (23). In this way, small aesthetic features when repeated become emblematic of larger sociopolitical conditions present across the Far North and the Deep South. Indeed, the aesthetics of the text reflect its sociohistorical concerns through what Hosam Aboul-Ela conceptualizes as the poetics of peripheralization—here those concerns include the impulse of the marginalized to bolster their comparative privilege through language. While these hierarchical dynamics are pervasive across numerous global borders, the Iceland-US connection illuminates particular aspects, such as the colonial liminality of certain spaces, parallel depictions of Whiteness and belonging, and mentalities built on exceptionalism—whether the US exempting itself from following the norms it promotes, the US South positioning itself as outside of the currents of the nation, or Iceland viewing itself as progressive and separate from colonial histories.

STEREOTYPES OF "WILD" NORTHS
AND "BACKWARDS" SOUTHS

Even within the discussion of Nordic exceptionalism, Iceland is placed in a uniquely liminal space: simultaneously neither/nor, as well as to an extent both/and. Located on the periphery of Europe, Iceland was yet "an integral part of western Europe" (Agnarsdóttir 30), with rich fishing grounds that attracted foreign fishermen and exported fish products benefiting the Danish economy (Agnarsdóttir 13). While neither an official colony nor colonial power, Iceland was both a dependency of Denmark and one of the poorest European nations for much of its history (Loftsdóttir, *Crisis and Coloniality* 4). However, Icelanders have also participated in settler colonialism by migrating to the Americas (Loftsdóttir, "Dualistic Colonial Experiences" 32), and they have reproduced racism against colonized people in cultural production like the Icelandic version of *The Ten Little Negros* (1922), illustrated by beloved Icelandic artist Guðmundur Thorsteinsson (Loftsdóttir, "Republishing" 301). Derogatory generalizations about people from Asia and Africa in both terminology and illustrations appeared in late nineteenth-century textbooks (Rúnarsdóttir 86), demonstrating how these stereotypes were accepted and sanctioned through the educational system, with school materials playing a powerful role in "maintaining stereotypes and transmitting an intergenerational world view" (Loftsdóttir, "Learning About Africa" 83).[3] At the same time, Icelanders have been aligned with stereotypes, unmasked by postcolonial studies, of colonized people as innocent, childlike, and one with nature, compared with more "civilized" and rational Europeans, and Icelanders were also seen as personifying their country's wild nature (Neijmann, "Foreign Fictions of Iceland" 486). Steve Garner writes that "Icelanders (colonised people), Greenlanders, Faroe Islanders and Sami (indigenous and backward), and Finns (Mongols) were constructed as lying lower down the ladder of white supremacy (below the Nordics)" (417), an association against which the Icelanders rebelled in the example of the Danish colonial exhibition. This complexity highlights the liminality of Iceland's coloniality, which Loftsdóttir describes as "lived and executed at the margins of Europe" (*Crisis and Coloniality* 4).

According to Henk van der Liet, while Iceland was a Danish colony (other scholars prefer the term *dependency*), the lack of ethnic difference between the Danes and Icelanders, the shared linguistic history, and a sense of Iceland's superior literary art led to Iceland not having "the same ring of exoticism to it" as was the case for both Greenland and the Virgin Islands (451, 450). This resulted in Iceland's complex colonial positioning in relation not only to Denmark, the US, and other nations of the so-called Global North, but also to formerly colonized spaces in the Global South. However, speaking to the exoticization of Iceland, Loftsdóttir notes that it is "more secure" due to the ways it is implicitly positioned as a "'White' country"; the tourism industry also plays into the notion of Iceland, alongside its fellow Nordic countries, as "outside of colonialism, and thus colonial imaginaries," with racialization becoming innocent and safe ("Dualistic Colonial Experiences" 47). Even further, Ann-Sofie N. Gremaud has demonstrated how Iceland leans into the stereotypes that it is pure, unspoiled, and natural as branding strategies, in not only the tourism industry, but also the energy sector and official policies ("Power and Purity" 79).[4] This is in line with "the forms of exoticism that characterize tourism marketing of non-western regions," as well as the paradox that tourism corrupts what it markets as "'pristine,' 'undiscovered,' and culturally 'authentic'" (Carrigan xiii), which applies not only to Iceland, but also to the Caribbean, Africa, and South Asia. The juxtaposition of these claims—van der Liet's of inbetweenness, Loftsdóttir's of a "safe" exoticism, and Gremaud's of "representations of nature as brand" ("Power and Purity" 79)—overtly illustrates the country's liminality and the complexity of Iceland's relationship to the stereotypes accompanying global positionings and postcolonial theories.

Comparable to the nuance required when applying postcolonial theories to the Far North, theorizations of the experiences and histories of Nordic nations require the creation of new locally specific language and concepts for the articulation of particular experiences within broader networks of power. For instance, Gísli Pálsson's term "arcticality" analyzes the specific discourses positioning the Arctic regions as "both exotic and domestic, emphasizing its lessons for 'us' (Westerners)" (275).[5] Kirsten Thisted applies the concept of "Arctic Orientalism" to the relationship between Denmark and Greenland, which, building on her work, Kristin Lorentsen and Jakob Stougaard-Nielsen describe as "an 'othering' of the Arctic periphery that expresses a cultural, political and economic asymmetric relationship also characterising other geo-political and cultural 'contact zones'" (133). "Borealism," coined by Icelandic ethnologist Kristinn Schram, incorporates the Latin *borealis* (or "the North") to describe "the cultural practices involved in exoticizing the inhabitants of the North," building on Edward Said's Orientalism, which refers to "the ontological and epistemological distinction between East and West" ("Banking on Borealism" 310). Schram investigates the shifting dynamics of the "liminal space of foreignness" inhabited by Icelanders abroad and the interaction with centers and margins of power (309), including the way that

A Statement on Nuclear Warfare.

Nuclear weapons are dangerous to humanity in the degree to which they are accessible to political desperados who think in terms of "positions of strength", and act accordingly. Some people say there will never be a nuclear war, because no politicians would dare to throw the H-bomb. The fact is, however, that power politicians, who are holding the fate of nations in their hands, ▨▨▨▨▨▨▨▨▨▨▨▨, have declared before the whole world that they are going to throw H-bombs on the towns and cities of the earth, and so wipe out human life indiscriminately, if and whenever they deem it necessary. Of course such procedure would not have much to do with war. Nuclear weapons have no meaning as factors in a war; their use would mean only the destruction of humanity and the extirpation of life on earth. In the same way nothing would have been more desireable than an H-bomb to Hitler in his last halt, so nothing is a greater matter of hope and joy to those political monsters that day and night, through their news agencies, press and radio, are castigating humanity with threats of annihilation.

Everybody knows that their absurd theories of a conflict between the peoples of East and West are an invention, serving its inventors as a pretext to justify their desire of destroying their own nation as well as other nations. The nations of the earth feel themselves bound to each other in friendship and in brotherhood.

There is only one conflict in the world that matters, the conflict between political desperados in possession of H-bombs on one side, and the peoples of the earth on the other side.

It is imperative to the peoples of the earth to get together and put out of commission those most malign agents of death that, since Life came to earth, have appeared on its surface.

Figure 1.1 A signed draft of a statement written by Halldór Laxness in 1955 on nuclear weapons. It was originally intended for the March 1955 meeting of the Soviet-controlled World Peace Council in Vienna. When it was not used, he submitted it for their meeting in Helsinki in June. It was also not used then, but Laxness published an Icelandic translation in *Gjörningabók*, a collection of essays, in 1959. Many thanks to Laxness's biographer Halldór Guðmundsson for the context of this document. For a comprehensive biography of Laxness, see Guðmundsson's *The Islander: A Biography of Halldór Laxness*. Laxness, Halldór. "A Statement on Nuclear Warfare." Laxness Special Collection, National and University Library of Iceland, Lbs 200 NF, "Halldór Kiljan Laxness: Skjala- og handritasafn," B. Handrit, BE. Ritgerdir og greinar.

not only media images but also Icelanders abroad portray "this perceived northern eccentricity through performances of tradition, 'primitive' origins, and seemingly archaic food traditions" to their own ends (323). Iceland's "post-colonial condition" might pale compared to other former dependencies or colonies in terms of wealth, culture, and identity, but "its historical and contemporary exoticism and marginalization is considerable" (Kjartansdóttir and Schram 65), demonstrated through the lingering impact of stereotypes.

Some of the enduring stereotypes about Icelanders—that they are eccentric and "primitive" with backward food cultures—serve to uphold their reputation as exotic others in the contemporary period. According to Sumarliði R. Ísleifsson, the creation of national identities occurs in a "dialectic relationship" to the images of "the Other" (6). Thus, this borealistic gaze on the Far North was situated with the European nations to the south that defined themselves in opposition. Ísleifsson describes general historic stereotypes of Icelanders as "uncivilized barbarians" (4)—even having "more in common with wild animals than humans" (10)—as well as more specific views of Icelanders as arrogant and ambitious (6); he also recognizes the long-held belief that people in the North are drunkards (7). These stereotypes would help to position the gazers' nations, such as Denmark, England, or Germany, oppositely.[6] Ísleifsson notes that cultural descriptions of the Far North "emphasized immorality in sexual practices, witchcraft, barbaric appearance and clothing, sexual confusion (the sexes were believed to have a similar appearance), small stature, stench, and speech—or lack thereof, since it was believed that many Northerners communicated by emulating the sounds of animals" (12). These negative representations existed alongside more positive and even sublime associations generated by romantic writers who "recreated the North as the birthplace of creativity, the desire for freedom, individuality, and human kindness. And the North, not least the far North, was defined as the home of heroism, masculinity, and poetry" (15).[7] Iceland has frequently captivated the imaginations of creative writers from more southern locales, including British poet W. H. Auden, Irish poet and playwright Louis MacNeice, and Argentine writer Jorge Luis Borges.

Similar to the theories of borealism applied to the Far North, the US South was often defined against the nation: "the retrograde South and a progressive nation" (Lassiter and Crespino 5). Although this southern exceptionalism has been exposed as a myth, it has served to continually distort understandings of US history (7). Viewed in opposition to the national ideal, the South is persistently associated with "slavery, white supremacy, under-development, poverty, backwardness" (Greeson 1), which in reality span the nation as a whole. Moreover, the broader stereotypes of the exotic, "wild" Far North can be put in productive conversation with generalizations about the likewise exotic, "backwards" US South. In both cases, stereotypes serve as a way to embed difference through discourse on a broad scale. Larry J. Griffin outlines how the US South was positioned as "America's opposite, its negative image, its evil twin" (7)—separating the characterization of the southern region from the rest of the nation. Griffin expands on common stereotypes of southerners as "courteous, religious, friendly, conservative, etc.," as well as "not hardworking, not intelligent, and violent" (14). Some of these have a long history, appearing in Thomas Jefferson's letter to the Marquis de Chastellux, in which he positions southerners as "fiery," "voluptuary," and "indolent," but also "generous" and "candid" (qtd. in Smith and Cohn 9). Aligned with the desire for freedom in understandings of the Far North is the representation of southerners as "zealous for their own liberties, but trampling on those of others" (qtd. in Smith and Cohn 9). As Griffin notes, this is what makes the White South in particular exceptional—for instance, the commitment to slavery and attempt at secession and nationhood, in addition to the military defeat and occupation it experienced (7), the latter of which is unique for a region of the United States but an experience shared with Iceland, along with many nations of the Global South.

Historically comparable though temporally distinct, Iceland endured a US military presence for the better part of the twentieth century and into the twenty-first. Until the British invasion of the island infringed upon its neutrality, Iceland had upheld its isolation and pacifism, since the 1918 Dano-Icelandic Act of Union (Deans 35). Iceland and the United States signed the Keflavík Agreement in the summer of 1946, which gave the US access to Keflavík airport and Icelandic soil, and the last US soldiers left in 2006 (D'Amico 460). The issue of the US military base, as well as Iceland's membership in NATO, dominated Icelandic politics; the main arguments against them were in support of national sovereignty (S. G. Magnússon 247), as well as Iceland's historic neutrality. Sigurður Gylfi Magnússon relates the Icelandic responses to this interference back to the nation's colonial ties to Denmark: "Icelanders' reactions in their disputes with foreign nations—in the Cod Wars [tensions with the UK over Iceland's fishing limits from the late 1950s to the 1970s] and over the Keflavík base—suggest an extremely brittle self-image, a hangover from the country's colonial past" (247). Illustrating the US's pseudo-neocolonial relationship to Iceland, Ástráður Eysteinsson adds that in terms of the debate over the US military base, "the American presence has constituted a highly 'useful' other, against and with which many Icelanders have thought of their cultural sovereignty" ("Icelandic Resettlements" 162), defining themselves in opposition to this invasive presence. For example, the intrusion of the US military in Iceland is central to Icelandic writer Laxness's *The Atom Station* (1961; *Atómstöðin*, 1948). Although the Americans remain primarily in the background, they hold symbolic weight as a force for Icelanders to define and assert themselves against.

INVENTED LANGUAGES AND INTERSECTING
HIERARCHIES IN *THE ATOM STATION*

The Atom Station, Laxness's Cold War novel (D'Amico 461), critiques US interference in Iceland. The plot involves two interwoven historical events: the 1946 treaty involving the US military base in Keflavík and the transfer of Icelandic poet Jónas Hallgrímsson's bones from Copenhagen to Reykjavík (S. A. Magnússon, "The World of Halldór Laxness" 460). As Giuliano D'Amico observes, the US is "represented as Iceland's one and only real colonial power," with the Danes and the British not even mentioned (472). US military representatives discuss the potential for a base in Iceland with Parliament member Búi Árland and other local politicians, which is characterized as "sell[ing] the country" (Laxness, *Atom Station* 28). This context is conducive to broader postcolonial readings of Iceland's positioning; however, the novel is also invested in examining the interaction of multiple, overlapping hierarchies in Icelandic society—including those of race, class, gender, and space (urban south versus rural north).[8] Laxness makes this clear from the opening scene of the novel, in which our central characters—the family of Árland and Ugla, a young woman from the north joining the household as a maid—are introduced to readers and each other with a combination of their Icelandic names and African nicknames or "barbarian names" (1).[9] The father expresses his distaste for the nicknames, stating that his family "cannot get by with less than Africa at its very darkest—bu-bu, dú-dú, bó-bó, dí-dí . . ." (4). The African nicknames used by the Icelanders can be considered in direct relation to the historic stereotype, noted by Ísleifsson, that northerners supposedly communicated "by emulating the sounds of animals." Through their very nature, nicknames are intended to be continually repeated until the word or sounds are enmeshed with the identity of the named individual. This is heightened through the sound patterns with these names, which, given the use of vowels specific to the Icelandic language, would appear to have been created by Icelandic speakers to approximate—or, more accurately, satirize—African languages.[10]

As demonstrated by the experiences of Helga Crane, the biracial protagonist of Nella Larsen's *Quicksand* (1928), when she moves to Copenhagen,

Black people need not be physically present in a space for there to be anti-Black racism (and similarly, Larsen does not need to depict colonization in the novel for its presence to be felt). Relatedly, Icelanders historically learned racism through discourse as opposed to experience (Rastrick, "Not Music" 102). Written in the 1940s, *The Atom Station* follows closely after the Harlem Renaissance in the US—a movement with global reach that simultaneously led to the wide recognition and consumption of Black American artistic and cultural production, as well as the commodification of Blackness, with anti-Black racism also positioned as a cultural export. While occurring in a different culture and part of the world, the literary resonances of the US movement may be explained by the changes in Icelandic society that accompanied the British and US occupations during World War II, such as their relation to the world beyond Iceland and the deep interest in the new and novel "to an almost unique degree" that accompanied the exposure to people, things, and ideas from abroad (S. G. Magnússon 233, 235). Therefore, Árland's family's creation of nicknames that exoticize Blackness function similarly to the way in which many Icelanders constructed their "cultural sovereignty," to return to Eysteinsson's term, against the intrusive US presence during this period—a presence that looms large in the novel—by defining themselves in opposition to cultural others like the US military or an invented African presence.

Árland, associating the names with "Africa at its very darkest," perpetuates stereotypes of an "uncivilized" Africa that are rooted in canonical Western literature, such as Joseph Conrad's *Heart of Darkness*, in which the language of Conrad's Congolese characters is frequently positioned as an incomprehensible "violent babble of uncouth sounds" (25). In response, it is essential to note that "Africa" here does not refer to a culture or even country, but an entire continent, which, according to the African Language Program at Harvard, is home to "approximately one-third of the world's languages" or between one and two thousand separate languages ("Introduction to African Languages"). However, Árland and his family are not interested in realistic representations of Africa and its specific languages or cultures. In reference to his son, introduced as "Bubu" rather than his Icelandic name Arngrímur, Árland states, "Yet another barbarian. . . . Apparently from Tanganyika, or Kenya; or the land where they decorate their hair with rats' tails" (Laxness, *Atom Station* 4).[11] In his example of rats' tails, Árland calls up grotesque, exoticized imagery unconnected, even in his mind, to any one African culture—"from Tanganyika [today's Tanzania], or Kenya"—and seemingly received through hearsay, as indicated by his use of "apparently."

Búi Árland is a complex father figure who maintains a certain distance in his familial relationships throughout the novel. However, while he criticizes their behavior, his references to "Africa at its very darkest" and "barbarian names" in this opening scene have a similar effect to the other family members' use of repetitive monosyllables as names. Both the family's naming activity and Árland's statements reify stereotypes of Africa as "uncivilized" and lacking language, culture, and history. Located on the periphery of Europe, and thus Whiteness, the family and those of their bourgeois class are eager to draw lines of racial distinction and solidify their own positioning as White, European, and "civilized," in part through activating stereotypes of other cultures. In this way, Árland and his family exemplify that "Icelanders participated in recreating and reaffirming racialized and dehumanizing images of colonized people elsewhere," in part in reaction to the historic stereotypes about their own culture that present Icelanders as "eaters of raw fish and meat" and "animal-like beasts," not generally as "complete savages but neither as fully belonging with civilized peoples" (Loftsdóttir, "Belonging" 60, 59). Though the nicknames are used in jest, I argue that on some level the family intends them to ironically emphasize their own Whiteness, distance from what they perceive as "Africanness," and elevated positioning in relation to the entwined hierarchies of class and space in Icelandic society. They intend to identify upward toward Europe and away from Africa in a tripartite system. Operating in a comparable way to the Icelandic student protests in Copenhagen, the nicknames signify that "we are this because we are not that."

The family's attempts to establish themselves as White, European, and "civilized" are underscored through a narratological lens. Subtly throughout the scene, the Árland family is associated with Whiteness and Europeanness through Ugla's first-person narrative voice.[12] Búi Árland, who makes her "feel funny in the knees" (Laxness, *Atom Station* 2), is introduced as "a tall, slim man with a Roman nose and a fine head" (1–2), highlighting his Roman features and thus the European associations of his physical body. The mother, whom Ugla refers to in the scene as Madam, describes the nicknames as being in style—again perhaps echoing the cultural interest in and global commodification of Blackness originating in the 1920s and 1930s: "'My husband isn't very *chic*,' said Madam. 'He would prefer to call the boy Grímsi. But modern times are *chic*. Everything has to be *à la mode*'" (4). The use of French phrases, in addition to the French-derived "madam" by which Ugla refers to her, contrast sharply with the nicknames—an overt attempt through the narration to underscore the differences between this Icelandic family and the African continent. Ugla describes the eldest daughter, who would prefer to be named Dúdú over Guðný or her Icelandic nickname Gunsa, as "newly confirmed" and as "looking as fresh-coloured as cream except for her black-painted lips and nails, adjusting with supple fingers her thick, blonde, cork-screw curls" (1). This description emphasizes her Whiteness through phrases such as "fresh-coloured as cream" with her "thick, blonde, cork-screw curls." However, Ugla portrays Guðný as electing to darken her lips and nails with black paint—an external "Blackness," self-imposed and à la mode, that only heightens the contrast with her natural cream-colored skin and blonde hair, illustrating that on some level, the family seems aware that "the power of whiteness rests in its ability to normalize certain bodies" (Loftsdóttir, "Dualistic Colonial Experiences" 35).[13]

While, knowingly or not, Ugla accentuates the family's White and European associations through her descriptions, her narrative voice also illustrates the cultural distinctions between Laxness's northern and southern Icelanders—another dichotomy of identity central to the novel alongside "an internal contrast between radicals and conservatives, and an external one, between Icelanders and Americans" (D'Amico 462). For instance, as a northerner, Ugla's worldview has been deeply impacted by the Icelandic sagas. She was taught not to believe what is written in the papers, "nothing except what is written in the Icelandic sagas" (Laxness, *Atom Station* 44). Ugla divulges to Árland's wife that "[i]n the country [or north], everything is read . . . beginning with the Icelandic sagas" (5), although Madam remains more concerned about who might be reading the Communist paper (6). As D'Amico observes, Ugla admits to having difficulty understanding abstractions like "soul" and "love" (68, 72), since there is no mention of them in the sagas (D'Amico 470). As a result of this aspect of her character and her position as narrator, *The Atom Station* includes ubiquitous references to Iceland's rich literary and cultural history, which on another level also writes back to stereotypes of Iceland as barbaric and uncultured through the form of the novel itself—the allusions challenging simplistic views of Iceland, speaking to a poetics of peripheralization. Ugla references Njáll's Saga (12, 68, 72, 129, 136), Egill's Saga (68, 128, 136), Grettir's Saga (68, 128), and the Edda (68, 69, 174), in addition to Icelandic folktales (79, 113, 145). Ugla and her northern community, including the church-builders who "discuss the saga heroes over their carpentry" (127), retain a deep interest in and reverence for the sagas, situating the northerners as less modern and more peripheralized than the southerners. This dynamic mirrors the spatial and cultural hierarchies reflected in the relationship between Iceland and Denmark—the latter considering the former as the keeper of their shared Norse heritage.[14]

In contrast, the southern Icelanders are more removed from this cultural history than the rural northerners and are more modern and global in their cultural interests, such as Guðný's mimicry of Hollywood fashions (Laxness, *Atom Station* 106). The novel's portrayal of "the atom poets"—a term coined by Laxness in this novel that came to be associated with the modernist Icelandic poets of the 1940s and 1950s—and their involvement with "sell[ing] the country, bury[ing] the bones" (Þorvaldsson 474; Laxness, *Atom Station* 169), heavy with satire, also exemplifies this distinction.[15] The campaign for the bones of Jónas Hallgrímsson, a plot point that has the added effect of amplifying the poet's reputation for non-Icelandic readers, is clearly intended to distract the public from other political machinations.[16] In the end, the atom poets steal the bones to bring them to the north where Hallgrímsson was from, yet the crates do not contain human remains but Portuguese sardines and Danish clay—a detail that also satirizes global capitalism. A previous side comment reveals the poets to have been aware of this. The antics of the atom poets, from stealing the crates to shooting a local farmer's lamb, are emblematic of the modernizing south and contrast sharply with Ugla's portrayal of her grounded, taciturn father and his calm rejection of their behavior. Due to her migration south and more ambiguous relationship to modernity (D'Amico 472), Ugla inhabits a liminal position in between rural and urban, traditional and modern, and northern and southern, which benefits her narration in her ability to describe and relate to both.

Returning briefly to the novel's opening scene, Ugla's introduction and positioning as a White, working-class northern woman in relation to the Árland household also illuminates the novel's spatial hierarchies beyond her narrative voice and saga references, as well as their entanglement with class and gender. Fresh from the north, Ugla's difference from the southern bourgeois family is highlighted throughout the episode, in addition to her association with innocence and purity, which I argue are gendered qualities. Árland's first line in the novel is to ask, "How is an innocent girl from the north to memorise these barbarian names?" (Laxness, *Atom Station* 1). He goes on to note that it was good of her "to come all the way from the north to help us here in the south" (2)—emphasizing the significant spatial and cultural differences. Árland references the "heathenish Parliament" (2), out of which he will attempt to wrangle money for Ugla's father's rural, northern church, introducing the fact that the north is also associated with the values of religion—specifically Christianity.[17] Árland demonstrates this directly: "You are from the north, from that unforgettable valley of Eystridalur, the daughter of Wild-horses Falur who is building a church: won't you please re-christen the children for me?" (4). In addition to associations with purity and religion, stereotypes of northerners include a lack of culture. Ugla reflects, "How ludicrous it was to hear a big, strapping north-country girl announce in a civilised home that she was going to learn to play the harmonium" (3). The southern home is characterized as "civilized," while as a northern girl, she is "big, strapping" and assumed to have no interest in culture beyond the northern interest in the sagas. Her interactions with the family's cook also demonstrate that northerners are looked down on by southerners even within the same class group: "'That's just like you northerners, to start talking to people,' said the cook when I returned to the kitchen. Rebellion stirred in me and I replied, 'I am people'" (3). Self-possessed northerner Ugla is positioned by Árland and his family as a pure though uncultured northern girl who can perhaps save them from the "heathenism" and debauchery of the urban south—a tension that will play out in the remaining sections of the novel. Not only through the repetitive use of nicknames, but also Ugla's narrative perspective and initial interactions with the family, intersecting hierarchies of race, gender, class, and space are introduced through the opening scene and remain central throughout the story.

THE CATEGORIZING, DEHUMANIZING POWER OF LANGUAGE IN *ABSALOM, ABSALOM!*

Like *The Atom Station, Absalom, Absalom!* (1936) is attuned to the webs of hierarchical relationships and the interrelation of the past and present, although Faulkner's novel takes place across the Atlantic in the US South.[18] While the novel was written less than ten years before Laxness's, it covers almost one hundred years, from the early 1800s to 1910. The Tidewater, Virginia, episode, my focus here, occurred in 1817, opening to transgeographical but also transhistorical readings of patterns of relations. Like the opening scene of *The Atom Station*, this episode of *Absalom, Absalom!* highlights the power of language to differentiate and dehumanize, a point emphasized through repetition. Keeping in mind the ways in which Whiteness takes different forms as a result of distinct histories and local traditions but is also "entangled within larger global discourses of difference and power" (Loftsdóttir, *Crisis and Coloniality* 6), I leave space for cultural and historical differences. For example, the Árlands likely react to stereotypes of Africans through media, whereas Sutpen reacts to the enslaved Black Americans his family lives alongside in Virginia. Nevertheless, this comparison reveals parallel tripartite systems with those in the liminal middle positions—the Icelandic family and Sutpen—identifying upward in their attempts to secure a degree of power.

Narrative perspective is significant to the Tidewater scene: there exists distance between lived experiences and their narration—actor and narrator. Thomas Sutpen, observed by Rosa Coldfield, tells his story of growing up in Virginia to his friend General Compson, who in turn tells his son Jason, who tells his son Quentin, who relates the events to (and with) his room-mate at Harvard, Shreve McCannon, and in turn to (and with?) the readers. Young Sutpen is interpellated into social relations through his interactions with others beyond his social identity groups, and he uses language in his attempt to understand his own positionality. At the same time, the story is not solely Sutpen's but reveals the narrators in turn as well. Thus, in contrast with Ugla's first-person account, there are layers of complexity to the narrative structures in this novel. Sutpen's repetition of dehumanizing language is also General Compson's, Jason's, Quentin's, and Shreve's (the sole narrator unambiguously from the Global North), revealing the ways in which hierarchical mindsets are passed down across the generations, cementing an intergenerational White supremacist culture.[19] The intentional narrative slipperiness reveals much about storytelling and the unknowable nature of histories, even our own, in a way that connects the novel's themes with its aesthetics, in line with Aboul-Ela's poetics of peripheralization, representing "multivocal, anti-Eurocentric histories of coloniality" (*Other South* 136).

As Susan Scott Parrish and Johannes Burgers have noted, the voice associated with Sutpen in this section is Quentin's narrative reconstruction and not technically Sutpen's voice, to which readers do not have direct access. Parrish and Burgers more accurately refer to this as words "used around" Sutpen.[20] As the novel calls into question the ability to know anything concretely about the past, I'll suspend disbelief to read the language patterns as originating with their speaker in order to offer a reading of the formation of identity through language. However, I acknowledge that this language is also Quentin's, as well as that of his father and grandfather (though to an unknown extent), from whom he inherits this episode of the story. In a similar way to the Icelanders solidifying their claims to Whiteness and Europeanness in comparison with other colonized people in the Global South, through the repetitive use of terms such as "monkey n***" (Faulkner, *Absalom, Absalom!* 186), this reconstructed version of Sutpen, perhaps unconsciously, attempts to establish his difference as White and working class from Black enslaved people, at least as imagined by Quentin, generations removed from the events.

Sutpen's "innocence" is referenced throughout the scene (Faulkner, *Absalom, Absalom!* 183), which I interpret as his ignorance of the intersectional social relations that he is unaware he possesses: "He had learned the difference not only between white men and black ones, but he was learning that there was a difference between white men and white men not to be measured by lifting anvils or gouging eyes or how much whiskey you could drink then get up and walk out of the room. That is, he had begun to discern that without being aware of it yet" (183).[21] In a sense, Sutpen's innocence of race and class relations ends up leading to his guilt. His ignorance causes him to experience shame at the door of the planter for whom his father works, which spurs him to pursue his "design" and replicate the South's colonial hierarchies with himself positioned as White enslaver (194). I focus here on the first step in this trajectory: Sutpen's interpellation into social relations.

After the family leaves the mountains—where "the land belonged to anybody and everybody" (Faulkner, *Absalom, Absalom!* 179)—to join Tidewater society in 1817, Sutpen awakens into an awareness of social hierarchies from what is depicted as a specifically White innocence/ignorance: "he no more conscious of his appearance in them [worn out, ill-fitting garments from the plantation commissary] or of the possibility that anyone else would be than he was of his *skin*" (185, emphasis mine). Here, Sutpen is unconscious of the fact that clothes might signify class status, as well as the social implications of his White skin. Interestingly, Sutpen's ignorance extends to his own birthplace and date: behind him was "the moment when he last could have said exactly where he had been born now weeks and months (maybe a year, the year, since that was when he became confused about his age and was never able to straighten it out again . . .)" (184). The uncertainty surrounding a birthdate is a common feature of many US slave narratives, which specify a place but often not a date for the birth of the formerly enslaved narrators (Olney 50). However, in Sutpen's case, he lacks knowledge of both. This blurring of the boundaries of race and class or the instability of social hierarchies, where enslaved Black people are materially better off than working-class White people, leads to the drive to emphasize race over class and to the racial violence we see in the episode.

Sutpen learns about the hierarchical distinctions between individuals at the same time he discovers that in some instances the enslaved Black people are materially better off than he is. For example, he describes the enslaved man fanning the White planter as wearing "every day better clothes than [Sutpen] or his father and sisters had ever owned and ever expected to" (Faulkner, *Absalom, Absalom!* 184), then notes that White people of their class "lived in other cabins not quite as well built and not at all as well kept and preserved as the ones the n*** slaves lived in but still nimbused with freedom's bright aura, which the slave quarters were not for all their sound roofs and white wash" (185). The racial tensions he observes in response to material distinctions transcend lines of gender, as he notes the hostile feelings his sisters and other White women hold toward the enslaved Black servants, shown through their "certain flat level silent way" of looking (186). While Sutpen recognizes the cloths and homes of the enslaved workers may be of better quality, he is able to some extent to comprehend the differences in relation to freedom and the system of enslavement.

In his observations about material goods and ownership, Sutpen—via Quentin, Jason, and the general—first refers to an enslaved man as a "monkey," listing him as a possession to be coveted, alongside shoes: "He coveted the shoes, and probably he would have liked for his father to have a broadcloth monkey to hand him the jug" (Faulkner, *Absalom, Absalom!* 184–85). His first use of this term is enmeshed with his understanding of the man as a possession. Sutpen both refers to the man as an animal—the weighted choice of "monkey," given the racist history of that term—and positions him as an object of utility, double-layered dehumanization. Throughout his reconstructions, Sutpen also includes multiple allusions to the materiality the man protects: "the monkey-dressed n*** butler kept the door barred with his body while he spoke" (187), "And now he stood there before that white door with the monkey n*** barring it and looking down at him in his patched made-over jeans . . ." (188), and "the plantation that supported and endured that smooth white house and that smooth white brass decorated door and the very broadcloth and linen and silk stockings the monkey n*** stood in to tell him to go around to the back before he could even state the business" (189). This leads to his own recognition, shame, and embarrassment that he is someone from whom the "smooth white"—repeated twice in the last passage—"Tidewater splendor" might need protection (180).

Sutpen's continuous replication of the term "monkey n***" (Faulkner, *Absalom, Absalom!* 186)—repeated so frequently it almost starts to deconstruct itself—emphasizes the Black servant's difference and de-emphasizes his humanity as not only "n***" but also as "monkey."[22] Indeed, Sutpen's language demonstrates his growing awareness of his Whiteness and the advantages that accompany it, alongside his lower-class status; his racist language in part constructs his envisioned position of privilege above enslaved Black people. However, while the enslaved Black people are considered lower on the racial hierarchies, they hold higher value to the White enslaver class. This layered recognition is also interwoven with Sutpen's humiliation at being turned away from the front door of the plantation house by the enslaved Black man and told "to go around to the back" (190)—his humiliation at someone else, and someone he considers below him, having the power to define him.

Although to the outside observer Sutpen's overreaction smacks of fragility, his continual replaying of this scene also brings to mind traumatic repetition—a coping mechanism through which he attempts to process the encounter.[23] According to Robyn Fivush and Beth Seeling, "Human beings seek meaning, and when experienced events cannot be understood, the human mind returns again and again to the event to try to make sense of it in a repetitive and compulsive way" (qtd. in Foster 104). In addition to Sutpen's replaying of the scene at the front door, the repeated retellings of the Sutpen family history may also be seen as an attempt to represent a psyche working through a traumatizing situation, as well as the deferral of the most "accurate" version of the story. Given the novel's narrative complexity, this begs the question of whose trauma response Faulkner is capturing by calling back to the shared language across the generations of narrators. Of course, the answer is unknowable, but the question reveals trauma as a contagion of White supremacist culture: from Sutpen, Rosa, and General Compson through Jason to Quentin and Shreve. According to Resmaa Menakem, "white supremacy is trauma" or a "traumatizing, organizing principle of America" that can appear incidental, as opposed to foundational, if not examined in these terms ("Resmaa Menakem"). Menakem asserts that trauma responses can become internalized and passed down over generations within groups and start to look like a culture, and both White and Black Americans hold forms of racialized trauma in their bodies (Menakem 9). Along with the repetition of the story, the reverberation of violent language across the generations, attempting to bolster wavering racial hierarchies, may also reveal a deeper level of racialized trauma beyond the embarrassment and shame that accompany Sutpen's recognition of his race and class position.

INTERPELLATING SUTPEN: RACIST IMAGERY AND VIOLENT DENIALS OF HUMANITY

After his experience at the front door, Sutpen grows more conscious of the differences between the White upper-class enslavers, the White lower-class laborers, and the Black enslaved people, as well as the tensions between these groups. He continues his repetitive use of racist imagery through an additional dehumanizing metaphor, describing enslaved people as "toy balloon[s]": You could hit them, but they were "not what you wanted to hit; that when you hit them you would just be hitting a child's toy balloon with a face painted on it, a face slick and smooth and distended and about to burst into laughing" (Faulkner, *Absalom, Absalom!* 186). In this passage, Sutpen reveals his growing awareness of the complexity of societal power structures and the inadequacy of violence in response to oppressive class hierarchies. While the enslaved Black people may be slightly better off in terms of clothes and housing, they are not responsible for these distinctions; however, since the underlying power structures themselves are not tangible enough to be hit, they sometimes stand in as scapegoats. His description of enslaved people as "a child's toy balloon with a face painted on it" and "a face slick and smooth" includes a slippage from a plural group to a singular toy, a singular face. In other words, "they" become "it"—further erasing the complexity of enslaved people's individual identities. Sutpen, again via the narrators, repeats this additional metaphor for Black people—toy balloons with painted faces—throughout the remainder of the section alongside "monkey n***." Moreover, through his focus on "laughing" and the fear of being laughed at, Sutpen also exposes that his humiliation at being turned away from the front door of the plantation home is entwined with his awareness of social relations. A few pages later when his father returns after "whupp[ing] one of Pettibone's n***s" (Faulkner, *Absalom, Absalom!* 187), Sutpen employs this balloon imagery to decenter and deny the enslaved man's humanity or to distance the man from his pain to also alleviate any guilt or concern Sutpen might himself feel.

Further, the way in which Sutpen comes into an understanding of his identity based on these primal scenes of interracial violence finds a counterpart in the *Narrative of the Life of Frederick Douglass, an American Slave* (1845). This is not to conflate in any way the protagonists' positionings or experiences; however, the mechanism leading to awareness is comparable, although the two men's identity positions—an enslaved Black man, and a working-class White man—are dissimilar. Early in the narrative Douglass witnesses the physical violence (and implied sexual violence) toward Aunt Hester and awakens into his identity as an enslaved person. Douglass describes in detail the violence experienced by his aunt, "whom [the enslaver] used to tie up to a joist, and whip upon her naked back till she was literally covered with blood" (6). Douglass positions the encounter as "the first of a long series of such outrages, of which I was doomed to be a witness and a participant" and "the blood-stained gate, the entrance to the hell of slavery, through which I was about to pass" (6), underscoring the important role this witnessing of violence had in the formation of his identity. While his positioning is in many ways oppositional to Douglass's, a parallel may be drawn to Sutpen's awakening into a sense of his identity as a young White man in a plantation culture through his relationship to this scene of racial violence—although less direct than Douglass's role as a personal witness. Perhaps a consequence unintended by Faulkner, these parallels between Sutpen's experiences and US slave narratives add depth to his depiction of identity development, elucidating patterns across social identity groups of race, class, and gender.

Additionally, through a denial of reality, Sutpen prolongs his own state of White innocence/ignorance:

no actual n***, living creature, living flesh to feel pain and writhe and cry out . . . the fierce hysterical faces of the white men, the balloon face of the n***. Maybe the n***'s hands would be tied or held but that would be all right because they were not the hands with which the balloon face would struggle and writhe for freedom, not the balloon face. (Faulkner, *Absalom, Absalom!* 187)

As Aliyyah I. Abdur-Rahman describes, the balloon face "was a grotesque form without human essence or individual interiority. The insinuation here is that, by law and by the logics of racial slavery, the enslaved black was mere bodily material to be animated and manipulated by the external will of the white" ("What Moves" 54). Sutpen—perhaps consciously—does not recognize the human essence or agency of the man. Recasting the violence of beating another human being as striking a balloon dehumanizes the man, denies his pain, and cleanses the violence of its horror. Refusing to recognize the man's pain, Sutpen disconnects the man from his body and the physical violence he experiences, as "they were not the hands with which the balloon face would struggle" and "not the balloon face"—underscored through the repetition of "balloon face." Comparable to the Icelandic family members' definitions of themselves in opposition—we are European because we are not African—Sutpen comes into knowledge of social relations through opposition in a tripartite system—I am poor White, because I am not rich or Black—as a result of these primal scenes of violence. In this way, he echoes the Árland family in their use of repetitive language patterns to reify lines of difference and deny the humanity of the people on the other side of the lines, an impulse extending across regions and cultures.

Similarly, considering violence in response to being turned away from the front door, Sutpen is aware that it is not the enslaved servant that he wants to shoot "anymore than it had been the n*** that his father had helped to whip that night. The n*** was just another balloon face slick and distended with that mellow loud and terrible laughing so that he did not dare to burst it" (Faulkner, *Absalom, Absalom!* 189). Again here, Sutpen denies the reality of violence and pain, as well as the man's humanity. This example conflates the two racist images used throughout the episode: the servant who turned him away, usually depicted as the "monkey n***," becomes the "balloon face." On the next page, in another compulsive reconstruction of the scene, "the balloon" guards the planter and his material splendor, "held barricaded and protected from such as [Sutpen]" (190). This conflation once again denies the individuality of Black people—functioning similarly to the slippage from "them" to "it." Consciously or not, Sutpen and the intergenerational narrators refuse to uphold even the singular objects of reference for their racist metaphors, in opposition to the one-to-one correlation required by nicknames, with singularity and individuality reserved for those on the other side of the lines of difference.

This scene stands out not only for the slippage in his depiction of the enslaved servants from animals to balloons, but also for Sutpen's recognition of his marginalized class position, again through the use of metaphor. Sutpen observes that he and his family are seen by the "rich man (not the n***)"—the parenthetical detailing that in his mind the rich White man can look down on him but not the enslaved Black man—as "cattle, creatures heavy and without grace, brutely evacuated into a world without hope or purpose for them, who would in turn spawn with brutish and vicious prolixity, populate, double treble and compound, fill space and earth with a race whose future would be a succession of cut-down and patched and made-over garments" (Faulkner, *Absalom, Absalom!* 190). Sutpen dehumanizes himself and his family here as heavy, graceless "cattle." Instead of leading purposeful lives, they are "brutely evacuated" with neither "hope" nor "purpose," other than to "spawn" with "brutish and vicious prolixity," or a seemingly animalistic frequency, until the earth is filled with others like them—a "race" linked by ill-fitting clothes. Through the animal imagery and repetitive use of forms of "brute," Sutpen dehumanizes himself and his family, alongside the Black enslaved workers, from the imagined mindset of the planter, but as "cattle" as opposed to "monkeys," with a different mental image and set of associations.

In this passage, we also see Sutpen's awareness of the split between how he sees himself and how he imagines the rich planter sees him, which I argue can be read as a type of poor, White southern double consciousness.[24] Similar to the lack of knowledge surrounding his birthdate and the primal scenes of violence that link his story directly to the slave narrative genre, reading double consciousness into this scene connects Sutpen to the genesis of the term: W. E. B. Du Bois's *The Souls of Black Folk* (1903). Du Bois's text delineates the dualities and conflicts in African American self-perception: the crux of Black Americans' struggles to identify themselves as Black and American with a "sense of always looking at one's self through the eyes of others, of measuring one's soul by the tape of a world that looks on in amused contempt and pity" (8). Du Bois writes, "One ever feels his two-ness,—an American, a Negro; two souls, two thoughts, two unreconciled strivings; two warring ideals in one dark body, whose dogged strength alone keeps it from being torn asunder" (8). This highlights the complexity of identifying as both Black and American, as a citizen of a nation that allowed one's ancestors to be enslaved for generations.[25] Important differences here include the fact that Sutpen's White working-class identity may be less immediately visible than Blackness, and while he is marginalized as a result of his poverty, this does not equate to the systemic anti-Blackness and racial violence experienced by Black Americans. Nonetheless, this cross-racial connection again highlights the instability of overlapping social hierarchies in the Tidewater community, which in turn leads to White violence in the urgent attempt by marginalized White people to preserve their status elevated above enslaved Black people on the social hierarchies—this violence existing alongside the intergenerational linguistic violence of the narrators.

In addition, the verb *spawn* is used by Sutpen multiple times earlier in this episode. Each instance reveals his worldview, with the uncertainty of the narrative voice again highlighting the degree of removal: "some people were spawned in one place and some in another, some spawned rich (lucky, he may have called it: or maybe he called lucky, rich) and some not" (Faulkner, *Absalom, Absalom!* 180). A similar sentiment is expressed a few pages later: "He still thought that that was just a matter of where you were spawned and how; lucky or not lucky" (183). This mentality demonstrates his naive understanding of social identity groups and societal structures. Throughout his fiction, Faulkner repeatedly uses the word *spawn*, which he tends to associate with the "threat" of a multiracial future. The ending of "Delta Autumn" in *Go Down, Moses* illustrates this clearly when Isaac McCaslin is horrified to imagine a future in which "*Chinese and African and Aryan and Jew, all breed and spawn together until no man has time to say which one is which nor cares*" (347). Isaac somewhat inexplicably links the blending of different ethnicities with the loss of these separate cultures or histories. Significant also is his use of "Aryan" here alongside more specific ethnic and ethnoreligious groups, such as Chinese, African, and Jewish—though comparatively still too broad, with "African" instead of "Nigerian" or even "Igbo" or "Yoruba," for instance. This may speak to the White supremacist inflections of the speech, as well as the prevalent view of Whiteness as the default, the norm, or the absence of ethnicity or culture. While he doesn't use the word spawn directly, the passage from *Go Down, Moses* is reminiscent of Shreve's monologue at the end of *Absalom, Absalom!* in which he is the mouthpiece for a fear that the "Jim Bonds are going to conquer the western hemisphere" until "in a few thousand years, I who regard you will also have sprung from the loins of African kings" (302). Faulkner highlights this fear of amalgamation to the point of individual groups becoming indistinguishable and all Americans passing for White with traces of Black ancestry through ending the novel on this image. While the Canadian Shreve likely intends to be tongue-in-cheek in his monologue, Isaac's speech is read as anything but, exposing his sincere fear of a multiracial future and the loss he believes it would entail.

Nevertheless, this emphasis on similarities, as opposed to differences, need not only represent the irrational fears of White southerners (like Sutpen or Isaac), but may also gesture toward a solution to the entrenched hierarchical race and class dynamics in the US South. The potential for collaboration across a multiracial working class would be a threat to the plantocracy and the power and privilege upon which it rests. Stated more directly, segregation laws were deliberately designed to separate working-class White and Black Americans, encouraging the White workers "to retain a sense of superiority over blacks, making it far less likely that they would sustain interracial political alliances aimed at toppling the white elite" (Alexander 34). The system, as Sutpen slowly becomes aware, was calibrated by those with power—upperclass White men—to preserve their privileges. A goal of this design was to prevent collaboration across the lines of difference that would disrupt the paternalistic, patriarchal, and racist social structures or, in Levine's words, the "dominant terms of hierarchical binaries [would] fail to align and coordinate" (86). However, this solution, connection across racial lines, lingers in the background of both Faulkner's and Laxness's novels—neither acknowledged nor given space to flourish. For texts in which racial distinctions are so central, Blackness is not absent or negated but remains subtly present through, for instance, the understated use of double consciousness and slave narrative tropes in Faulkner and the commodification of Blackness as "*à la mode*" in Laxness.

SELF-DEFINITIONS, GENDERED EXPECTATIONS, AND THE FUSING OF BODIES IN "THE LODGER"

According to Levine, "the privileged term in each binary reinforces the privileged terms in all of the supposedly foundational binaries" to ultimately "consolidate power and agency in the hands of white, male subjects" (83). For an added wrinkle and to end on a more fully intersectional note, I turn briefly to another example from twentieth-century Icelandic literature, incorporating a gender-based analysis to complicate the mechanics of defining oneself in opposition to another. If the Árland family asserts that they are Icelandic because they are not African (or American!), and in a similar way Sutpen positions himself as poor White because he is not rich White or poor Black, what happens when an outside party fails to recognize the self-proclaimed differences due to multiple interlocking forms of domination not always granted visibility? In Jakobsdóttir's "The Lodger," from the collection *The Lodger and Other Stories* (2000; *Leigjandinn*, 1969), an unnamed wife witnesses her Icelandic husband, Peter, and an uninvited, foreign houseguest that she refers to as "the lodger" physically merge into one being—a critique of outside influences on Iceland functioning less on a thematic level and more symbolically through aesthetics and imagery in a poetics of peripheralization.

All three central characters are racially unmarked and thus equated with Whiteness given the context—"the Icelandic body always assumed as 'White'" (Loftsdóttir and Mörtudóttir 215). Because of the ease with which he assists the couple financially, the lodger can be considered of a higher class. Like the US military remaining on the island from the 1940s to 2006, the uninvited guest leaves the Icelandic couple unsure of how long he will stay: "of course the man would leave, especially as he was a foreigner: home ties . . ." (Jakobsdóttir 24).[26] The uncertainty surrounding his visit is emphasized, as well as the repetition of the fact that he did not knock—instead, he is depicted oddly pounding on the door and the walls from the inside (22–23)—and that the wife hadn't offered any resistance (37). Bodily mutations are introduced early in the novella, with the woman fearing and "almost certain even" that "her whole existence was being reversed: the inside turning outwards, the outside inwards, and just as she felt she was losing herself in this ominous reversal, he stopped his pounding" (14–15). With his knocking from the inside out, she believes her existence would be reversed, anticipating a later scene when she fears she would be divided into two. Unlike her husband, however, the woman experiences no corporeal transformations—at least until the last line, when her arm turns to stone.

While in terms of national hierarchies, granted particular emphasis during the occupation period, the men's positions are contradictory, in other ways they are indistinguishable as White men of a certain body type living in the same household. Eysteinsson describes the novella as an allegorical story of a nation "about to acquire its much desired independence but is then occupied by a foreign power that shows no signs of leaving" and asserts that the thread of a woman "desperately trying to find her place, her sanctuary, in a male-dominated world" gives the narrative added complexity ("Icelandic Prose Literature" 431, 432). Likely the Icelandic husband and foreign lodger would define themselves in opposition to each other, in the same manner as Sutpen and the White planter or enslaved servant. However, by the end of the story, the wife is literally unable to distinguish between them as their physical bodies fuse together, destabilizing these identifications through difference when refracted through a third party. The consideration of this example alongside the others emphasizes that identity is always multiple, shifts according to perspective, and encompasses both how you see yourself and how others see you.

According to Sigurdur A. Magnússon, "the episodes set forth have their parallels in Iceland's destiny since the foreign occupation during World War Two until the present day" ("The Modern Icelandic Novel" 143).[27] Emphasizing his otherness as "foreign occupier," the lodger doesn't have a strong understanding of Icelandic history or culture. This is only brought to the fore twice: once when the wife decorates the Christmas goose with little Icelandic flags (Jakobsdóttir 76), retaining a semblance of national identity and affiliation, and then when Peter describes why separate bedrooms have importance to Icelanders.[28] He notes that "bodies have been separated to be sure, but a spiritual communal life has never been abandoned" (63), to which the lodger responds with interest. However, Peter's historical explanations regarding "how Icelanders had all lived, slept and communed in the same room, day and night, for centuries" are interrupted by his wife banging her fist on the table to demand the lodger stay in his own room (63). The wife's strong reaction here speaks not only to her growing power in the domestic situation but also to her underlying concern with security, defense, and privacy throughout the story, which connects to Iceland's experience of occupation and history of more communal living, as well as her social position as a woman, portrayed as more vulnerable to both physical and sexual threats and societal expectations. The story begins with her often repeated line, "You are so insecure when you rent" (13). She expands on this sentiment, stating that her landlord had an extra key, so there was no point in even locking the front door. In terms of security, the woman believes moving from the rented apartment to the new house will be an important change, and only her dream of the house "is capable of wrapping her in the security she desired" (25). She feels free after the move—"Now the house could be locked" (60)—and she states, "Better to live alone with the knowledge of one's freedom and hold on to it rather than jeopardize it by relating it to others" (71). In a similar way, the symbolism of the melding bodies can be read as interwoven with both the history of communal living and of foreign occupation, the formal reflecting the thematic.

To a careful reader, the men's fused bodies at the conclusion of the story, while shocking, will not come as a total surprise.[29] For example, an earlier surreal scene anticipates this unusual ending: the husband consumes milk directly from his wife's breast, another symbolic gendered expectation, and this brings him calm and peace. When he "only emptied one breast!" she is filled with rage at being forced to empty the other herself—"what right had he to all this?" (Jakobsdóttir 33). Moreover, Jakobsdóttir carefully folds in clues concerning the men's fusion early on, such as when the wife notices the lodger loosening his tie "in the same manner her husband usually did when he came home from work" (14); when the two men meet for the first time, she watches "Peter's hand enclose the lodger's; their hands became entwined, and for a moment their palms remained so tightly clutched that it was as if they had grown together" (21). Later, it is their gendered behavior that reflects their similarity: "at first she was unable to distinguish the one man from the other: just this masculine behavior as soon as they settled in their seats, how they hitched up their trousers at the knees, ran their hands along the creases, their legs spread apart, fully stretched out. Two men basking in the glory of the world" (41).[30] The physical transformation itself is not sudden. Part way through the story, each man has one leg that begins to shorten, making mobility a challenge, until the wife begins to refer to them as a collective entity: "Where on earth had she stuffed *their* slippers?" (61, emphasis mine).[31] Eventually, the shortened legs disappear:

> Only the toes stuck out, as if grown from the groin. She saw them fumble for each other for support, saw them groping for a handhold while they approached each other. For a moment she thought she saw anguish appear in Peter's eyes, but only fleetingly, and then they sidled into each other, coalescing as one man. That is how they stood facing her, one man with two heads and four arms on two legs. (77–78)

This grotesque description of toes seemingly growing from their groins emphasizes that their joining is the result of each individual man's lack— literally of a disappeared leg. The merging thus results from the physical impairment of each man as they are "fumb[ling] for each other for support" and "groping for a handhold"—depictions layered with homoerotic connotations—before ultimately sidling up to each other to form one whole man, which would also be productive to consider from a disability studies perspective. On the axis of gender, the unnamed wife is apart from the men and able to view this transformation for what it is: understanding, shared financial support, and physical proximity leading to the melding of two nationally oppositional entities.

In contrast to the fusion of the men, there are references throughout to the splitting of the woman's identity. She feels "she would soon be divided into two and forced to look herself in the face" (Jakobsdóttir 73). This line follows two earlier scenes featuring similar concerns. In the first, worried about sound carrying between the hallway and the bathroom, "her consciousness was divided into two," and with "the ears of the lodger," she listens to everything she does there (45). A few pages later, she views her mirror image as separate from herself—"she stretched out her hand and touched the hard and cold surface of the face opposite her . . . but the image did not flinch from her intimate touch"—and envies the "complete power [that] the image [had] over its surroundings" (48). This dividing in two relates to a gendered double consciousness that compels her to view herself through the eyes of others throughout the story, as her domestic role as an Icelandic woman is constantly subject to the judgmental eye of her community, splintering her sense of herself. For instance, the women she encounters at the store continually "wanted to get her to talk, to sweep back the curtains from her home-life for everyone to see," and she knows her relationship and domestic life "would be judged and seen in relation to" the lodger (47).[32] In the final scene, however, she does not fully split into two but loses feeling until "her whole arm had turned to stone" (78).

Glancing back once more to *Absalom, Absalom!* reveals productive resonances between the unnamed woman in "The Lodger" and the character of Rosa Coldfield in Faulkner's novel, particularly around this doubling. The juxtaposition of the woman's face and her mirror image recalls Rosa recounting her first confrontation with Thomas Sutpen's biracial daughter Clytie on the staircase at Sutpen's Hundred when they "*seemed to glare at one another not as two faces but as the two abstract contradictions which [they] actually were*" (Faulkner, *Absalom, Absalom!* 111). In contrast to the unflinching mirror image in Jakobsdóttir's story, Rosa recoils from Clytie's touch, "*that black arresting and untimorous hand on my white woman's flesh*" (111). Rosa's description highlights the racial difference between the women, with this distinction emphasizing an external separation, while the unnamed woman and her mirror image signal a merging or loss of distinction. Rosa is also the subject of much gossip in her community and interacts with a "lodger" of sorts through her father's self-imposed exile in the attic of his home, electing to starve to death "rather than look upon his native land in the throes of repelling an invading army" (47). And *Absalom, Absalom!* opens itself to spatial allegories as Sutpen's Hundred stands in for the South more broadly, just as "The Lodger" positions the merging men as symbolic of Iceland under foreign occupation—another point of connection between these two seemingly dissimilar texts.

In conclusion, whereas characters in Laxness and Faulkner attempt to clearly delineate difference through the power of language—and, more specifically, repetition and stereotypes—assertions of masculine difference are challenged or even undone in Jakobsdóttir from a woman's perspective, and the complexity of the roles granted to women in Icelandic society, explored further in chapter 3, comes to the fore. As White, male subjects from a certain class background, the men are used to being differentiated and recognized for their specificities and singularities, yet Jakobsdóttir challenges this privilege of individuality from the viewpoint of her narrator while simultaneously exploring the difficulties of negotiating the domestic expectations foisted on Icelandic women.

To pull back once more, the potential for recognition, understanding, and allyship across intersectional lines of difference, spanning gender, race, nation, and class, connects directly back to Iceland's liminal positioning in relation to Europe and the Global South. Former president Ólafur Ragnar Grímsson stated that Iceland's history as "once the poorest country in Europe" could position Icelanders to understand the predicaments of other colonized countries (qtd. in Loftsdóttir, "Belonging" 66–67), which Loftsdóttir accurately unmasks as an example of Icelandic exceptionalism. She writes that Grímsson's comments acknowledge "the affinity with the racialized 'others'" while simultaneously serving to "absolve Iceland from any share in colonialism as a producer of it" (67).[33] Nevertheless, if readings of Icelandic history and culture, such as Loftsdóttir's scholarship, were more widely accepted and centered, and the ways in which Iceland has benefited from colonial hierarchies acknowledged, then perhaps in this complexity Icelanders might deliver on Grímsson's words. In this way, Iceland would be uniquely positioned to understand the predicaments of other marginalized countries across the globe while simultaneously recognizing the ways it has benefited as a nation from global structures of inequity, bringing a unique perspective to international discussions and diplomacy. Building on these points of connection, as opposed to fixating on the lines of difference reified through language, may not dismantle social hierarchies but might nevertheless make possible greater awareness of the structures and their impacts, leading to more robust, sustained solidarities across lines of difference.

Chapter 2

AESTHETIC RADICALS

White Violence as Exclusion in Guðbergur Bergsson, William Faulkner, and Jean Toomer

In an interview discussing depictions of race in US literature, Toni Morrison examines how

> Faulkner in *Absalom, Absalom!* spends the entire book tracing race, and you can't find it. No one can see it, even the character who *is* black can't see it. . . . Do you know how hard it is to withhold that kind of information but hinting, pointing all of the time? And then to reveal it in order to say that it is *not* the point anyway? It is technically just astonishing. As a reader you have been forced to hunt for a drop of black blood that means everything and nothing. The insanity of racism . . . (qtd. in Denard 74)

In this chapter, I investigate William Faulkner's portrayal of this insanity, interpellating the reader into a racist mentality while simultaneously depicting its fanaticism. I explore Faulkner's and Jean Toomer's depictions of Whiteness in the US South alongside Icelandic writer Guðbergur Bergsson's portrayal of sanctioned forms of anti-Blackness and violence in Icelandic society, a connection that reveals much about each region's history and the complexity of colonial and neocolonial dynamics. A comparison between case studies from regions associated with the Global North and the Global South emphasizes the multiplicity within each, as well as the far-reaching negative impacts of colonialism. Both spaces challenge the binaristic concepts common to early

Figure 2.1 This copy of *A Fable* was signed by Faulkner and gifted to Icelandic publisher, Ragnar Jónsson. Faulkner, William. *A Fable*. Random House, 1954. Massey-Faulkner Collection, Albert and Shirley Small Special Collections Library, University of Virginia.

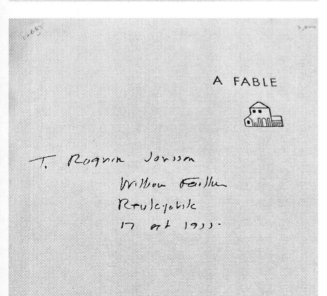

Figure 2.2 Faulkner inscribed the book, "To Ragnar Jonsson. William Faulkner, Reykjavik, 17 Oct. 1955." Faulkner, William. *A Fable*. Random House, 1954. Massey-Faulkner Collection, Albert and Shirley Small Special Collections Library, University of Virginia.

iterations of postcolonial theory, such as core versus periphery, colonizer versus colonized, and even Global North versus Global South. A consideration of these texts in tandem exposes racism as "a global hierarchy of human superiority and inferiority, politically, culturally and economically produced and reproduced for centuries" (Grosfoguel et al. 536) across cultures and societies. In centering depictions of Whiteness in a novel from the Far North alongside three works set in the deep US South, I expose the complex impacts of colonial histories, such as the far-flung webs of racialized violence, as represented in literature from these diverse regions not typically considered together, which in turn complicate global understandings of space.

BERGSSON'S CLOSED MALE WORLD

A prolific writer and societal provocateur whose work spans many styles, Guðbergur Bergsson published his first books in 1961, poetry volume *Repeated Words* (*Endurtekin orð*) and novel *The Mouse That Skulks* (*Músin sem læðist*); his last novel, *Þrír sneru aftur* (*Three Men Return*), was released in 2014.[1] Only two of Bergsson's novels have been translated into English: *Svanurinn* (1991), translated by Bernard Scudder as *The Swan* (1997), and *Tómas Jónsson, metsölubók* (1966), translated by Lytton Smith as *Tómas Jónsson, Bestseller* (2017). To my knowledge, scholarship has yet to analyze *Tómas Jónsson, Bestseller* alongside Faulkner's work, despite the fact that Bergsson's depictions of complex family dynamics and a mythic, Icelandic village in his Tangi cycle have been described as "Faulknerian" in character: "Like Faulkner, Bergsson unveils the ruthless realism that characterizes much human intercourse, however idealistic it may seem on the surface; and rudely realistic and macabre scenes are woven into a modernist text that is disjointed in its occasional employment of the stream-of-consciousness technique and its sometimes absurdist dialogues and descriptions" (Eysteinsson, "Icelandic Prose Literature" 425). Both writers employ similar aesthetic techniques, including the fragmentation and stream-of-consciousness mentioned here, to depict a combination of the realist and macabre, or, in Hosam Aboul-Ela's terms, they use the poetics of peripheralization to convey meaning about the historiography of these peripheralized spaces through form, to which I will return.

Additionally, Bergsson translated Latin American and Spanish fiction into Icelandic. In his afterword to the Icelandic translation of Gabriel García Márquez's *One Hundred Years of Solitude* (1967), he writes, "These are family tales inspired by pure Lutheran or communist thought, but fiddle in a strange and degenerate way with sin, and have the objective of being national symbols, a form of punishment, and a declaration of love to the fatherland, all at once. The best known authors of such love-hate fiction are Hamsun, Faulkner, Laxness, Rúlfo (*sic*), and Marquez" (qtd. in Bjarnadóttir 4). Here Bergsson directly discusses the complexities of Faulkner's work along with those of fellow Icelander Halldór Laxness, discussed in chapter 1; Norwegian Knut Hamsun, whose work—such as *Pan* (1894), set in Norway and India— also lends itself to postcolonial readings; and Mexican Juan Rulfo, whose *Pedro Páramo* (1955) deals with the colonization of Mexico by Spain. According to Birna Bjarnadóttir, Bergsson claims to lack the ability to compare Faulkner's characters with García Márquez's: "fictional worlds that he calls closed, male worlds that smell of rutting and biblical tragedy" (4). Nevertheless, this afterword reveals the extent to which Bergsson read and reflected on Faulkner's work in conversation with other great world writers, particularly his fellow Nordic authors and Latin American writers. The work of Latin American writers, such as García Márquez and Rulfo, have been reciprocally linked to Faulkner's legacy since the 1980s and 1990s, as highlighted through the publication of "A Latin American Faulkner" (1995–1996). This special issue of the *Faulkner Journal* edited by Beatriz Vegh includes articles on Latin American literary responses to Faulkner, as well as reflections by writers like Mexican writer Carlos Fuentes and Argentine writer Juan José Saer on their relationships with Faulkner's writing. The "closed, male worlds" steeped in sexual intrigue and tragedy might have linked García Márquez's novels to Faulkner's in Bergsson's mind, yet this is a connection to his own work as well.

More specifically, in *Tómas Jónsson, Bestseller*, Bergsson literally creates a "closed, male world" within the mind of the titular narrator where all the events of the novel transpire. The entire novel is composed of the ramblings, writings, and surreal vignettes of fictional character Tómas, a retired bank clerk who is writing a memoir from his basement apartment. The novel both parodies and subverts the conventions of biography, which was at the height of its popularity as a genre in Iceland at the time (Eysteinsson, "Icelandic Prose Literature" 423). *Tómas Jónsson, Bestseller* represents "the paradigmatic modernist revolt in the novel lasting the rest of the decade and into the 1970s," remaining "a landmark in Icelandic fiction" (423).[2] Described as "fragmentary" and a "story in compartments" (Bjarnadóttir 192; Sigfús Daðason qtd. in Bjarnadóttir 192), scholars such as Ástráður Eysteinsson have also viewed the novel as Tómas's "collected memory, in its own way encyclopedic in the spirit of enlightenment" (qtd. in Bjarnadóttir 193). Building from Eysteinsson's analysis, Bjarnadóttir describes Tómas as a "satire on the critical, informed, and independent bourgeois citizen" (193), emphasizing the more satirical aspects of the novel as a whole, which are also crucial to my reading.

54 CHAPTER 2

First, I examine the surreal episode Tómas invents during the US occupation of Iceland in World War II, building from the historical agreement that no Black soldiers would be stationed on the island nation to the government-sanctioned murder of a mixed-race baby. This episode, like the novel as a whole, is couched in the narrator's own decrepit White, male body, introducing the decay and degeneration that accompany exploitative cisheteropatriarchal systems. Then I relate this history and the accompanying fiction to the racial codes governing the "protection" of White women's sexuality in the US South via the lynchings of *Light in August*'s Joe Christmas and *Absalom, Absalom!*'s Charles Bon and the corresponding forms of toxic Whiteness and racial fanaticism they reveal. In their failed alignment with the "myth of the Black rapist," both Christmas and Bon unmask Whiteness in all its grotesqueness—spotlighting the perpetrators from Percy Grimm to Henry Sutpen, the latter of whom preserves the memory of this violence in his own decaying White body. These scenes in turn find a parallel in Toomer's "Blood-Burning Moon," which concludes the first section of his Georgia-based collection *Cane* (1923) with an ill-fated interracial love triangle. White violence consumes the story—intentionally thwarting Black male lineage. The types of exclusion enabled by these episodes of violence expose what is valued in each culture grounded in their specific colonial and racial histories: the erasure of Blackness for an imagined "racial harmony" in Iceland versus the endemic exploitation of Black women central to the system of slavery (and its resulting White wealth) in the US South. Black futures are extinguished in Bergsson's Iceland, and the potential for Black love is thwarted in Toomer's South, leaving only White male exploitation imagined as rape. In this way, transhistorical and transgeographical approaches to US southern literature open toward *radical* re-readings—that which Angela Y. Davis defines as simply "grasping things at the root" (*Women, Culture, and Politics* 14). Arising from different social and historical contexts, these examples of racial violence and exclusion, almost to the point of nonexistence, expose the anti-Black, paternalistic, and patriarchal underpinnings of the social, political, and economic systems not just in the United States in the 1860s and the early twentieth century, but also midcentury Iceland, which remain relevant in both countries today.

RACE, GENDER, AND SEXUALITY: ICELAND AND THE US DURING WORLD WAR II

Iceland, a former dependency of Denmark that was occupied by the US military to different degrees between 1941 and 2006 (Hall 22), has been negatively impacted by its complex colonial history, as explored in chapter

1. However, historian Guðmundur Hálfdanarson asserts that Iceland's relationship to Denmark "bore limited resemblance to the imperialist relations between the 19th-century European metropoles and their African and Asian colonies" ("Iceland Perceived" 56). Icelanders benefited from the racial prejudices fueling European imperialism, since they were definitely White, which "sheltered Iceland from the colonial gaze" (Hálfdanarson, "Iceland Perceived" 56). Magdalena Naum and Jonas M. Nordin illustrate Iceland's ambivalent colonial positioning—"identifying itself with imperial Europe and being treated as a colonial subject"—through a comparison with areas like Greenland that were "subjected to the full-blown policies of economic exploitation and civilising quests, similar to those practised in Sámpi" (8). Historically, Icelanders drew on associations of Whiteness with "civilization" and utilized racist stereotypes to differentiate themselves from inhabitants of globally southern colonies, as demonstrated in the previous chapter. Underscoring this liminal positioning, Katla Kjartansdóttir and Kristinn Schram argue that "while Iceland's 'post-colonial condition' can only be a modest counterpart to the gross appropriation of many former colonies in terms of culture, identity and wealth," the exoticism and marginalization Iceland experienced both historically and in the present period is significant (65). Still, Icelanders took advantage of their Whiteness to situate themselves as Europeans, despite their exoticized position at the margins of Europe.

Additionally, Iceland's colonial liminality connects to the colonial ambiguity of the US South, depicted as a colony of the federal government during Reconstruction and as a site of internal colonization of the Black population. Indeed, the US South is a bivalent space, existing within the borders of both the Global South and a "First World" nation. However, neither the US South nor Iceland were officially colonized. According to Ann-Sofie N. Gremaud, postcolonial theories are not precise enough to encompass the complex view of Iceland from a Western perspective ("Iceland as Centre" 89)—"a curious mixture of identification and exotification" and simultaneously core and periphery in relation to Europe (95, 101). Gremaud asserts that Herzfeld's crypto-colonial approach helps to recognize the ways in which Iceland's "primary international relations and dominant cultural narratives" are obscured (101). In addition to its relevance for Iceland, I argue that this recognition may also be useful in examining the social fictions and liminality of the US South as exposed through literature.

It is worth noting a more direct colonial connection between Iceland and the US: while Iceland had broken free of direct Danish influence in 1944 during the Nazi occupation of Denmark, it was invaded by British military forces, which were later replaced by the US military (Loftsdóttir, "Republishing" 300).[3] In 1941, the population of Reykjavík doubled, primarily owing to young

British servicemen and transplants from elsewhere in Iceland; there were over 50,000 soldiers in Iceland at the height of the war, and the population of the country at the time was 120,000 (Oxfeldt et al. 46). This transformed Icelandic society and led to a "strong fear of everything that was new, different or alien" (S. G. Magnússon 233–34). More specifically, according to Kristín Loftsdóttir, the fear that soldiers might corrupt Icelandic women "gained more direct racialized focus with the secret agreement that the Icelandic government made in 1941 with the USA that no 'black' soldiers would be stationed in Iceland" ("Republishing" 300).[4] Giuliano D'Amico notes that "intercourse between Icelandic women and girls and American soldiers was strongly stigmatized" and that this "feeling of otherness also took on racist tones" (463). Regardless of the race of the US soldiers, the drive to "protect" the sexuality of Icelandic women took on a racialized quality in the overzealous response to *Ástandið* ("the Situation") of Icelandic women spending time with Allied troops. Reactions ranged from "the wish to protect young girls from sexual violence to the unabashed eugenic desire to protect the 'Icelandic race' from foreign 'pollution'" (Oxfeldt et al. 46). According to Valur Ingimundarson, this "public policy was never acknowledged openly. What occurred was an attempt to silence a particular truth, to hold aloft myths of tolerance and open-mindedness and then to deny having been in agreement with the policy when the truth eventually came out at the end of the 1960s" (qtd. in S. G. Magnússon 234). This episode in Icelandic history would need to be suppressed to uphold the self-image of the nation as tolerant and progressive. Moreover, while the Icelandic state requested that no Black soldiers were allowed in Iceland during the occupation, the US agreed to this racist policy of exclusion—linking the two spaces through a government-sanctioned anti-Blackness. In fact, the desegregation of the US military did not happen until President Harry S. Truman's executive order in 1948; the US was both agreeing to racist policies abroad and maintaining them within its own ranks. Bergsson's novel spotlights this historical episode and underscores the linked participation of Iceland and the US, which proponents of the vision of Iceland as open-minded and inclusive would prefer to forget.

As the policy was formed specifically to prevent sexual or romantic interactions between Black US soldiers and White Icelandic women, it crystallized the anxiety surrounding interracial sex and mixed-race children, which is mirrored during the same period in the US.[5] The intensive sexual policing of Icelandic women included an all-male "Situation Committee" developed for this purpose; women were "vilified and labelled as traitors to the Icelandic race and the purity of the nation" (S. G. Magnússon 233).[6] Paraphrasing Kristinn Kristjánsson's scholarship, Daisy L. Neijmann notes that "women provided a convenient scapegoat for a national sense of resentment and guilt, as they were a far easier target than the army" ("Soldiers and Other Monsters" 98). She argues that sexual relationships between Icelandic women and soldiers were blamed "almost squarely on the uncontrollable lust of women" (110).[7] This mentality is seen in literary depictions of this period, such as Indriði G. Þorsteinsson's *North of War* (1981; *Norðan við stríð*, 1971).[8] In Þorsteinsson's novel, readers do not get a developed sense of the interiorities of the women involved with soldiers, here primarily the British. One exception to this might be Imba of the Forge, who upon feeling a soldier's hands on her body has "the distinct feeling that she's beginning to be a person" (Þorsteinsson 46)—her sense of identity born from these relationships. For the most part, the narrative voice lingers with the male characters, such as Jon Falkon's misogynistic musings: "Women were like that. They could remain content with shit-asses, thieves, drunks, morons, and good-for-nothings. Otherwise, they got bored" (36). Falkon struggles with his wife's affair with a platoon leader, employing misogynistic terms in reference to her, thinking, "Then, perhaps, she will have to sit up and take notice, that slut. That god-damned slut" (51–52), and later saying, "Shut up, you British whore; you sell yourself for sixpence!" (78). This casual misogyny is echoed by the Communist paper, which later dismisses a missing woman as "a nationally known trollop" (100), and by bus drivers, who when questioned say their vehicles "are full of blonde females in red coats, fur collars, and white boots; they no longer distinguish one from another" (101).[9] Þorsteinsson's physical descriptions of women characters also raise questions about the degree to which this misogyny is critiqued or simply reproduced by the novel—a complexity echoed through Bergsson's depictions of racial stereotypes, to which I will return.[10] Nevertheless, the novel exposes the misogyny present in Icelandic society at the time, which existed alongside the racism and nationalistic fervency discussed above.

Elisabeth Oxfeldt and her collaborators discuss the treatment of Icelandic women during World War II in terms of the value placed on reproduction and maternity as these relate to national identity: "By having sex with foreign men, Icelandic women neglect their duty to bear *Icelandic* children with *Icelandic* men and thus to transmit the perceived national culture and values from one generation to another" (48). This interconnection between family and nationality is also visible in a US context. For instance, Walter Benn Michaels explores what he refers to as "nativist modernism," characterizing some works of American literature from the 1920s, including Faulkner's *The Sound and the Fury* (1929) and Willa Cather's *The Professor's House* (1925). Michaels examines the ways in which ideas of American identity shifted from "the sort of thing that could be acquired (through naturalization) into the sort of thing that had to be inherited (from one's parents)," with family becoming a site of national identity and nationality an effect of racial identity (8). Nativism, positioned as a desire to retain "national culture and values," is intertwined with the presentation of family dynamics in twentieth-century representations of life in both Iceland and the US South, yet it also elucidates hierarchies of identity.

The pressures surrounding the intergenerational transmission of national culture within a family are not only gendered but linked to race and sexuality. In Iceland, these gendered pressures connect to the *Fjallkonan* or the Lady of the Mountain, a figure in Icelandic culture set up as a model for women in terms of faithfulness to nation, culture, and heritage and often depicted in traditional Icelandic national dress (Oxfeldt et al. 44). A countersymbol to the Danish king, the *Fjallkonan* was depicted as an independent mother figure who both embodied and possessed the land (Björnsdóttir 109). During *Ástandið*, this figure was used to shame Icelandic women in their failure to live up to her ideal (Oxfeldt et al. 45). One contemporary commentator argued that women who had relations with soldiers revealed their "'Eskimo and Negro character', claiming that their unpatriotic conduct put them on a level 'with their primitive and half-wild sisters in the South Seas or in Greenland', the absolute opposite to the qualities of the *Fjallkonan*" (Oxfeldt et al. 45). These sentiments expose the way that attempts to control Icelandic women's sexuality were entwined with understandings of national identity and sexualized racial stereotypes. This sexual control over women and the accompanying racial anxieties connect directly to the cult of southern womanhood in the antebellum US South. Through this ideology, White men attempted to retain power over White women—who were seen as "the repositories of white civilization" (Jordan 148), charged with maintaining "pure" lines of descent—while simultaneously institutionalizing the exploitation of enslaved women, illustrating the intersectional nature of racialized sexual policing.[11]

BERGSSON AND WRIGHT: FICTIONALIZED INTERRACIAL INTERACTIONS

Bergsson incorporates the secret historical agreement between Iceland and the US regarding Black soldiers into *Tómas Jónsson, Bestseller* through an italicized vignette entitled "The Black Sheep: A Folk Tale." This episode occurs about halfway through the novel and begins with the line "*As is well known, iceland was occupied during the World War II, first by the dirty British, then later, by request, by a select American army*" (Bergsson 217).[12] Like Faulkner, Bergsson plays with aesthetics in this novel through, for example, the use of capitalization and italics. Iceland is frequently represented with a lower-cased "i," which I argue signals Bergsson's interest in what Eysteinsson describes as "explode[ing] mythic notions that Icelanders have regarding their identity, culture, and independence" ("Icelandic Prose Literature" 424), marrying form and content in line with the poetics of peripheralization.[13] Referred to by Vésteinn Ólason as a "radically modern" writer (86), Bergsson constantly deconstructs "the speech and writing of predecessors and contemporaries, attempting, as I see it, to shock us into awareness of our language" (101). Bergsson's radical modernism emanates from his deconstruction of Icelandic identity and its connections to Whiteness, masculinity, and nationalism, along with his parodies of form and established Icelandic literary conventions, underscoring his use of satire as critique.

More specifically, the scene, positioned as a folk tale, combines a surreal quality with crass descriptions—in line with narrator Tómas's broader style—to describe a sexual encounter between a White Icelandic woman and a Black American sailor, recalling the historical agreement many Icelanders would prefer remained buried. The repetition of phrases such as "*as is well known*," "*it is believed*," and "*the story says*" helps develop the folktale aura with tellers disagreeing on some aspects of the story, such as when and how the interracial couple had "*sexual intercourse*" (Bergsson 217, 218). This speculation incorporates the crasser aspects of Tómas's narration: "*Some say they were in the back seat of an automobile and pulled the seat forward and had their heads and legs sticking out the open door*" and "*some want to maintain that he put the woman up against the mudguard to show off*" (218). Although she consents, the woman, named only once as Anna, does not have much by way of agency in the scene as it is narrated: "*accompanied by a girl he got to follow him*" (218). Similarly, the man is unnamed and referred to only as "*the sailor*" or "*the negro*" (219, 218), highlighting these disruptive aspects of his identity for the insular Icelandic society at this time. As explored in chapter 1, characters and narrators in Faulkner's *Absalom, Absalom!* use dehumanizing language to reify hierarchies of identity, which likewise centers White, male narrative voices while de-emphasizing the stories and experiences of women and people of color.

While the unnamed Black soldier remains undeveloped in Bergsson's novel with neither a voice nor narrative viewpoint, one can look to Richard Wright's short story "Big Black Good Man" (1958), which focuses on the experience of a Black sailor in Copenhagen, to perhaps gain some understanding of his experiences. Although the sailor in Wright's story is not given a narrative perspective either, he both speaks and is central to the story, unlike the sailor in Bergsson's novel, whose main purpose in the plot is to impregnate a White Icelandic woman. Olaf Jenson, a White hotel clerk who interacts with the well-dressed Black sailor in "Big Black Good Man," describes him using repetitive, problematic phrases, such as "the biggest, strangest, and blackest man he'd ever seen in all his life" (Wright 95), "the living, breathing blackness looming above him" (98), "the black mass of power" (103), "the devil of blackness" (103), and "the black giant" (102); this last phrase is repeated three times, and "giant" appears alone another four times on the same page (102). Here another White, male narrator employs dehumanizing language in the attempt to secure his own position of racial privilege. To the same ends, Wright's narrator Olaf alternates between using the pronouns "he/his," and "it/its" for the Black sailor (96), with the latter pronouns calling his humanity into question. The man tells Olaf to write "Jim" on the envelope containing his money before locking it in the safe; it is unclear whether this is truly the man's name or a reference to the Jim Crow system in the US—especially given the man's use of American slang like "Daddy-O" (109), popular in the 1950s and 1960s.

More directly, Olaf notes that "he didn't seem human" (Wright, "Big Black Good Man" 96), which is underscored through his comparison to nonhuman entities throughout his initial depiction: "His chest bulged like a barrel; his rocklike and humped shoulders hinted of mountain ridges; the stomach ballooned like a threatening stone; and the legs were like telephone pools" (96). This description also includes a reference to "its buffalolike head" (96). This relation to the nonhuman both echoes and contrasts with Imba of the Forge in Þorsteinsson's *North of War*, who declares that she only begins to be a person when she feels a soldier's hands on her but also demonstrates more control over how she is positioned. Here, Wright's entire story hinges on Olaf's misreadings of the Black sailor. His racist expectations of the man as violent—"Too big, too black, too loud, too direct, and probably too violent to boot" (96)—culminate in his own violent fantasies of the man's death, wherein everyone on the ship is sacrificed so that "a shark, a *white* one" can eat him (105). The anxiety surrounding interracial sex between Black men and White women is present here as well: although Olaf often sends sex-workers to the rooms of the sailors staying in the hotel, he feels the need to repeatedly describe the man as "big" and "black" to Lena and is uncertain as to why he is "so damned worked up and nervous about a n*** and a white whore?" (100). His language demonstrates the interconnected racism and sexism described above, as well as the dehumanizing power of language itself. The story turns as the reader discovers that the man did not intend to threaten and embarrass Olaf by putting his hands around Olaf's neck before leaving the hotel, and was in fact, not sizing him up but literally sizing him to have "six nylon shirts" made to fit him—one for each night he was with Lena (108). The Black sailor also exchanges letters with Lena while he is away, indicative of deeper feelings that surpass Olaf's assumptions of him. Importantly, while the Black sailor is still externally narrated in Wright's story, he is humanized through Olaf's misreadings, positioning the story as an important correlative extension of Tómas's tale. Faulkner utilizes a similar technique in his story "Pantaloon in Black" in *Go Down, Moses* (1942), in which the protagonist, a similarly large and strong Black man named Rider, is humanized in the readers' eyes through a White sheriff's misreadings of Rider's pain in response to the death of his wife. Misreadings like Olaf's or the sheriff's emphasize the humanity of these characters as a result of the disconnect or gap between the narrators' depictions and the readers' own layered understandings.

In returning to Bergsson's unnamed Black sailor, however, it is clear that the prose de-emphasizes his humanity, as well as that of Anna—"*who had or did not have sex with the sailor*" (219)—through the language and structure of the passage, narrated in Tómas's voice. After Tómas relays eyewitnesses' disagreements over what happens between the sailor and Anna, the sailor disappears entirely from the story without any speculation regarding what has become of him, leaving Anna pregnant "*after this ended*" (219). The dehumanization extends to the baby, who is referred to as "*it*" when not called "*the child*" (219)—although he is described once as being held by "*his*" feet (219)—echoing Olaf's use of both "it" and "he" to refer to the sailor in Wright's story. Most strangely, the doctors diagnose the child as "*manifest[ing] some kind of perversion*" (219): he is supposedly born White but becomes Black in the doctor's hands, which they deduce occurs as a result of contact with the atmosphere. Practically speaking, this distances Anna from accusations of interracial sex, since a more direct acknowledgment that the child was born Black may have put the mother at risk. This change also has the effect of both increasing the surreal feel of the scene and the suspension of disbelief required, harkening back to the blend of the realist and the macabre described earlier, as well as the use of poetics to amplify the meaning—here drawing attention to the anti-Blackness unacknowledged by official accounts. Wright's and Bergsson's comparable techniques, such as pronoun usage and particularly situated White male narrators who showcase anti-Blackness, highlight the overlap in the projects of two writers shaped by southern and northern spaces, respectively.

62   CHAPTER 2

IMAGINED SCENES OF VIOLENCE:
PRESERVING RACIALLY HOMOGENEOUS ICELAND

Although he is the narrator, Tómas also positions himself as a character in
the scene. His involvement is not revealed until halfway through the episode
when he attempts to interrupt the murder of the newborn child: "*Hold off
on any intervention, the office worker Tómas Jónsson answered*" (Bergsson
220). It is unclear throughout whether this is a memory or invented episode;
however, given the tone and the other fantastical episodes among which it
is positioned, it is likely the latter. The doctors do not listen to Tómas and
decide to "*cut the baby's cord and then off it*" (221):

> *The umbilical cord was severed and the body was thrown into the milk
> bucket on the floor and bled to death. But there was so much strength
> to the circulation that the umbilical cord swung to and fro around the
> pail rim like a jet from a powerful water hose and it twisted and buzzed
> on the floor not dissimilar to a wriggling articulated earthworm. The
> body was burned, with its limbs cut off, in a special oven that hospitals
> have, connected to the central system. After that, everyone had a cup of
> strong bitter coffee.* (221)

The grotesque and almost carnivalesque descriptions of the umbilical cord
emphasize the newborn baby's body as a physical threat with "*much strength
to the circulation*" and the comparisons to a "*powerful water hose*" or "*wrig-
gling articulated earthworm.*" Given that the baby is a newborn infant, these
descriptions require the same suspension of disbelief as the baby's changing
skin color. Harkening back to Morrison's quote about the fixation on a drop
of "black blood," the circulation of the infant's blood—here imagined also
as "black blood"—is described as so "strong" that he must be drowned in
white milk.[14] The sexual connotation to the umbilicus, linking to the Black
phallus that created the child in the first place, highlights the connection to
Joe Christmas's castration, discussed below. In this way, the depiction of the
baby's "threatening" body unmasks the racism present in Tómas's telling—
echoing his descriptions of the woman's difficult birth with the "*negro child*"
having "*too large a head for the Icelandic woman's frame*," which, according
to Tómas, demonstrates that "*stubbornness and reluctance were innate in
negroes*" (220). The racism underlining his depiction exists alongside his
censure of the violence and disturbing juxtaposition of the doctors burning
the body of an infant and then enjoying a strong cup of coffee. Consuming a
sudden jolt of black liquid—the figurative opposite of drowning the baby in

white milk—might seem contrary to the goals of expelling a Black presence from Iceland but speaks symbolically to the complications, tensions, and inconsistencies embedded in racist mentalities, here situated with Tómas. The degree to which Tómas is replicating or truly subverting racist tropes remains unclear, like so much else in the narrative, and the extent to which Bergsson's critique is intentional is obscured in this ambiguity.

The fact that the baby is burned and his limbs taken off connects cross-culturally to imagery of lynching in the US, central to both Faulkner's and Toomer's texts, that continued throughout the 1940s when this episode occurs, which I will return to shortly. The child's cremation, or more directly the destruction of evidence of this brutal killing of an innocent baby, ensured there was "*no irrefutable proof that it had been anything other than the brain-child of the office employee who answered the phone*" (Bergsson 222), Tómas, who is promptly fired. The readers are led to position this as Tómas's invention but, as they frequently are throughout the novel, are denied that certainty—realistically reflecting the blurring of memories and imagination heightened with age. As an extension of the bizarre focus on bodies in this episode, the entire vignette exists in his mind and is couched in his decrepit, White male body—its own grotesqueness underscored by the novel's scatological emphases, with an extended focus on bodily functions running throughout the text as a whole. Entrenched hierarchical social formations, represented by and layered within Tómas's body, are themselves revealed as grotesque.

The violence and disturbing tone of the scene highlight the irony of the following paragraph through which Tómas's critique becomes more apparent:

> 'Thus, with snares and sleight of hand, the tendency toward racial hatred and discrimination that would otherwise loom large within the nation, and which other countries must confront and seek a way past, was erased. Had it not been, the birth of this one child would have brought upon our defenseless people the threats racial fanaticism creates'; so read a secret report to the authorities on the matter. (Bergsson 221)

While the subversion is subtle, the flippant tone emphasizes the irony in the fact that the murder of a newborn child was necessary for preventing "*racial hatred and discrimination*" from "*loom[ing] large within the nation,*" which "*other countries must confront and seek a way past.*" Tómas suggests here that through the aggressive absence of racial diversity, including the brutal killing he witnesses and the real-world historical context of the government-sanctioned exclusion of Black soldiers, Iceland avoids directly confronting its underlying racism, which as a result permeates this entire vignette. The irony is heightened through the use of "*defenseless*" to describe not the innocent, coldly slaughtered child but the Icelandic people who might be subject to "*the threats racial fanaticism creates*." Tómas's telling of this episode suggests that the "myths of tolerance and open-mindedness," often linked to Icelandic society in the collective imagination, rest on the violent suppression of otherness. Further, the naive notions that the afore-mentioned secret report relied upon are countered by Ólafur Rastrick's work on the negative reception of jazz in the context of social reform and identity politics ("Not Music" 92). As opposed to simply conservative responses to change, Iceland's negative response to jazz specifically engaged racial themes, such as the stereotypical linkage between Africa, African American music, and "unrestrained eroticism" (Rastrick, "Not Music" 102). Iceland's monoracial demographics did not mean that the society was free from racial prejudice, but that "Icelanders had learned racism not through the intersection of discourse and experience but solely via discourse, because only a small proportion of the community had ever met an African or an African American person, let alone experienced any social conflicts between racial groups" (102). Rastrick's scholarship demonstrates that the absence or suppression of difference does not equate to racial harmony.

RACIST SYSTEMS WITH DIFFERENT INTENTIONS: US SLAVERY VERSUS NAZI GERMANY

Before his dismissal, Tómas somehow gains access to and makes a copy of the letter the Icelandic government sent to the US military administration. The letter contains the following disturbing, illogical passage that, perhaps willfully, entirely mischaracterizes US history, emphasizing Bergsson's use of satire in this episode:

> . . . *you Americans should have adopted such ingenious solutions at the beginning of slavery, and castrated the blacks so none of that dark race outlived their life. A sizable herd of them were taken so as to get some-thing for your ancestors in Africa. Had you applied an equally radical approach against the multiplication of blacks, you would not only have been able to prevent the present and future chaos of racial tension, but also, with time and pillaging, managed to clear the whole of Africa of blacks and thus with that removal and your descendants have removed the old colonial troubles.* (222)[15]

First the racist imagery of the letter, such as the dehumanizing, animalistic language of "*that dark race*," "*a sizable herd*," "*the multiplication of blacks*," connects to Tómas's descriptions of the baby and his unruly umbilical cord, as well as harkening back to the language of Wright's Olaf. A tension exists between the use of irony as critique and the problematic language and imagery of the whole episode, raising again the question of the intended extent of the critique. A generous reading positions this as Bergsson's censure of the underlying racism linking the Icelandic officials' letter to Tómas's broader account, as both are situated in a society unable to "*confront and seek a way past*" this destructive mentality, while an ungenerous reading questions the intentionality.[16] Although narrator Tómas's condemnations are tempered by his replication of stereotypes and problematic imagery, another layer to Bergsson's critique may also exist in his portrayal of Tómas himself, a narrator situated in an Icelandic society that, due to the decisions of government officials, never confronted its racism.

The use of the term *solutions* here also recalls the language of the Nazi regime. "Final Solution," coined by Franz Stuckart as undersecretary of the Reich's Ministry of Interior, refers explicitly to "the general liquidation of the Jews" (Grossman 56, 55). This linguistic connection, in addition to the imagery of burning the infant's body in an oven, links the Icelandic government to the Third Reich, as the bodies of hundreds of thousands of people killed in concentration and extermination camps were cremated in ovens (Van Baar and Huisman 1034). Linking the governments in this way emphasizes the layers of critique in the scene and highlights a broader project of the novel—playing with conceptions of Whiteness, nationalism, and masculinity in relation to Icelandic identity. Bergsson signals this intention from the first page: Tómas's autobiography begins with the lines "I am descended from the bravest, bluest-eyed Vikings. I am related to courtly poets and victorious kings. I am an Icelander" (3).[17] Opening the novel with the narrator's view of his lineage, "descended from the bravest, bluest-eyed Vikings," also underscores associations often drawn between Viking and Norse imagery and Whiteness and more specifically White supremacy. Groups associated with White supremacist ideologies, from the Nazi Party in the 1940s to alt-right groups in the 2020s, have drawn on this imagery, seemingly unaware that Vikings were multicultural and multiracial (Kim).[18] References to the Third Reich appear elsewhere in Bergsson's novel—most memorably in another surreal segment, also italicized, in which an Icelandic opera singer, Katrín Jónsdóttir, is pursued by a young Adolf Hitler. Tómas seems to blame Katrín for Hitler's later actions. Her rejection causes him to hiss, "*If I cannot win you with goodness, I will conquer the world with evil*" (Bergsson 248), and following the episode, we are told *"the Führer's armies advanced into that pigpen, Poland"* (251). This scene illustrates the misogyny characteristic of the text—Tómas himself having been accused of rape—as well as anti-Polish sentiments, with Poland described by Tómas as a "pigpen," another example of the dehumanizing effect of animal imagery.

Additionally, the Icelandic officials composing the letter found by Tómas conflate the Nazi regime's "Final Solution" with the enslavement of Black people in the US: racist systems that had very different intentions, as the former focused on annihilation and the latter on exploitation. The *"multiplication of blacks,"* mentioned here as negative—as it would have also been seen by the Third Reich—increased the wealth of the White enslaver class; castration would not have been in their financial interest, undermining the system as a whole. The vague phrase *"as to get something for your ancestors"* mystifies the purpose behind slavery: the extraction of labor from Black bodies. Thus, the Icelandic officials reveal themselves to be ignorant of the entire purpose of the slave system in the US, in which enslaved Black people fill the role of property or capital while the White plantocracy extracted wealth from their bodies, their labor. This underscores Bergsson's satire of the Icelandic government and their racist—and in this episode, murderous with the death of the baby—policy, and by extension the US government as well. The officials' incongruous understanding of the history of race relations in the US leads them to propose that the castration of enslaved people in the past, like the murder and exclusion employed in Iceland in the present episode, could have somehow eradicated racial tensions in the US (yet, as we know from Rastrick's work, absence does not equal acceptance). This suggestion, however, calls to mind the dismemberment, including castrations, often involved in the lynching of Black Americans, which was endemic in the post-emancipation period when the destruction of enslaved people, who doubled as property, was no longer tantamount to economic loss. Therefore, the Icelandic officials' absurd revision of US history resonates with the very real racial violence rampant during the same period in the US.

In spite of Bergsson's Icelandic officials and their ignorance, readers knowledgeable about the history of enslavement in the US are nevertheless left with a sense of connection between violence and exclusion. This includes the forms sanctioned by the Icelandic officials in this episode and historically through the agreement that no Black servicemen would be stationed in Iceland, as well as the lynch culture pervasive in the US South in the same period and explored in a number of Faulkner's novels. A 2017 report by the Equal Justice Initiative documents that there were at least "4084 racial terror lynchings in twelve Southern States between the end of Reconstruction in

1877 and 1950" (*Lynching in America*), and in 2020 the same group reported at least 2,000 lynchings during the twelve years of Reconstruction alone (*Reconstruction in America*). Moreover, "the last known spectacle lynching" occurred in 1981 in Mobile, Alabama (Lightweis-Goff 15), more than a century after Reconstruction. Aliyyah Abdur-Rahman describes White racial violence as "*a will to whiteness*": the "routinized, ritualized violence of the lynching act" and pervasive White participation expose the need for evidence that the racial order of slavery was intact, reflecting "profound insecurity around the stability and supremacy of whiteness in the post-Reconstruction era" ("White Disavowal" 189). The lynch culture and reinvigorated White violence in this era resulted from the destabilization of hierarchies that was feared to accompany emancipation.

READING FAULKNER THROUGH BERGSSON: RACIAL VIOLENCE AS EXCLUSION

How, then, does reading Bergsson change how we read racial violence in Faulkner? Reading Faulkner through the lens of Bergsson may cause us to focus anew on the ways in which the deliberate murder and castration of Black men should be understood not only as an attempt to reinforce plantation hierarchies, but also as a form of racial exclusion through thwarting the generations to come. Most overtly, Joe Christmas of *Light in August* is castrated as well as lynched—in line with the "solution" to racial tensions in the US proposed by the Icelandic officials. Murder as exclusion becomes explicit in this example through the destruction of genealogy and lineage, preventing the present generation from thriving and future generations from existing. In other words, while castration limits the possibilities for interracial sex, it is also a preventative against procreation—eliminating the need for the murder of a baby, as in the Bergsson episode. This connection is made plain in the surreal segment toward the end of Ralph Ellison's *Invisible Man* (1952): an imagined castration causes the narrator to be "*free of illusions*" (569), watching his "*generations wasting upon the water—*" (570). Through this fictional mutilation, the narrator is relieved of any illusions of inclusion in the nation's future, a goal he pursues throughout the novel. If future generations are destroyed, then differences are flattened and biases are seemingly removed, in line with the mentality of the Icelandic officials who believe that the only way to protect the community from "*racial hatred*" is by excluding or destroying everyone racially different—reverberations of the Nazi regime's "Final Solution." This comparison to the overt exclusion in Bergsson reveals similar fears and sentiments underlying both examples. With the failure of the US government to make lynching a federal crime until 2022, this racial violence and exclusion should be seen as sanctioned by the US government, echoing the state-sponsored violence depicted in Bergsson's novel.[19]

Reading Faulkner alongside Bergsson causes us to reconsider the stakes of lynching on both individual and communal levels, particularly because Faulkner's portrayal of lynching in his novels centers the mania of White racism. Bergsson too emphasizes the roles of the White perpetrators in the violence they inflict, with more attention granted to the doctors, nurse, and Tómas than the Black soldier or the biracial baby, who are neither named nor humanized. Both Charles Bon's death at Henry's hands as reconstructed by Quentin and Shreve in *Absalom, Absalom!* and Joe Christmas's death and castration by Percy Grimm in *Light in August* emphasize the link between violence and exclusion through the impact of these deaths on future generations. Bon, Christmas, and their descendants will not be included in the national imaginary—an outcome that also highlights grotesque White hatred and fear of difference.

Faulkner's *Absalom, Absalom!* centers on the experiences of the Sutpen family before, during, and after the Civil War, including the patriarch Thomas and his children, Judith and Henry. Henry, White male heir to the Sutpen plantation, repudiates his inheritance for Charles Bon, his friend and Judith's fiancé, who is later revealed as the siblings' half brother, before shooting Bon. In the final retelling of Bon's death, Henry is depicted as racially motivated, which is made overt through Bon's statement that he is not Henry's brother but *"the n*** that's going to sleep with your sister. Unless you stop me, Henry"* (Faulkner, *Absalom, Absalom!* 286). Generations later, Sutpen's biracial daughter Clytie sets fire to the plantation, Henry, and herself. Faulkner's *Light in August*, meanwhile, focuses on the journeys of a pregnant White woman, Lena Grove, and a racially ambiguous man passing for White, Joe Christmas; the novel ends with his death. Like Bon's statement to Henry, Christmas's murderer, Percy Grimm, makes Christmas's purported sexual threat explicit. Grimm asks Reverend Hightower in the moments before shooting and castrating Christmas, "Has every preacher and old maid in Jefferson taken their pants down to the yellowbellied son of a bitch?" (Faulkner, *Light* 464). Just after, he "sprang back, flinging behind him the bloody butcher knife. 'Now you'll let white women alone, even in hell,' he said" (464). The fact that the preachers and old maids have the agency to take down their pants implies that it is not a lack of consent that Grimm finds threatening but what he imagines to be the expansive nature of Christmas's sexual partners, crossing lines of race and gender. Faulkner describes Christmas's "pent black blood" that rushed "like released breath" (465), which echoes the *strong circulation* of the baby's "black blood" in the Bergsson vignette and the mania surrounding a "drop of black blood" that, according to Morrison, "means everything and nothing." This fixation on blood showcases the anxiety surrounding the infiltration—or, alternatively framed, the inclusion—of Black individuals into White families and communities, which links the twentieth-century US southern and Icelandic societies.[20]

In my previous work, I've analyzed how Faulkner subverts the myth of the Black rapist in these scenes of lynching through the characters' racial ambiguity and the absence of rape, yet, like all of Faulkner's most complex moments, a multitude of contradictory layers is built into these scenes.[21] For instance, in their disruption of racial and gendered stereotypes, Christmas and Bon redirect focus toward the perpetrators of the violence they face, as well as the ways in which the perpetrators' misreadings serve as justification for this violence. In this way, they expose the devastating and self-destructive effects of Whiteness—ranging from the systematic vigilantism of Percy Grimm to Henry Sutpen's disavowal and ultimate annihilation of Charles Bon. After shooting his beloved friend and brother to prevent his sister from having interracial sex, Henry disappears from the novel, only reemerging the night Quentin solves the mystery of who or what is hiding at the old Sutpen place: "the wasted yellow face with closed, almost transparent eyelids on the pillow, the wasted hands crossed on the breasts as if he were already a corpse; waking or sleeping it was the same and would be the same forever as long as he lived" (Faulkner, *Absalom, Absalom!* 298). The weight of Henry's racialized violence has been submerged under the skin of his aging White body for generations, again calling attention to the corrosive impact of cisheteropatriarchal structures. Henry's "wasted yellow face" also calls to mind the phrase "high yellow," representing a light-skinned biracial person in the US, which ironically links Henry visually to the interracial mixture he detests. As a pivotal secret around which the novel is structured, Henry and his decaying Whiteness take up residence in the center of this circuitous novel, emphasizing the novel's focus on the impact of racial violence on the White characters.

Faulkner also centers the White perpetrator of violence in the scene of Joe Christmas's lynching. The entire episode leading up to his death focuses on the character of White supremacist, Percy Grimm, with Christmas only appearing briefly from the perspective of Grimm and other men with him. Critics have interpreted Percy Grimm and his actions in a variety of intersecting ways, positioning him, for example, as a "protofascist" or "a sadly unironic forerunner to the militarized 21st-century Caucasian" (Lightweis-Goff 83; Worley and Birkhofer 336). Abdur-Rahman argues that Grimm functions "as the white phallic authority that attempts to rejuvenate and restore white racial hegemony" ("White Disavowal" 189), and indeed, other critics have analyzed the intersection of race, sexuality, and gender here. Jay Watson builds on John N. Duvall's suggestion that the scene engages "the problematic of male homosexual panic" (Duvall 60), connecting the town's "panic" over Christmas with Judith Butler's conceptualization of "gender trouble," culturally incomprehensible behavior that reveals the constructedness and performativity of gender (Watson 150). Rebecca Nisetich, meanwhile, refers to Grimm's murder and castration of Christmas as "a profoundly violent attempt to stabilize Christmas's identity by defining his race. And yet, the scene itself underscores Christmas's pan-sexuality and his protean racial identity. Grimm's act of castration does not stabilize his victim's gender identity but permanently blurs it" (60). This reading centers the instability of intersectional identity categories in the novel and the distress it causes White male characters like Grimm, which I agree is a central element of this scene: Christmas's identity is blurred through the focus on White reactionary responses.

Reading Faulkner through the lens of Bergsson also brings Grimm's proto-Nazi tendencies to the fore through the linked projects of White exclusion and destruction. Daniel Spoth describes Faulkner's own awareness of Grimm's fascist associations, depicting him in a letter to Malcolm Cowley as a "Fascist galahad who saved the white race by murdering Christmas" and claiming he had "created a Nazi before [Hitler] did" (Spoth 239). Chuck Jackson emphasizes that "the novel's simultaneous articulation of and collapse between the National Guard and the Southern lynch mob [is] a representation of whiteness as a racialized force of history and terror" (194), and Paul M. Worley and Melissa Birkhofer assert that Grimm "represents the structural realities of a system that normalizes violence against black and brown bodies" (336). This emphasis on the systemic implications of Grimm's violence is in line with my own reading of Grimm through the lens of Bergsson, emphasizing his fixation on "preserv[ing] order" by containing the disruptive aspects of Christmas's identity (Faulkner, *Light* 451). Grounding the violent death of Christmas, a main character, within the subjectivity of Grimm, the proto-Nazi embodiment of the White cishetereopatriarchy, forces readers to read Christmas on Grimm's terms.

Grimm's mentality in this scene illustrates Jennie Lightweis-Goff's definition of pathological racism as "dedicated to perpetuating the lie that empowered racial others constitute a 'common danger' that will infiltrate and destroy the community via sexual and cultural miscegenation" (13). Both Grimm's final words to Christmas about White women and Bon's words to Henry, in which he situates himself as potential Black rapist, highlight the perceived "common danger" and sexual threat to the community embodied by these racially ambiguous men. The misreadings of these men have high stakes, resulting in their deaths. Just as Anna, while consenting, is an absent presence whose agency is obscured in Bergsson's vignette, the agency of the White women in these examples—Joanna Burden, Christmas's consensual lover, and Judith Sutpen, Bon's betrothed—is masked or even ignored to uphold the illusion of threat to White women's sexuality. Granting more attention to these absent voices would help readers to understand characters like Christmas, Joanna, Bon, and Judith, as well as Bergsson's Black solider and Anna, on their own terms, as opposed to within a White patriarchal mentality. However, I'd argue that neither Faulkner nor Bergsson intend to reconstruct overlooked presences but instead work to emphasize the impact of White violence and racism on the White male characters.

Through the decision to narrate Christmas's death via Grimm's perspective, Faulkner spotlights Grimm's White southern pathological mindset and its resulting violence, situating readers within his "sublime and implicit faith in physical courage and blind obedience, and a belief that the white race is superior to any and all other races and that the American is superior to all other white races . . ." (*Light* 451). Faulkner underscores Grimm's measured, methodical response to what he views as a sexual threat to his community through the repetition of certain phrases in this section. Grimm is described as having a "cold and detached expression" and as being "without heat" twice on the same page (454, 455), as well as "indefatigable, restrained yet forceful" and "indefatigable, not flesh and blood" (453, 462), with " blind and untroubled faith in the rightness and infallibility of his actions" (459). Deliberate and controlled, Grimm's violence is positioned opposite a frenzied mob mentality: he is methodical and unemotional, with a simplistic and single-minded belief in his actions and "nothing vengeful about him either, no fury, no outrage," a dispassion even Christmas can see (461). This act of violence is not personal for Grimm but part of what he sees as his responsibility to his White community. Grimm's pathological combination of nationalism, White supremacy, and their violent effects takes center stage with the death of Joe Christmas. By narrating the murder through the perspective of this seemingly minor character, Faulkner emphasizes Grimm's fanaticism and exposes the cold brutality of White violence, while simultaneously leading us to read Christmas within Grimm's White pathological frame. Connections back to the Icelandic government's policy of exclusion and the echoes of Nazi ideology, fascism, and extremism examined above amplify the stakes for the disruption of White supremacist mentalities and structures across cultures—stakes that have major implications for our current moment.

By centering White violence and the resulting exclusion of racially inde-terminant men from the national imaginary in both novels, Faulkner might recognize his own complicity as a White southerner. However, this recogni-tion doesn't actively challenge the structures of anti-Blackness, paternalism, and patriarchy in any concrete way. Similarly, Henry Sutpen's rejection of his father's wealth—or, a more fitting example, Isaac McCaslin's repudiation of his family's legacy in *Go Down, Moses* (1942)—can be viewed as acknowl-edgment of his complicity in an unjust system, yet neither action leads to structural change. Ending on Henry's "wasted yellow face" and death in the fire again centers the decrepit White male body and the impact of racial violence on White people, similar to the effect of narrating Christmas's death from the perspective of a fanatical White supremacist, who reads it as "pent black blood" rushing "out of his pale body" (465). Centering Whiteness (and maleness) in this way and zeroing in on the actions, reactions, and complicity of White male characters—from Tómas, the doctors, and govern-ment officials in the Bergsson vignette to Henry, Percy, and Ike in Faulkner's novels—unmasks its destructive power.

A SHIFT IN EMPHASIS:
RACIAL VIOLENCE IN TOOMER'S "BLOOD-BURNING MOOD"

To conclude this chapter, I turn to a final example of White violence as exclusion in the short, lyrical story closing the first section of US writer Jean Toomer's *Cane*, set in rural Georgia. While the insidious effects of Whiteness are central to the story, Toomer grants more space to the experiences of the Black and biracial characters than the previous examples I have explored, providing an essential correlative or even corrective. Toomer only visited the Deep South twice, for a total of less than three months (Ramsey 74), yet his depiction resonates profoundly with others, including his friend and fellow writer Waldo Frank, who declares in the foreword, "This book *is* the South" (Frank 138).[22] Toomer, a multiracial writer, described himself as "Scotch, Welsh, German, English, French, Dutch, Spanish, [and] some dark blood" (qtd. in Banks 293), echoing the fixation on blood as racial-ized in Morrison, Faulkner, and Bergsson. He refused to subscribe to the Black/White binary or identify as either Black or White, instead claiming to be a member of the American race (Banks 293), which offers a complex nuance for the idea of racial purity that Icelandic and US southern ideolo-gies glorified. "Blood-Burning Moon" reveals the lingering attachment to White supremacist and misogynist mentalities in place in the US since the days of enslavement—comparable to both the murder of the biracial baby in Bergsson's novel and the lynchings in Faulkner's. The White lynch mob's violence in Toomer's story has the effect of preventing the coupling of a Black man, Tom Burwell, and a presumably biracial woman, Louisa, destroying the potential for Black male lineage and reproducing the forms of exclusion discussed above. The force of the White mob's violence overpowers the story, taking agency away from Louisa and ending Tom's life. This example elucidates even more clearly that these moments of exclusionary violence take different shapes based on the specific racial and colonial histories of each space. In this way, the depictions of sexualized racism found in Bergsson and Faulkner can also be traced through "Blood-Burning Moon." While the effects of White violence spotlighted in Bergsson and Faulkner remain central in Toomer's story, through his aesthetics and representational choices, he invests more in the experiences of Black and biracial characters and the impacts on their lives and futures. Indeed, the form of Toomer's story amplifies its sociohistorical concerns in line with the poetics of peripheralization.

Louisa, a light-skinned woman positioned as Black in the story, is simultaneously pursued by both Bob Stone, the White son of the factory owner, and Tom Burwell, who typically works away from her in the fields. Each man wants to possess her independently of the other, and neither seems to give much credence to her desires. The story takes a turn when, after discovering "the huddled forms" of Tom and Louisa together (Toomer 33), Bob instigates a fight, takes out a knife, and ultimately has his throat cut by Tom. The racial codes of the US South dictate that Tom, a Black man, must die as a result, and he is soon "swarmed" by the White men in the community, who burn him alive at the factory (34). As Susan L. Blake notes, the chaos in the story "results from the conflict between natural and social laws": the former allow the Black and White men to each compete for Louisa, yet the latter prevent the Black man from winning, even if the White man himself doesn't win (523). However, when the violence of the White mob takes over, its destruction leaves us with no story, no future for the characters.

As described above, both Tom and Bob want Louisa to be their "gal" or "girl," claiming to love her, though neither holds much care for her wishes in the situation. For example, Tom dismisses Louisa's protest to his claim that he will "cut" Bob (on which he delivers) with "I said I would an there aint no mo to it" (Toomer 30–31). Allan G. Borst draws on Eve Sedgwick's analyses of homosocial desire to argue that "Stone and Burwell's sexual fantasies about Louisa boil down to fantasies about each other" (19), which silences her voice and turns Louisa into an object to be won (16–17), echoing the love triangle between Judith, Henry, and Bon in *Absalom, Absalom!* In trying to possess her, Tom and Bob can prove their masculinity to themselves and to each other. Beyond this, the men also use Louisa to position themselves racially, in line with the community's efforts to stabilize Joe Christmas's identity in *Light in August* by treating him in accordance with racial stereotypes.[23] Robert Arbour asserts that "Louisa becomes a site of interracial contact, although each man ostensibly sees in her an opportunity for the assertion of his own racial identity" (322), and the story emphasizes the interplay between the men in terms of their racial difference. In Louisa's mind, "[Tom's] black balanced, and pulled against, the white of Stone, when she thought of them" (Toomer 28), and yet the men are not physically described beyond their respective Blackness and Whiteness. However, Louisa's skin and breasts are emphasized, in accordance with the sexualization of light-skinned biracial women, dating back to the trope of the "tragic mulatto": "Her skin was the color of oak leaves on young trees in fall. Her breasts, firm and up-pointed like ripe acorns" (28). Although never directly positioned as biracial or multiracial, since we are not given access to her family history or backstory, the readers can deduce as much from the comparison between her skin and "the color of oak leaves." Additionally, the odd inclusion of her breasts as "ripe acorns" links this description of her physical body directly to the beauty of the natural world and trees specifically, a trope running through many of the poems and vignettes in *Cane*.

As the object of desire for the two men, Louisa would seem to be at the center of the narrative. Yet, as Blake argues, while Toomer's stories appear superficially to be about the women, the real interest "is in the men who labor to possess them," with the "silent, passive, elusive" women representing "the experience that the men are trying to grasp" (517).[24] This places more emphasis on the women's impact on the men—as something intangible they want to hold on to—than on the women as fully formed, knowable entities, similar to Bergsson's vague portrayal of Anna. The language of possession is used to refer to the men's feelings for Louisa. While the narrator states that Bob "loved her," he continues that "[b]y the way the world reckons things, he had won her" (Toomer 28). This sounds less like the love of another human being than the acquisition of a prized object through sport, dehumanizing her in line with Bergsson's and Wright's use of animal imagery. Moreover, Tom has a visceral physical response to a comment about Louisa and Bob: "Blood ran up Tom's neck hotter than the glow that flooded from the stove. He sprang up. Glared at the men and said, 'She's my gal'" (29), before instigating a physical altercation. Bob has a comparable reaction, though layered with his own racist language and sentiments: "No sir. No n*** had ever been with his girl. . . . Some position for him to be in. Him, Bob Stone, of the old

Stone family, in a scrap with a n*** over a n*** girl. In the good old days . . . Ha! Those were the days. His family had lost ground . . ." (32). For Bob, these feelings of possession regarding "his girl" are entangled with his nostalgia for his family's more overt privileges under the system of enslavement—in his mind, "the good old days." His musings reveal his complicated senti-ments: at the same time that he wants to own "his girl" Louisa, he recognizes her humanity (although "girl" is a less respectful acknowledgment than "woman"). This differentiates his from a true enslaver mentality, according to which she would be property, an object along with livestock and furniture, with whom he could never claim to be in a relationship as "his girl."

Tom draws connections to the past when he suggests that "White folks always did do for n*** what they likes" (Toomer 30), yet he also believes some of the dynamics present during enslavement have fallen away: "An then besides, white folks aint up t them tricks so much nowadays" (30). Tom implies that in the present setting of Toomer's text, White people do not take advantage of their unrestrained sexual access to women of color to the same extent as they did during enslavement. However, he also seems unable to envision nonexploitative relations between a White man and bira-cial woman (Williams 96), which is arguably what exists between Bob and Louisa. Complicating the relationship dynamics further, Bob also appears to yearn for the simplicity of the days to which Tom alludes. Passing the house that served as the "plantation cookery" during enslavement, "his mind became consciously a white man's," and he envisions Louisa bent over the hearth: "He went in as a master should and took her. Direct, honest, bold. None of this sneaking that he had to go through now" (Toomer 31).[25] While I disagree with the narrator that Bob in fact "loves" Louisa, given the lack of care mentioned above, his feelings seem to be more layered than even he is able to acknowledge: "He was going to see Louisa to-night, and love her. She was lovely—in her way. N*** way. What way was that? Damned if he knew" (31). For him, her loveliness is enmeshed with her racial identity and his understanding of its connotations. He doesn't understand why he is drawn to her or what role her racial difference plays in his attraction: "She was worth it. Beautiful n*** gal. Why n***? Why not, just gal? No, it was because she was n*** that he went to her. Sweet . . ." (32). I agree with scholars like Charles Harmon, who argues that Bob is "attracted to Louisa precisely because her race connotes for him images of tabooed sexual release" (95); however, I'd leave space for more complexity here as well. The ambiguous core of Bob's feelings for Louisa defies any neat formulations. Drawn to her difference, he alternately dehumanizes her as a prize or a possession, while also claiming her as "his girl." If his mind at times becomes "consciously a white man's," then what is it the remainder of the time? The mind of a less self-aware White man?

Regardless of the nuances of individual feelings, Bob Stone's imaginings and direct connections back to his family's position during enslavement illustrate the linkage between sex and property, Black labor and White wealth. Exploitative sex with Black and biracial women was a White male privilege, in addition to its economic advantages in producing more Black bodies/ laborers (A. Y. Davis, *Women, Race, and Class* 183). Adrienne Davis argues that "enslaved black women gave birth to white wealth" (117), while Jennifer Morgan asserts that the "reproductive lives" of enslaved women were "at the heart of the entire venture of racial slavery" (4). Thus, in the words of Kimberly Juanita Brown, there is "no telling of this story without making black women central, no way to see the indexical force of the horrendous event of transnational slavery unless the way of seeing, the sight and the sound of it, is rearticulated and black women are at the center of the frame" (17). By focusing on a biracial woman—whose own body and lineage are a testament to this sexual violence—Toomer is able to critique both the exploitation of Black and biracial women and the violence toward Black men without reinscribing the myth of the Black rapist.[26] In Brown's terms, of the examples surveyed in this chapter, Toomer's story would come closest to accurately depicting the histories of slavery, due to the more central role given to Black and biracial women's experiences—although still narrated from without. Jennifer Williams, for example, asserts that Toomer "challenges popular narratives of lynching by placing a black woman at the center of the conflict and crafting a black man as a protector" (96). At the same time, the "patriarchal underpinnings of chivalry do not go unnoted," and Toomer's story "recasts the players in the lynching drama consistent with a history of sexualized racism" (Williams 96). While his representations still leave much to be desired, Toomer attempts to make central the experiences of a biracial woman in this depiction of interracial violence. He tries to complicate more typical representations of the violence of lynch culture in a way that emphasizes the destructive aspects of this violence on Black and biracial bodies in the present, as well as on future generations, that is, as a way to extinguish Black male lineage as a form of exclusion. Toomer's formal choices in the final scene of the story, including the representation of the White mob and the impact of violence on Tom's body, stand out in contrast to the episodes explored previously. Whiteness still has a nefarious part to play in Toomer's story, and its destruction overwhelms the narrative, yet as a result of his aesthetics, the impact of this violence on the White perpetrators is given less space than its effect on the Black recipient.

The power of the White mob at the end of this story decimates all traces of the love triangle, as well as the characters' individual agency, emphasizing the story's "clear indictment of Southern racial codes" that emerged from the US South's specific racial histories (Ramsey 85). The dominance of the White mob is depicted:

> White men like ants upon a forage rushed about. . . . Shotguns, revolvers, rope, kerosene, torches. . . . They came together. The taut hum rose to a low roar. Then nothing could be heard but the flop of their feet in the thick dust of the road. The moving body of their silence preceded them over the crest of the hill into the factory town. It flattened the Negros beneath it. It rolled to the wall of the factory, where it stopped. (Toomer 34)

And as Tom dies the mob is described yelling like "a hundred mobs yelling" (34), emphasizing the frenzied power of this communal force. We are never introduced to any individual White participants beyond the collective, denying them that specificity in the reverse of a core racist tenet; instead, Toomer offers only the visual force of them as foraging ants rushing about, their low roar, and the power of their rolling silence, which has the impact of flattening the Black people present. They "poured down" on Tom and "swarmed" like wasps now instead of ants, binding him and dragging him to the factory where he is burned alive and can be "seen within the flames" (34). The fire here links back to Clytie's burning of Sutpen's Hundred and Henry's death in the flames, as well as the burning of the biracial baby's body in Bergsson. Each story, novel, vignette ends on this specific form of destruction, symbolizing the layering of loss—here, not only of Tom's life, but also his and Louisa's agency and capacity for love. While his use of fire imagery parallels that of the other writers, Toomer's use of animal imagery reverses the textual dehumanization with the White characters depicted as wasps and ants.

Whereas the power of the White mob is significant here as a composite entity, Toomer provides narrational space to Tom as an individual and the physicality of his experience when he is caught. Toomer centers Tom's experience of shock, stiffening, and flight: "Tom knew that they were coming. He couldnt move. And then he saw the search-lights of the two cars glaring down on him. A quick shock went through him. He stiffened. He started to run" (34). The depiction of the scene of the baby's death in Bergsson is told from the viewpoint of Tómas, and Joe Christmas's lynching is situated by Faulkner through Percy's perspective; however, the gaze on Tom here is not fixed within a particular White subjectivity. Given the anonymity of the

White bodies in the mob, more narrational weight is given to Tom's singular experiences. The depiction of his death emphasizes the impact on his body: "Tom's wrists were bound," and "his breast was bare. Nails' scratches let little lines of blood trickle down and mat into the hair. His face, his eyes were set and stony"; ultimately, with the flames engulfing him, witnesses can see "only his head, erect, lean, like a blackened stone. Stench of burning flesh soaked the air. Tom's eyes popped. His head settled downward" (34). Alain Solard argues that in accepting his death "stoically, a silent victim," Tom is positioned as "a Christ figure whose hair is matted with blood as if he were wearing a crown of thorns" (559), adding even more weight to the significance of his death.[27] Toomer does not let the reader turn away from the physical ramifications of this violence on Tom's body—from his bound wrists and the cuts on his head to the impact of the heat on his eyes. In this way, Toomer's depiction can be taken as a corrective to those of Faulkner and Bergsson through its focus on the Black recipient of the violence, more so than the White perpetrators or decaying White male bodies. His emphasis centers the residual impacts on the generations to come, such as the erasure of the potential for love and the decimation of any hypothetical future generations, while also representing a space for questioning and resisting the structures and scripts presently in place.

As Williams succinctly states, Toomer's scene of lynching reveals "anxieties around race, gender, class, and nation at a moment in which these categories were being recodified," with the racial legislation resting upon "the regulation of sexual desire through both extralegal forms of violence as well as legal forms of segregation and anti-miscegenation statutes" (96). As depicted by Toomer, the racial violence specific to the US South during this transitional early twentieth-century moment is overwhelming and destructive. However, in addition to calling attention to the impacts of the legacy of plantation slavery in the US, Toomer's account simultaneously leaves space for individuals' attempts to resist the scripts that history has written for them. According to Harmon, while Tom and Bob live and die according to "Southern racial orthodoxies," there might be the roots of something positive in both men's seeming skepticism, revealing a change: "instead of unquestioningly identifying with racial norms, people in Toomer's South lynch and are lynched out of a sense of obligation toward what they think they ought to feel as blacks and as whites" (95). For Harmon, Toomer creates space for individuals to question their own entrenched mindsets. A step beyond this questioning of historical racial dynamics is an acknowledgment of one's own positioning within them and the potential for more impactful shifts away from the status quo.

To conclude, while from a twenty-first-century perspective, neither Bergsson's nor Faulkner's subversions take the critique of racism in Iceland and the US South far enough, they do shift the needle incrementally in the direction of progress. In comparison, Toomer's story extends this work in more overt and comprehensive ways, unmasking the colonial histories and White supremacist structures linking the two distinct spaces.[28] Though flawed, Toomer's essential inclusion of Black and biracial women's experiences and his focus on the heavy impact of racial violence on Black bodies alter the White-centric narrative around lynch culture, avoid the reinscription of the myth of the Black rapist and White women as victims, and clear space for shifts in individuals' relationships to history. I'll continue to explore the unmasking of colonial histories and hierarchical structures in chapter 3, where I analyze the interaction of gender nonconformity and sexual fluidity in novels by US southerner Carson McCullers and Icelander Halldór Laxness. While the novels explored in the next chapter are less overtly concerned with the violence of colonial histories, the aftereffects of these hierarchical dynamics remain present, as revealed through a focus on liminal characters in these liminal spaces.

Chapter 3

"I'M SICK OF BEING A GIRL!"

Nonconformity and Intersecting Hierarchies of Identity in Halldór Laxness and Carson McCullers

Mick Kelly, the young protagonist of US southern writer Carson McCullers's *The Heart Is a Lonely Hunter* (1940), refuses the traditional position of woman as wife after her first spontaneous sexual experience with Harry Minowitz. Following the act, during which Mick felt like "her head was broke off from her body and thrown away" (McCullers, *Heart* 274), she emphatically states, "I didn't like that. I never will marry with any boy" (275). Salka Valka, beloved heroine of Icelandic writer Halldór Laxness's novel *Salka Valka* (1931, first translated into English in 1936 and again in 2022), reacts to her mother Sigurlína Jónsdóttir's mistreatment by her fiancé, Steinþór Steinsson, as opposed to her own direct experience.[1] Steinþór's continual rejection of her and simultaneous desire for Salka leads Sigurlína to take her own life. When friend, tutor, and future love interest Arnaldur Björnsson asks why she is wearing "such an ugly jacket" (Laxness, *Salka Valka* 95), described earlier as "a man's jacket" (86), Salka does not cite her poverty but thoughtfully replies, "I'm going to get some trousers soon, too, and stop being a girl" (95). Through this comment she demonstrates an understanding of gender as a social construct that predates Judith Butler's formulations of gender as performative or "the stylized repetition of acts through time" by almost sixty years (520). It also conveys Salka's belief that she has the agency to "becom[e] a boy" (Laxness, *Salka Valka* 105), as well as a distinction between gender and biological sex. Salka later reveals a direct connection between this impulse and her mother's treatment: "I'm sick of being a girl! I will never, ever become a woman—like my Mama!" (120). In their rejection of what they consider to be feminine roles and behaviors, from having sex to wearing skirts, these girls refuse to be caught within the confines of approved womanly behavior sanctioned by their societies. Mick and Salka also share this impulse with another of McCullers's infamous gender nonconforming heroines, Frankie Addams in *The Member of the Wedding* (1946). Considering the gender nonconformity and broader queerness of McCullers's young protagonists alongside Salka Valka centers the interaction of multiple forms of liminality in the novels, spotlighting connections between gender, sexuality, race, and coloniality.

These young heroines disidentify from traditional understandings of what it means to be a girl in their respective societies to carve out their own space within the confines of gender roles. Despite their limited means and inability to fit in with their communities, Salka, Mick, and Frankie reject their societies' versions of girlhood and have the agency to invent their own. Even in literature not blatantly about colonialism, its aftereffects are present in the hierarchical societal dynamics depicted in these coming-of-age novels, spanning gender, class, race, and sexuality. In McCullers's and Laxness's novels, parallel examples of resistance link two societies not typically considered together. Exploring these novels in tandem brings to the fore corresponding intricacies of each girl's identity, such as gender nonconformity and sexual fluidity, spotlighting nondominant identities within liminal spaces. While these intricacies of identity have been centered more fully in previous scholarship on McCullers than that on Laxness, this comparative reading not only brings them to light in Laxness's work through the proximity between the two, but also encourages a reading of these literary tomboy figures as a metaphor for the colonial liminality of the spaces featured.[2]

NONCONFORMITY, DISIDENTIFICATION, AND QUEERNESS IN LITERATURE

Salka, Mick, and Frankie are embedded in the social contexts of the time, identifying as girls, albeit gender nonconforming girls, who embrace more masculine qualities and subvert the binary associations of gender. While in the contemporary period these characters are recognized as gender diverse or as fitting broadly into the category of trans, which can include "anyone who feels misaligned with the gender attributed to them, regardless of how they identify and how they choose to express themselves" (Mesch 9), in the 1930s in the US, they would have been considered "tomboys."[3] Although at present a more controversial term, I believe it is productive to consider these characters and their nonconformity within a history of literary tomboyism to illuminate their challenges to societal norms within the context of their times and places.[4] I will historicize the concept of the literary tomboy and explore how Salka, Mick, and Frankie perform female masculinity to reject the rigid gender expectations and confinements common to US southern and Icelandic societies. I follow Karin Quimby's understanding of queer as "what undermines or exceeds the fantasy of stable identity categories of gender and sexuality" (1). The tomboy figure embodies this definition by shunning feminine for masculine identifications and exposing categories like male/female and masculine/feminine as unstable (1).[5] Accordingly, I frame my discussions of queerness more specifically through a disruption to the belief in normative understandings of gender and sexuality. Salka, Mick, and Frankie demonstrate a queer resistance to patriarchy and the societal limitations imposed on femininity.

Through examining how comparable characters from similar time periods across these diverse societies diverge in their life trajectories, I explore the role the subject positions of the authors might play in these distinct approaches. How might their identities—Laxness a White, often assumed straight, Icelandic man and McCullers a White, queer, US southern woman—impact their depictions, particularly regarding representations of sexuality and sexual violence, as well as the entanglements between identity and community, queerness and postcolonialism. The term queer has been linked by scholars like Heather Love and Ásta Kristín Benediktsdóttir with the margins, as well as concepts like exile and alienation, which are also associated with modernism (Love 745). Therefore, liminal or peripheral spaces are embedded with the potential for queerness.

According to José Esteban Muñoz, disidentification is a "third mode of dealing with dominant ideology, one that neither opts to assimilate within such a structure nor strictly opposes it; rather, disidentification is a strategy that works on and against dominant ideology" (11). In contrast to identifying with and assimilating to dominant ideology or trying to entirely "break free of its inescapable sphere," to disidentify is to attempt to "transform a cultural logic from within" (11). Laxness's and McCullers's young tomboys do not reject societal understandings of femininity outright or attempt to function outside of normative gender roles, but they operate in this third space, attempting to alter the system from within. Indeed, disidentification as a third mode for dealing with ideology relates here to Homi Bhabha's concept of a Third Space, or "the 'inter'—the cutting edge of translation and negotiation, the *inbetween* space—that carried the burden of the meaning of culture," through which we "may elude the politics of polarity and emerge as the others of our selves" and sink into a culture's hybridity (56). The colonial liminality common to Iceland and the US South, flourishing in a Third Space, directly correlates to the protagonists' third mode of rejecting certain aspects within the structures themselves, emphasizing the connections between the focus on gender and sexuality in this chapter and this book's broader postcolonial frame. To understand both what Salka, Mick, and Frankie absorb and what they reject, I will turn to the context of each space—Iceland and the US South—in the 1930s. An analysis of the different though comparable ways that gender nonconformity in the form of tomboyism manifests in literature from each space also elucidates the patterns resulting from their various histories and experiences of colonization.

"We have no queer literature in Iceland," states Icelandic writer Sjón (qtd. in Portwood). Although scholars such as Benediktsdóttir have demonstrated a subtle thread of queerness running back to the Icelandic sagas, Sjón's statement is striking and speaks to a certain lack—perhaps of visibility. Benediktsdóttir expands that "[queer literature] is a part of our history and culture that has not really, with some very important exceptions, been documented or studied thoroughly" (Cohen). In particular, Benediktsdóttir points to the work of Elías Mar writing in the 1940s, yet to be translated into English, in addition to work by later twentieth-century writers Guðbergur Bergsson (whose work is central to chapter 2), Vigdís Grímsdóttir, Nína Björk Árnadóttir, Kristín Ómarsdóttir, and Lilja Sigurðardóttir (Cohen). In a recent article, Benediktsdóttir also positions Laxness's *The Great Weaver from Kashmir* (2008; *Vefarinn mikli frá Kasmír*, 1927) as "the earliest outspoken queer novel written in Icelandic" due to its direct reference to homosexuality, which led to discussion in the media, and the role of queerness in the protagonist's life ("The Spirit" 222). Benediktsdóttir asserts that Laxness lived "a heterosexual family life and no available sources prove that he was queer or had sex with men—but the sources do not rule out that possibility either" ("The Spirit" 222–23). While the examples are exceptional and not well-documented, queer literature exists and has existed in Iceland, and the ways in which queerness is represented are significant to discussions of Iceland's colonial history and national identity.

More specifically, discernible patterns exist in the depiction of restrictive approaches to sexuality and gender identity in Iceland in the first half of the twentieth century, which relate to the unstable positioning of the nation. A set of recent historical novels depicts Icelandic culture during these periods as conservative, repressive, and quick to tamp down on anything that deviates from sexual and gendered norms: Sjón's *Moonstone: The Boy Who Never Was* (2016; *Mánasteinn, drengurinn sem aldrei var til* 2013), imagining the life of a young, gay cinephile in 1918 Iceland, and Auður Ava Ólafsdóttir's *Miss Iceland* (2020; *Ungfrú Ísland*, 2018), following an aspiring woman writer in 1960s Iceland. Sjón has referred to Copenhagen as the capital of Iceland, and like other capitals of former colonial powers, Copenhagen was "a place of exile for homosexuals and a place of education for young Icelanders" (Moberg et al. 219), relating Iceland's environment of restriction back to colonial power dynamics. *Miss Iceland*'s Jón John, a gay man, lived in Copenhagen for a while, and *Moonstone*'s protagonist Máni Steinn ends up in London, another capital of a former colonial power, which Sjón positions as a place of escape for queer exiles.

In another sense, as the outsider to national narratives, Iceland is already associated with nonnormativity or queerness in relation to Denmark through its alternativeness, leading to the strict need to disassociate from anything different that may detract from the fight for nationhood.[6] According to E. Paul Durrenberger and Gísli Pálsson, few nationalisms "grant women and men equal access to resources," and they legitimate "male dominance over women and [have] a special affinity for male society, the passionate brotherhood that requires the identification, isolation, and containment of male homosexuality to protect its proper homosociality" (11). For example, Benediktsdóttir argues that Máni's sexuality in Sjón's novel is "associated with 'unnatural foreign practices' that are not only a threat to the reputation of Iceland and Icelanders but incompatible with Icelandic national identity" ("'Rise'" 138). Through unmasking national identities and borders as unstable and not natural, homosexuality is seen as threatening to the family and the nation: "nationalist discourses often place high emphasis on rejecting and repressing homosexuality," positioning it as foreign and dangerous, particularly when national identities are being shaped and contested (Benediktsdóttir, "'Rise'" 140). As the North Atlantic nation remained a Danish dependency until 1944, the complex reaction to these colonial ties and the simultaneous lack of and desire for independence resulted in more restriction and the policing of normative social roles, as depicted in the literature.

Additionally, scholars like John Howard, Jaime Harker, and Michael P. Bibler have demonstrated that the US South was always already queer. According to Howard, in the first half of the twentieth century, "homosexuality and gender insubordination were acknowledged and accommodated with a pervasive, deflective pretense of ignorance" before the "queer empowerment foreclosed the quiet accommodation of difference" later in the century (xi, xvii). Harker asserts that "sexual deviance is one of the South's most successful exports; indeed, from the 1930s through the 1950s, the southern grotesque made queer transgressive decadence a key part of the southern literary brand" (100). Thus, a queer literary undercurrent was allowed to flourish if, as Bibler argues, the relationships did not upset other hierarchies of power, such as race (*Cotton's Queer Relations* 18). The difference in these approaches may have something to do with the subtle but important shift from considering a nation (Iceland) to a region (US South), the latter having less to prove; in contrast, in early twentieth-century Iceland, queerness was taken as an affront to national independence efforts. Examples from even the most canonical southern literature, such as Henry Sutpen and Charles Bon's layered relationship in William Faulkner's *Absalom, Absalom!* (1936), which is mirrored in that of Quentin and Shreve across *Absalom, Absalom!* and *The Sound and the Fury* (1929), and John and Freddie's connection in Ernest Gaines's *Of Love and Dust* (1967), reveal passive acceptance of queer relationships and atypical gender performances.[7] Due to the predominance of the confining structure of the plantation in the US South, even passive acceptance of queerness functions as resistance in its embrace of antihierarchical ways of interacting.[8] In this chapter, I will focus on nontraditional gender roles by centering literary tomboys, the liminality they represent, and their resistance to hierarchical social formations. If confining women to the role of wife and mother can be seen as a means of securing their inferior positions in the gender-hierarchy, then an acceptance of alternative gender roles operates against hierarchy. The work of this comparison highlights issues both specific to and spanning societies of the Global North and South, such as cisheteropatriarchal social formations and the sexual threat they hold to young girls, as well as forms of resistance like disidentification. Through a focus on liminal figures in liminal societies, these novels illuminate the social pressures and conventions of their times and places, revealing that, despite our assumptions, Iceland and the US South in the 1930s are not worlds apart.

GENDER ROLES IN ICELAND
AND THE US SOUTH IN THE 1930s

Although having become a "sovereign state in a personal union with Denmark" in 1918 (Loftsdóttir, *Crisis and Coloniality* 7), Iceland was still a dependency of Denmark in the 1930s. Iceland was also one of the poorest countries in Europe until the World War II period: Europe's perception of "nineteenth-century Iceland as backward was ambiguously both a colonial and a class issue" (Lucas and Parigoris 97). In addition, the 1930s in the US saw the economic hardship of the Great Depression. This shared period of financial difficulty serves as the backdrop to the work of both Laxness and

McCullers and the challenges to restrictive gender roles held in common by both. The example of the *Fjallkonan* or lady of the mountain, discussed in chapter 2, demonstrates the connection between Icelandic gender ideologies and nationalism. Represented in Icelandic national dress, the *Fjallkonan* "served as a model figure for the personal conduct of Icelandic women set on being faithful to their nationality and heritage" (Oxfeldt et al. 44), and she remains a central symbol in Icelandic nationalist discourse (Björnsdóttir 109). Constructed to counter the symbol of the Danish king as the "father," the *Fjallkonan* was "an independent mother, royalty in her own right and the embodiment and the possessor of the land" (Björnsdóttir 109).[9] This link between nationalism and traditional representations of womanhood devolved during *Ástandið* and the endemic sexual policing of Icelandic women during World War II discussed in chapter 2. Coterminous with the suppression of homosexuality during times of national development were attempts to contain sexuality, and specifically women's sexuality, within the family structure (Benediktsdóttir, "'Rise'" 139–40). Icelandic women, seemingly falling prey to fashions from abroad such as the use of cosmetics and bobbed hair, were considered in relation to the traditional gendered expectations linked to the *Fjallkonan* (Oxfeldt et al. 40).[10] This is seen in Laxness's novel through the juxtaposition of Salka with Herborg, Arnaldur's aunt, who dresses in "her respectable national costume" and considers the wearing of trousers by women to be "unseemly behavior" (*Salka Valka* 169, 170). However, Laxness's depiction of Herborg as the ideal of the *Fjallkonan* is revealed as more complex. The fact that she takes off her national costume as soon as she enters her house, opting instead to wear "a pretty morning gown" (172), may reveal her association to be more performative, and her implied extramarital affair with Arnaldur's father, Björn, supposedly resulting in her pregnancy, also complicates the connection (202).

Iceland's colonial relationship to Denmark also impacted understandings of gender in the early twentieth-century period through the importation of shifting domestic ideologies from mainland Europe in the eighteenth century (Ellenberger 1079). These ideologies, such as the positioning of the home as the central site of female identity, were disseminated to Iceland, demonstrating the role gender played in "directing the flows of certain ideas from the European metropoles to its margins" (Ellenberger 1079). Unnur Dís Skaptadóttir notes that maritime households in Iceland specifically can be termed woman-centered, whether the men are present or not: "Women run the household from day to day and are usually more involved in maintaining kinship relations and relations between households" (93). Women take care of the household and its finances without their husbands, yet this does not give them a higher status (Skaptadóttir 96). As depicted in *Salka Valka* through the powerful merchant Jóhann Bogesen and his Danish wife, many women occupying the top of the social hierarchies in Iceland were of foreign descent—typically from Denmark, Scotland, or the German state of Prussia—illustrating in particular the flow of people, goods, and ideas between Iceland and Denmark during this period (Ellenberger 1079).[11] And connecting back to the previous discussion, Bogesen positions Salka's atypical gender performance as a direct threat to the nation. He wonders out loud to Salka, "If all the pretty, shapely girls stopped thinking of house and home, wore trousers on Sundays and founded all sorts of unions? Yes, what would happen? What would that do to our nation?" (Laxness, *Salka Valka* 335), demonstrating the entwinement of ideologies of gender and nation.

In the US South of the 1930s, the lingering impacts of "the South's most iconic institution, the plantation" were still felt (Bibler, *Cotton's Queer Relations* 2), revealing the intricacy of multiple overlapping constraints left in its wake, with White, rich, cisgender patriarchs retaining power over those beneath them on the social hierarchies. During the post-emancipation period, White men feared losing control over the sexuality of White women, which led to the cult of southern womanhood. White women were expected to be the submissive sustainers of White civilization while White men were off satisfying their lusts elsewhere (Jordan 148), often through rape and exploitation. This dynamic exposes the interacting plantation hierarchies of race, class, gender, and sexuality. Tamlyn Avery asserts that "McCullers's fiction bears witness to psychological and ideological plantation legacies still enclosed within the household hierarchy, where the atavistic divisions of race and gender remained hegemonic long into the twentieth century" (70). McCullers, herself a native of Columbus, Georgia, sets her two novels "in the middle of the deep South" (*Heart* 6), which in the post-emancipation period felt the lingering impacts of the plantation system and remained affected by the cotton industry. Alongside the racial hierarchies inherited from the plantation structure are the confining domestic expectations for women, whose central role was to produce White heirs. Sarah Gleeson-White notes that in both *The Heart Is a Lonely Hunter* and *The Member of the Wedding*, there is a "tension between Mick's and Frankie's tomboyishness and the ideal of the southern belle or lady" (13), hearkening back to plantation ideologies of gender.

Various forms of this gendered emphasis can be found across both the US and Iceland in the early twentieth century. More specifically, Alison Graham-Bertolini, speaking to US culture in the 1930s, states that the "tragedy" is that "growing up" required that girls "be codified into a system of submissive behavior that rendered them financially dependent on men, and had a devastating impact on their sense of self, their sexuality, and their ability to embody power and manifest joy" (3), which I argue is an inheritance from the plantation ideologies of gender described above. Graham-Bertolini describes McCullers's fiction in particular as including examples of the normalization of this gendered conditioning in the US in the 1930s and 1940s, where sex was used to control women and confine them to a social system "in which they are defined exclusively as objects of male pleasure" (3). While McCullers's novels have been analyzed productively through the lens of gender and power, there is little feminist criticism in English on Laxness's novel to date—although a long history of such work exists in Icelandic by scholars such as Helga Kress, Soffía Auður Birgisdóttir, and Dagný Kristjánsdóttir.[12] *Salka Valka* has been more often positioned as a "politically charged novel" that zeros in on "major economic and social problems of contemporary Iceland," especially "Marxism and class antagonism" (Van Deusen 57). As a social realist text, it is Laxness's "first attempt at writing a novel where Icelandic society is analyzed in terms of class struggle and where a modern sociohistorical approach is in evidence" (Jóhannsson 381).[13] McCullers, also known for her investment in the political, has been described as "one of the first white writers in the late 1930s and early 1940s to relate the South's racial practices and politics to European fascism" (González Groba 67). Deeply distraught over the situations of the cotton mill workers, she "expresses a strongly proletarian sympathy and denounces the oppression of American capitalism" in *The Heart Is a Lonely Hunter* (González Groba 66). However, I'll focus less on large-scale politics and more on the experiences of individual characters within the structures critiqued. This comparative reading of Laxness and McCullers brings to the surface central aspects of the texts that may otherwise be overlooked, such as cross-cultural patterns to gendered constraints and societal expectations in the 1930s and also resistance to such patterns.[14]

What does examining these texts together do for an understanding of each? Considering Salka Valka, Mick Kelly, and Frankie Addams alongside each other with a focus on their nonnormativity as resistance changes our understanding of each girl. Extending the queer feminist lens often applied to McCullers's work to Laxness's *Salka Valka* highlights in particular the gender nonconformity and queerness of this beloved Icelandic heroine. Indeed, the tomboy figure is usually understood as fundamentally female but performatively masculine—which can be seen as a parallel to a colonial space that might dress itself up and perform otherwise. As I will discuss in chapter 4, colonial rhetoric often positions colonial spaces as feminine, the land itself described as a woman's body. This is demonstrated more specifi-cally in the US southern context by postbellum reunion romances, a body of literature popular from the late 1800s to the 1920s that featured "a love affair between a Northerner and a Southerner whose relationship stands in for the nation as a whole," typically including a Union officer and a "young unreconstructed Confederate women" (Keely 624).[15] The basic structure of these reunion novels and plays relied on this gendered framework and stereotypes of women as emotional and submissive, "making rebellious but ultimately compliant southern women the main subjects of sectional bonding" (Silber 109–10). Here, we see the US South imagined as an explicitly conquered colonial territory and the figure of the young woman representing this space as resisting her proscribed role as a heterosexual lover: an image of colonial liminality in postbellum US fiction. Thus, a comparative reading suggests the tomboy figure's liminality may extend to both spaces' layered and complex colonial histories and, at the same time, may illuminate the interactions of tomboyism with other identity markers, including class, sexuality, and race, revealing much about the interrelation between identity and community.

THE TOMBOY FIGURE IN LITERATURE:
FRANKIE, MICK, AND SALKA

Although the tomboy figure emerged in US culture earlier in the nineteenth century (Abate ix), the late nineteenth and early twentieth centuries are often hailed as the "heyday of tomboy narratives" in the US (Abate xv), which aligns also with the heyday of reunion romances in the US South, underscoring that connection. In her work on the literary tomboy, Michelle Ann Abate notes that the figure is "an unstable and dynamic one, changing with the political, social and economic events of its historical era" (xii). The turn-of-the-century period in the US saw many important national changes and, by the end of World War I, "women were voting, engaging in such formerly masculine activities as smoking and drinking, and even asserting their right to participate in the 'male' world of work" (Abate x), resulting in an increased interest in the figure of the tomboy. Abate examines the liminality of the tomboy, which existed on "the border between masculinity and femininity, heterosexuality and homosexuality, whiteness and blackness" and symbolized the era's anxieties around shifting hierarchies of gender, race, and sexuality, or the "crumbling wartime distinctions between normality and abnormality" (159). While much of the theorization of this figure has occurred in a US context, I will extend this work through a consideration of Laxness's Icelandic tomboy, Salka Valka, the ways in which she adheres to and subverts the US version, and what is revealed about the distinct societies in question.

Tomboyism is defined by Jack Halberstam as an extended childhood period of female masculinity (155); according to Dianne Elise, the phenomenon involves the girl disidentifying from the mother (140). The tomboy experiences "the feminine norm as a place of constriction and the male one as a place of action" (Zevy 186), situated within the socially engrained gender binary. The traits most often associated with tomboys in the US are "a proclivity for outdoor play (especially athletics), a feisty independent spirit, and a tendency to don masculine clothing and adopt a boyish nickname" (Abate xvi). Described by Abate as "arguably the most popular literary tomboy after Jo March" of Louisa May Alcott's *Little Women* (154), twelve-year-old Frankie Addams of *The Member of the Wedding* has also been named as a quintessential example by scholars like Halberstam and Lisa Selin Davis. McCullers's novel follows Frankie around town in the days leading up to her brother's wedding, after which she dreams of joining the couple and traveling the world with them, stating, "*They are the we of me*" (*Member* 42). Frankie is introduced to the reader as having grown so tall for her age "that she was almost a big freak," and additionally, she "wore a pair of blue black shorts, a B.V.D. undervest, and she was barefooted. Her hair had been cut like a boy's, but it had not been cut for a long time and was now not even parted" (4). Through her nickname, clothing, haircut, and, we are soon to learn, her "feisty independent spirit," Frankie rejects the constraints of femininity in her society for a more active masculinity. She will also alter her name twice throughout the narrative: first, to the more feminine F. Jasmine, the opening letters "Ja" aligning her with her brother Jarvis and his bride Janice, and later to the more mature-sounding Frances.[16] Frankie's initial reflection in the mirror is described as "warped and crooked" (4), as if exposing her own underlying view of herself and her concern that as "a big freak" (4), her compatriots are to be found in the Chattahoochee Exposition's House of Freaks. She recalls her perception that "all the Freaks" (20)—among them "the Giant," "the Wild N***," and "the Half-Man Half-Woman" (19)—looked at her in "a secret way" as if to say they know her (20). This introduces a central concern of Frankie's throughout the novel, in addition to representing her society's anxiety around changing racial and gender norms and the accompanying fluidity of identity.

Whereas *The Member of the Wedding* is essentially Frankie's coming-of-age story, Mick Kelly, the tomboy figure in *The Heart Is a Lonely Hunter*, shares the center of the novel with a series of other misfits who are all connected through their deaf confidant John Singer. Around Frankie's age when the novel opens, Mick is described as a "gangling, towheaded youngster," who was "dressed in khaki shorts, a blue shirt, and tennis shoes—so that at first glance she was like a very young boy" (McCullers, *Heart* 18).[17] When asked by Biff Brannon, owner and bartender at the New York Café, if she had been to the Girl Scouts, she responds in the negative, adding, "I don't belong to them" (18)—a response either revealing her disinterest in belonging to any group or introducing her ambiguous relationship to binary gender distinctions. Mick feels apart from her peers but joins in with the neighborhood play at times and invites her fellow vocational students to her home for a successful prom—that is, before the local kids overrun the party. Similar questions of belonging feature in *The Member of the Wedding*: although in the novel's present Frankie is "an unjoined person," who "belonged to no club and was a member of nothing in the world" (3), she had previously been a younger member of the local girls' club until she was considered "too young and mean" (12). Both girls are outsiders in the novels' present periods, but they have also experienced acceptance in their respective societies.

In direct contrast to Mick's and Frankie's experiences of community, Laxness's Salka Valka has never been accepted by her peers or included in any group play. Divided into two volumes, the novel follows Salka's life in a small fishing community in Western Iceland and describes her "personal growth from being a poor child to becoming a grown woman, a worker, and a boat owner, in fact, one of the more influential figures in the small coastal town of Óseyri" (Jóhannsson 381). A true outsider as a child, Salka has some tomboy characteristics that are chosen aspects of her identity, while others are genetic or result from her lack of opportunities—an important difference between herself and Mick and Frankie. At eleven years old, her body roils with "unruly vitality"; her "deep voice, which sounded almost like a man's" is not within her control and positions her as more masculine than typical young girls (Laxness, *Salka Valka* 10).[18] She will cut her hair short as a young adult, but when we meet her, she has "ash blond" hair woven into braids and "limpid, almost water-colored eyes," and she is described as "big-boned, like a calf or foal" and graceless, with long and lanky limbs (22). Her name, Salka, which is short for Salvör, genders her in a way that Mick and Frankie's more gender-neutral nicknames do not,[19] and her homelessness and extreme poverty at the novel's start, responsible for her dressing in a masculine jacket, also distinguish her even before she more actively chooses to dress in trousers.

According to a UK-based study by Samantha Holland and Julie Harpin, "the tomboy identity encompassed a sense of freedom, mobility and physicality," and the tomboy feels that "she has more physical agency than a girly-girl, [as] even her clothing choices make her feel physically freer" (296). In opposition to Mick and Frankie, with their respective solo jaunts around town, Salka does not display much interest in mobility. Unlike the

Bogesens and their links to the cultivated society of Denmark, she has no interest in going abroad (Laxness, *Salka Valka* 609), having "been born with a peculiar indifference toward everything distant and foreign" and being "so deeply rooted to her village" (328). Contrastingly, Mick and Frankie both desire to escape their communities—a deep-seated drive for mobility that directly differs from Salka's acceptance of stasis. It is worth noting that in their fantasies of escape, both Mick and Frankie dream of Arctic climes and, as Jennifer Ann Shapland notes, resistance to social expectations is first possible for Frankie through imagined places (140). Feeling caught in their southern communities, they fantasize about empty, frozen landscapes, like those Salka inhabits for much of the year—a transtextual bond between these young heroines, linking them across the novels through realities and fantasies of snow. Frankie constantly dreams of Alaska, where her brother is deployed, but an undeveloped Alaska: "the snow and frozen sea and ice glaciers. Esquimau igloos and polar bears and the beautiful Northern Lights" (6). She does not like hearing about the reality of her brother's experience of swimming and battling mosquitoes in the summer (McCullers, *Member* 7).[20] Mick also dreams of snow, telling Harry during their sexual encounter that she wants to see "cold, white drifts of snow like in pictures. Blizzards. White, cold snow that keeps falling soft and falls on and on and on through all the winter. Snow like in Alaska" (McCullers, *Heart* 274). Her imagery echoes Frankie's: "far up in the north there were deep forests and white ice igloos. The arctic region with the beautiful northern lights" (307). While scholars such as Anna Young and Elizabeth Freeman provide convincing readings of McCuller's fixation on Alaska, the girls appear to desire the blankness and anonymity that accompany their fantasies of desolate snowscapes. The inclusion of Alaska is less about the reality of the place and more about the dreams of escaping beyond the limits of their known worlds—peripheralized norths representing respite from their own marginalized southern experiences.[21] The poetics of this northern imagery, symbolizing a desired escape, link these two novels each to the other, as well as cross-culturally to Laxness's, in a transtextual aesthetics of shared peripheralization.

Further, we follow Salka into early adulthood when she becomes a leader in her community, whereas we are only with Mick and Frankie for about a year. Historically, tomboyism has been considered a temporary phase that girls are supposed to outgrow: the inclusion of "boy" in the label reflects that "this is not yours, you as a female cannot keep it" (Elise 150). In this way Salka deviates from US-based conceptualizations, as she continues to wear pants into adulthood and doubles down on her masculine appearance by cutting her hair short.[22] The gender binary is still widely engrained, with masculinity more heavily guarded than femininity due to its alignment with privilege in US society (Halberstam 164).[23] Tomboy identities are seen as "benign forms of childhood identification as long as they evince acceptable degrees of femininity, appropriate female aspiration, and as long as they promise to result in marriage and motherhood" (Halberstam 156), or the normative domestic expectations for women and subservience to men. In contrast to this stipulation, Salka finds more social acceptance in her young adulthood—even though she is never domesticated through marriage. No longer alienated in the same way by class, thanks to anonymous money sent to her from America, she becomes the owner of Steinþór's family's home, Mararbúð, as well as a motorboat (305), and she helps to found the fisherman's union, of which she is the secretary (306), all of which are uncharacteristic behavior for a woman of her time. At the same time, however, Salka has an affair with a man, Arnaldur, and serves as a surrogate mother to the four older children of Magnús Book after his wife Sveinbjörg passes (462), making her more legible as a woman in the community in line with gendered expectations.

Nevertheless, in many ways Salka remains an outsider throughout the novel, referred to as "peculiar" so often that it almost deconstructs her peripheral positioning (10).[24] As noted above, she desires to disassociate herself from her mother's version of womanhood. Mothers in tomboy literature tend to be missing or emotionally absent (Abate xviii), which is the case with both of McCullers's characters: Frankie's mother has died, and Mick's is an absent presence. While she does not act like a traditional mother, Sigurlína is very present in Salka's life, and indeed, many of Salka's choices are made in reaction to her mother's. In her nonconformity, Salka does not align with the typical gendered associations for girls. She becomes a day laborer at eleven, washing fish with the village fish industry women, who, like Salka, are known for their strength and independence (Skaptadóttir 91). She never plays with the local children but on Sundays watches their outdoor games from a bridge, where she is laughed at and called "the daughter of a whore" while mud is flung at her (115, 151). This level of ostracization surpasses the alienation felt by McCullers's young heroines. Salka's poverty, arriving in the town of Óseyri with few possessions and no place to live, has a direct impact on her early experiences and the formation of her identity. Mick Kelly feels a version of this economic pressure at the end of *The Heart Is a Lonely Hunter* when she leaves school to support her family with the job at Woolworths, wondering what good all her plans and her passion for making music were when "all that came of it was this trap—the store, then home to sleep, and back at the store again" (350). Both Salka's and Mick's lives are deeply affected by the poverty of their families and their need to work at young ages.[25] While

Salka's poverty is linked to her first experience with masculine clothes, Mick's family's need for money forces her to abandon her aspirations to be a world-famous composer, atypical for women in the 1930s, for a more conventional job at a department store counter. Both examples demonstrate the entanglement of gender and class hierarchies across the novels.

Importantly, Salka's outsider status does not simply result from her marginalized class position, but also from her own active decisions—more in line with Mick and Frankie's disidentifications from society's rigid understandings of gender. For instance, through wearing shorts and pants, which directly correlate to a more active lifestyle, all three girls "resist and confound socially prescriptive patterns of identification" (Muñoz 28)—that is, the wearing of dresses and high heels—without operating outside of the community's understanding of gender in its entirety. Disidentification is, therefore, "a survival strategy that works within and outside the dominant public sphere simultaneously" without attracting the potentially violent repercussions of a more active resistance to gender roles and domesticity (Muñoz 5). By rejecting aspects of socially defined femininity from within the system, Mick, Frankie, and Salka "must work with/resist the conditions of (im)possibility that dominant culture generates" (Muñoz 6), which each does in her own ways through her nonconformity, pluralizing the category of girlhood and depicting nonnormativity across characters identifying as female. Gleeson-White notes that "notwithstanding the insistent social demand for conformity that the novels register, McCullers's adolescent portraits embody a dynamics of possibility and thus challenge any notion of female limits" (11). Mick, Frankie, and Salka each normalize difference by resisting certain standards, such as style of dress, from within society's gendered framework.

In another disidentificatory move, all three young heroines reject feminine expectations around cleanliness, in addition to dress. However, each later alters her hygiene routine for more traditionally gendered reasons: to look pretty at formal events or attract the interest of boys. Comparable to the way Salka revolts against her mother's version of femininity, Mick rejects that of her sisters, Etta and Hazel. When Etta states it makes her sick to see Mick "in those silly boy's clothes," Mick responds that she wears shorts because she doesn't want their hand-me-downs. She doesn't want to be or look like them and would "rather be a boy any day" (42). However, when throwing her prom party, Mick borrows Etta's "long blue crêpe de chine evening dress" (106), along with white pumps, a rhinestone tiara, and even one of Etta's brassieres, "just for the heck of it" (107). She scrubs her heels, knees, and elbows, making "the bath take a long time" before standing "for a long time before the mirror" (107), her intentionality underscored by this repetition. Her first time in an evening dress, she decides that she looks beautiful, while also feeling like she was "somebody different from Mick Kelly entirely" (107). Mick, however, learns firsthand about the restricted movement of feminine dress, sliding in high heels where "she would have landed like a cat" in tennis shoes, tearing the dress, and losing the tiara (116). After this night she will no longer wear shorts, demonstrating the existence of tomboyism in US culture as primarily a temporary phase to be outgrown when girls become women expected to subscribe to patriarchal expectations, such as impractical but aesthetically pleasing clothing. Mick plans to wear a silk dress and necklace when seeing Harry—perhaps to impress him (268), as she has been socialized to believe dresses and jewelry have the power to do. And like Mick, Frankie doffs her shorts for a more formal ensemble in preparation for her brother's wedding. However, as scholars like Gleeson-White have observed, the result is a parody of femininity with an "orange satin evening dress" that the family's house-keeper Berenice observes does not mix with the "brown crust" on her elbows, making her look like a human Christmas tree (89, 90). Frankie's desire to join the wedding causes her to want to subscribe to what she believes is normative femininity, in line with her taking the name F. Jasmine in this section.

As Mick wants to wear a dress due to her interest in Harry, Salka's blossoming feelings for Arnaldur activate her attention to cleanliness and her clothing. His first words to her are "Why are you so filthy" (Laxness, *Salka Valka* 95). Arnaldur does not comment on her washing after this, but as the narrator observes, "Nor, perhaps, was she ever really filthy after that" (116), as she begins to wash and comb her hair every evening. Moreover, Salka takes her job as a means to secure new clothing in part to impress Arnaldur: "Would she always have to be filthy and wear ugly clothes, in the sight of Arnaldur and the whole world, despite having gotten a job washing fish?" (106). After her mother steals her pay for her own Easter dress, Salka cries on the steps of the store, and her grief causes Jóhann Bogesen to take pity on her. She returns home "washed and combed, well-fed and cheerful, wearing a light blue dress that reached down to mid-calf, with numerous wonderful pleats here and there, black piping, and a bow . . ." (113). Her young love for Arnaldur feminizes her in this instance. Nevertheless, like Mick, this doesn't mean that Salka necessarily buys into normalized femininity, so much as that she knows what is positioned as attractive in her society. Natalie Van Deusen notes that "after wearing it every day, Salka Valka's new dress eventually becomes worn and tattered and she is forced to return to reality and the position to which she has been assigned in society," which Van Deusen views as "a stinging commentary on the possibility of social mobility in such a culture" (63). Clothing and appearance in Salka's community are tied closely to class in addition to gender.

Like her American shorts-wearing counterparts, Salka's style of dress is atypical of young girls and remains a topic of much discussion in her community. While Salka may not have chosen her first item of masculine clothing, the man's jacket referenced earlier, she shortly thereafter resolves to get trousers in order to "stop being a girl" (95)—demonstrating more agency. She is also accidentally in step with foreign trends, as revealed when the stylish Gústa Borgeson, recently returned from Denmark, mockingly tells Salka, "From what I can see, you're very much in vogue. That is considered the finest way to dress at seaside resorts in Germany and America—all the ladies there wear trousers" (160). While fashionable in the elite, international spaces in which Gústa circulates, trousers would not be in style in Salka's village where "Icelandic women would normally wear three different skirts at the same time, not trousers" (Guðmundsdóttir 39). Gústa's comment highlights the wide gulf between Salka and the fashionable, modern tourists at seaside resorts, at the same time that it cements Gústa's association with foreign (read: elite) cultures. However, although Salka is nothing like the privileged tourists, shades of her rejections of gendered norms can likewise be detected in the fashion shifts of the 1920s and the adjacent appearance of the gender-bending flapper.[26]

While they are first conceived as a way to differentiate herself from her mother's version of womanhood, Salka appears to feel the most comfortable wearing trousers, as we see her regret wearing a dress that has slipped above her knee at one point (Laxness, *Salka Valka* 541). However, if she wears them to take emphasis away from her body, Salka's trousers seem to draw more attention toward it. Throughout the novel, Salka's trousers spark an aggressive and invasive curiosity about her anatomy. While she is teased by Gústa's brother, Angantýr Bogesen, and a group of boys at a dance that want to "grab her and pick the lice off her" (218), one of them suggests "maybe then they would find out whether she was a man or a woman" (219). She thinks about shouting nasty words back but instead just escapes. At another point, a Norwegian skipper stops Salka on the square to ask "what gender she was; he even took hold of her, the damned lout, and she slapped his face" (365). And later, while trying to charm her into joining the offensive against the communists or "Bolshies" (387), Angantýr reveals that he has "often thought of asking [her] one thing," whether she wears suspenders or just a belt to keep her trousers up, at which point she yanks her hands away from him and almost slaps his face (385).[27] In each instance, these intrusive lines of inquiry are accompanied by a physical aspect—whether threatening to grab her, in the example of the boys at the dance; actually grabbing her, as in the case of the Norwegian skipper; or holding her wrist in a manipulative ploy, as with

Angantýr in the final example. Salka typically responds to these assaults on her privacy and physical well-being with either force or the consideration of it, and in this way Laxness shows readers, as opposed to telling us, about Salka's distress in these instances. Indeed, in the 1930s in this remote Icelandic town, there is no concept of a gender identity separate from one's biological sex until Salka wears trousers and contemplates becoming a boy, resisting the aggressive impulses of the men in her community who feel entitled to police her gender presentation.

QUEERNESS IN LIMINAL SPACES

By calling into question the alignment of gender and sex, Salka resists the cisheteronormative expectations of her Icelandic community in a similar way to Frankie and Mick in the US South, underscoring the entanglement between queerness and liminality. Much has been written about queerness in both of McCullers's novels, and that frame can be usefully extended to Laxness's. For instance, Rachel Adams claims that the "improbably frequent repetition of the word 'queer'" throughout *The Member of the Wedding* leaves "traces for a reader open to its suggestion that, rather than occupying any singular or normative position, sexuality is composed of multiple identifications and erotic possibilities" (561), which is comparable to Laxness's "improbably frequent" repetition of "peculiar." I'm interested in the ways that this queerness, or "sexuality [as] composed of multiple identifications and erotic possibilities," intersects with belonging as well as other identity markers in the novels, leaving space for disidentification with their feminine and, to different extents, heterosexual identities. Graham-Bertolini offers that McCullers's work in particular "demonstrates exactly how gender is learned over time and why those learned behaviors are so dangerous to the social development and human liberties of girls in our culture" (2), and Elise adds the possibility that "heterosexuality as it is constituted under patriarchy isn't always good for girls," supported by the dive adolescent girls take in relation to their self-esteem (150). Just as these gender diverse heroines challenge cisgender expectations, reading a sexuality beyond the heteronormative in the novels can make possible more expansive understandings of the characters and their intersecting identities within their US southern and Icelandic communities.

Berenice views the extent of Frankie's interest in her brother's wedding as abnormal: "I never before in all my days heard of anybody falling in love with a wedding" (McCullers, *Member* 82). Berenice's choice of the phrase "falling in love with" positions Frankie's interest in the event as existing outside of the heteronormative sphere, especially when she avers that what Frankie needs instead is "a beau. A nice little white boy beau" (82).[28] A reverberation of her interest in the wedding, Frankie's pairing with her new friend Mary Littlejohn at the end of the novel overtakes her dreams of the future and of escape: "They read poets like Tennyson together; and Mary was going to be a great painter and Frances a great poet—or else the foremost authority on radar" (159); furthermore, "when Frances was sixteen and Mary eighteen, they were going around the world together" (159). McCullers shows as opposed to tells readers what Frankie's relationship with Mary means to her, echoing Laxness's showing of Salka's distress. The ambiguity present in the descriptions, however, opens a debate in the scholarship over whether the ending represents Frankie giving up or embracing her queer identity through this new relationship with Mary.[29] Frankie seems to trade in her less categorical interest in the wedding for this new pairing with Mary, making her sexuality more legible; this ending, then, symbolizes the continuation of both her dreams of belonging and escape.

While Frankie finds a fulfilling relationship with Mary and may soon satisfy her dream of travel, other aspects of the novel's ending are not so positive. Honey Brown, a Black man coded as queer, closes the novel "locked in the jail, awaiting trial," after breaking into the store of a White man who had been selling him drugs (161). As Graham-Bertolini asserts, there is "no future for a genderfluid John Henry West, who dies abruptly from meningitis, just as there is no future for a loved and respected Black friend or mother figure in this racist white world," with Frankie indicating her belief in White superiority through a slight toward Berenice in the last pages (16). The novel may close hopefully on Frankie's queer future traveling with Mary Littlejohn but is less optimistic in terms of Frankie resisting the racism embedded within her society or the continuation of other less definable forms of queerness.[30]

Although there are also multiple readings of how the novel leaves Mick Kelly, overall, they are collectively less hopeful than views of Frankie's future. Louise Westling notes that even though McCullers herself moved to New York after the success of her first novel, *The Heart Is a Lonely Hunter*, "she was never able to project such a solution for her characters or to celebrate the kind of escape from gender which her own way of life implied" (55), later adding that like Flannery O'Connor, McCullers couldn't "envision any positive, active life for women of her own generation" (176). Westling connects the "smothering of Mick's ambitions" to be a composer with her "acceptance of womanhood" (117). Constance M. Perry relates this to her sexual experience with Harry, averring that Mick believes it's not possible "to be both a confident artist and a sexually adult female because in her culture female sexuality is shameful and dirty, meant to be mocked in graffiti" (44). According to Perry, this identity has been waiting for Mick symbolically since the scene in which she "ironically prophesies her fate as 'PUSSY M.K.'" (44), adding this graffiti to an empty house. Locating some positivity in Mick's otherwise bleak ending, Graham-Bertolini agrees that Mick's gender socialization prevents her from fulfilling her artistic potential yet affirms that Mick is aware of this (12). Angry over the social pressures to conform, Mick resists this oppression through planning to put two dollars each week toward buying a piano (McCullers, *Heart* 12). Although her circumstances—needing to work to help support her family—lead to her being more "caught" than Frankie, Mick also does not submit to the limitations that society places on her identity.

However, while Mick takes on more normative feminine qualities toward the end of the novel with her skirts and job at Woolworths, we've seen no evidence that we should discount her nonheteronormative assertion that she "never will marry with any boy." The depiction of her sexuality is even more ambiguous than Frankie's, yet I argue that there is space to read queerness here as well. Mick describes the connections she feels to different individuals, which could be read as pansexual crushes—although not necessarily erotic in nature. For example, she remembers in detail Celeste, a girl whom she would lie awake thinking about in the sixth grade and wanted to talk to "more than anything else" but never did: "The way she felt about Celeste would never let her go up and make friends with her like she would any other person" (242). After that, she thought about a boy named Buck, the lady who sold raffle tickets, Miss Anglin who taught seventh grade, Carole Lombard, and of course, Mister Singer, with whom she believes she shares "this secret feeling between them" (243). This last fantasy of connection is more developed, with Mick planning from her bed how she would be an orphan living with Mister Singer, "just the two of them in a foreign house where in the winter it would snow" (243). Thus, just as her interest in wearing either "a red dress spangled with rhinestones" or "a real man's evening suit" when conducting the orchestra in her imagined future breaks down binary associations of gendered clothing (241, 240), Mick cannot be confined by heteronormative expectations for her desired interactions or binary understandings of sexuality.

As a result of the novels' corresponding characters and themes, we can extend this scholarly discussion around queerness in McCullers's fiction through a turn to Laxness's *Salka Valka*, illuminating new angles from which to view the novel's protagonist. Even though the narrative voices position her feelings for and affair with Arnaldur in the highest of romantic terms, the bare facts are that Salka convinces him to leave at the end of the novel and has no interest in the heterosexual trappings of marriage once she is a financially secure adult. When a recently returned Steinþór mentions that she could have been married, Salka responds, "Married? Me? Why the hell would I be married?" (Laxness, *Salka Valka* 482), echoing Frankie's disinterested statement, "I don't want any beau, what would I do with one?" (McCullers, *Member* 82). David S. Baldwin offers a feminist reading of the novel: "the progressive emancipation of Salvör Valgerður ('Salka Valka')—as she first becomes a prominent local activist, then distances herself from the competing attentions of aggressively preying or dependently needy men—may reflect a growing awareness of her own sexuality." While Árni Sigurjónsson and others have read the ending more negatively—seeing Arnaldur as controlling Salka as her superior before betraying and deserting her (Guðmundsdóttir 58)—Baldwin proposes a different slant. Instead of reading Arnaldur's California journey as an abandonment contrary to her own desires with shades of martyrdom accompanying her actions, Baldwin's view argues that once Salka is aware of "the feckless serial infidelity of the impractically idealistic Arnaldur (and despite some lingering affection for him), she reluctantly but determinedly ends their relationship by encouraging him to pursue his dreams in America," leaving her "finally free of unwanted male attention" from "both barbarous Steinþor and immature Arnaldur." Additionally, Soffía Auður Birgisdóttir reads Salka sending Arnaldur away both as a declaration of independence and a reaction to watching the impact that living for another had on her mother (19), and Jón Yngvi Jóhannsson observes that Salka is stronger for being left behind and also "liberated after her sexual—and possibly political—awakening with Arnaldur" (383). While she still has feelings for him, Salka's desires are not as contrary to Arnaldur's as a more tragic reading of her sacrificing her own fulfillment for his might assume. In this view, Salka has the agency and takes the initiative to end the relationship, regardless of Arnaldur's wishes.

In addition to Salka's decisive actions that shift the novel away from a cisheteronormative marriage plot, a few moments in her youth make possible a more complex understanding of her sexuality. Her wardrobe choices are understood by Herborg as reflective of "somewhat unnatural views . . . to be a properly made girl, yet not wanting to be a girl" and already positioned by the community as abnormal (Laxness, *Salka Valka* 172). The phrase "properly made girl" is striking and would seem to imply a more expansive view of womanhood, leaving space for "less properly made" girls or perhaps those girls whose sex and gender do not align. In one instance, the narrative voices leave space to read a pansexuality mirroring Mick's into her interactions. Jóhannsson describes the novel's complex narrative structure with "variations in style and point of view" (384), and I'd add that the narrator's alignment with certain characters' perspectives can be revealing. For instance, as mentioned above, the return of the stylish and sexually uninhibited Gústa Bogesen from Copenhagen is the talk of the town. The narrator describes Gústa's body in detail, seemingly from Salka's perspective. The section is framed by Salka's failure to recognize Gústa and includes mention of her "stocky legs and muscular calves, an upturned nose and pale skin, full, red lips, and gleaming white teeth, and eyes that shone splendidly and self-confidently from her white face, steeped in foreign experience" (Laxness, *Salka Valka* 157). This gaze, recounted by the narrator but positioned with Salka, lingers on Gústa's legs and face, making note of her sensual lips. While witnessing a flirtatious interaction between Gústa and Arnaldur, Salka is perceived by Gústa as "the tall, adolescent-looking girl in men's trousers standing by the door" and described as "staring with such impertinent greed at the young lady, the candy, and Alli [Arnaldur's nickname], that it seemed as if she wanted to devour all three with her eyes" (160). Notably, Salka's voraciousness does not stop at Arnaldur and the candy.[31] Later Gústa is described as having "better teeth, whiter skin and a prettier nose than any other girl Salka Valka had seen" (216), and watching her dance drunkenly with the storekeeper's son "stirred up a sinful unrest" in Salka's breast (217). This reading creates space for an alternative, more sexually fluid reading of Salka, frequently interpreted as a peculiar heterosexual tomboy abandoned by her more worldly lover. It positions her sexuality, which she begins to discover by the end of the novel, as—like her gender—less beholden to cisheteronormative constraints.

Finally, I'd like to note two failed opportunities for queer resistance to heteronormative expectations in the novel and the possibility they nevertheless hold. The first is an intriguing side character with the promise of being developed as more empowered and less stereotypical. At one gathering, a "truculent spinster" is described speaking to a housewife, "yet often interrupting the men's conversation with harsh comments of her own, intended to set the men straight" (Laxness, *Salka Valka* 536). This character has the potential to represent another way to be a woman in this society, yet she is never elaborated on beyond this line. Another example is the pleasure Salka fails to find in her own body—a failure that may result from the blind spots or obstructed view of a male author representing female sexuality. As a young adult Salka experiments with autoeroticism, but these explorations bring her nothing but negative emotions: when "she touched herself between the sheets in the evenings, she was often seized with hatred, and fell asleep feeling sorrowful" (366). Later, her "strong, mature body [is] spread out before her eyes like a landscape; no one knew it but she herself"—an important distinction with "landscapes" often associated with depictions of women as ripe for the conquering in colonial narratives—yet when she touches herself, "even with the greatest of care, she ordinarily became frightened of herself and all of life" and is "seized with anguish" (547).[32] In contrast to Salka's view of her body as her own private landscape, Arnaldur essentializes Salka as one with the land, gazing out at the sea and chewing grass: "the landscape merged with her person, the essence of the winds with her breaths" (552). Once again here, the idea that colonial spaces are often positioned as feminine reverberates through this imagery, and those liminal locations resisting their coloniality might then echo the tomboy figure in a performative masculinity. Nevertheless, what could have been an opportunity to find pleasure in her body independent of the men in her life only fills Salka with pain. These moments of unfulfilled potential in the text might connect to the limited knowledge that cisgender male writer Laxness has of the inner intricacies of female sexuality, as well as a failure to imagine layers of complexity existing within "truculent spinsters."

What does uncovering potential moments of queerness do for an understanding of these novels depicting peripheralized societies? The backdrop of this 1930s period of shared financial difficulty in an Iceland dependent on Denmark and the US South during the Great Depression illustrates the anxieties surrounding gender ideologies and nationalism in the former and changing social structures in the latter. A comparative reading emphasizes the various overlapping forms of liminality circulating in this moment in terms of gender, sex, class, race, and coloniality. Investigating these examples of literary tomboyism alongside other identity markers allows for the possibility of more expansive readings focusing on the characters' agency and challenging of cisheteronormative narrative expectations upheld for liminal characters in liminal spaces. According to Karin Quimby, "the tomboy's 'perverse' detours away from the marriage plot—and the attachment of some readers to such emplotted figures—signify the presence of other significant forms of desire and identification that, for many girls and women, are ends in themselves" (5). For instance, *Salka Valka's* ending "detours away from the marriage plot," and the novel ends with her as an unattached, politically empowered woman with the freedom to decide what she wants next for herself. While there is debate on how enfranchised we leave Frankie, eager to travel the world with Mary Littlejohn, or Mick, working at Woolworth's yet saving up for a piano, their tomboy plots, like Salka's, "provoke desires and identifications that exist outside of heterosexual narrative trajectories" (Quimby 6). All three novels open up understandings of these characters and their dreams, goals, and desires, offering alternatives beyond the constraints of societal expectations for characters assumed to be straight, cisgender girls in peripheral spaces that are in many ways parallel.

THE PRESENCE OF RACE IN MCCULLERS AND LAXNESS

Just as an exploration of tomboyism alongside colonial hierarchies of gender, class, and sexuality opens the novels to deeper layers of understanding, an examination of race is also revealing and can be seen to reflect each society's distinct approach to racial relations, discussed in previous chapters. For instance, McCullers's candid representations of race in her novels mirror the more immediate, tangible interracial interactions in the early twentieth-century US South, where multiple races have inhabited the same communities for centuries through the history of plantation slavery. However, while immigration from African countries to Iceland, for example, has increased in the contemporary era from 176 people in 1996 to 668 people in 2008 (Loftsdóttir, "Imagining Blackness" 17), the nation was relatively isolated until the World War II period. During this era, Iceland had an insular and overwhelmingly White population—though it is worth noting that transnational migration always had some role in Iceland's history as a Danish colony (Loftsdóttir and Mörtudóttir 219). The anxiety around *Ástandið* or the "Situation" of Icelandic women pairing with foreign soldiers and the unofficial policy excluding Black soldiers from being stationed in Iceland during World War II reveal that this erasure of difference was to an extent intentional. This absence was especially pronounced in the more rural regions, demonstrated by a newspaper headline from 1977, "Negro in Þistilfjörður": as Loftsdóttir notes, the reporter considered the existence of a Black man in this remote area significant enough to warrant a special column ("Imagining Blackness" 17).[33] As a result, race is less apparent as a theme in *Salka Valka* than in *The Heart Is a Lonely Hunter* and *The Member of the Wedding*, yet its significance is implicit.

Scholars and her contemporary writers alike have praised McCullers's layered depictions of Black characters, including *The Member of the Wedding*'s Berenice Sadie Brown, the cook of the Addams household; T. T. Williams, her suitor; and her cousin Honey Brown, often read as queer and paired with Frankie through his inability to find a place for himself in the community; as well as Portia Copeland, her brother William, and her father Dr. Copeland, local intellectual and medical doctor, in *The Heart Is a Lonely Hunter*. McCullers demonstrates an understanding of the intersections of race, gender, sexuality, and class through her characters' interactions. For instance, when describing how everyone is caught in one way or another, Berenice notes that it is different for her because she is Black: "But they done drawn completely extra bounds around all colored people" (119).[34] In his review of *The Heart Is a Lonely Hunter*, Richard Wright voices what he considers "the most impressive aspect" of the novel: "the astonishing humanity that enables a white writer, for the first time in Southern fiction, to handle Negro characters with as much ease and justice as those of her own race" ("Inner Landscape" 18).[35] He accounts for this ability not in McCullers's politics or style, but "an attitude toward life which enables Miss McCullers to rise above the pressures of her environment and embrace black and white humanity in one sweep of apprehension and tenderness" (18), which Wright views as distinguishing her from her contemporaries (Mass 230).

In *Playing in the Dark: Whiteness and the Literary Imagination*, Toni Morrison identifies a "carefully observed, carefully invented, Africanist presence" (6), which looms also in US literature less directly engaged with Black characters and communities than McCullers's work. Morrison investigates "the ways in which a nonwhite, Africanlike (or Africanist) presence or persona was constructed in the United States, and the imaginative uses this fabricated presence served" (6), exposing "the entire range of views, assumptions, readings, and misreadings that accompany Eurocentric learning about these people" (7), as opposed to realistic reflections of Black people and cultures. She explains that coded language used to deal with "the racial disingenuousness and moral frailty" at the heart of the nation also infiltrated literature, extending into the twentieth century and reproducing the need for codes and restrictions (6). Moreover, while "the signs and bodies" of this "fabricated Africanist presence" were essential to the formation of US literature into the twentieth century (6), Morrison notes that other global spaces—"South America, England, France, Germany, Spain" (7)—also participated. And though it is not expressly named, I'd add Iceland to the Western nations on this list.

One explicit example of an Icelandic novel that exemplifies the coded approach to race described by Morrison is Einar Már Guðmundsson's compelling *Angels of the Universe* (1995; *Englar alheimsins*, 1993), which follows a young schizophrenic Icelander named Paul from childhood to early adulthood and is based on the experiences of the author's brother (Arnarsdóttir). While the novel includes no characters of color, I argue from my US-based cultural frame that teenage bully Omar, with his "criminal tendencies" (E. Guðmundsson 156), is placed in conversation, intentionally or not, with certain racialized stereotypes. Omar is a common name in Iceland and is of Arabic and Hebrew origin ("Omar 1"), associating the character with non-Whiteness. Omar's nickname, "Omar the Black," is not revealed until the end of the novel. While *Angels of the Universe* offers no explanation for it, the nickname seems to derive from the association of Blackness with criminality in the novel. What we get of the backstory of "Omar the Black, that cool gaolbird" also places him in conversation with other common Western racialized stereotypes (159). For instance, in their recent study interviewing Icelanders identified as "mixed, in terms of both race and origin" (215), Loftsdóttir and Mörtudóttir describe racial stereotypes of Blackness, such as "being good at physical activities and rapping," as "well-familiar" in Iceland (222). Raised in poverty, Omar is not interested in sports, yet he is described as "both nimble and athletic and later became a good dancer who would charm the girls off their feet" (157), in line with common stereotypes. Omar the Black's "voice was hoarse"; he has "deep creases down his face, scars from fights" (158); and he describes himself as having "loads of" children (159). Whether intended by the author or not, stereotypical associations of Black men not only with criminality, but also athleticism, violence, and absent fatherhood seem to have permeated this novel to provide layers to this minor character, whose reappearance nevertheless has a lasting effect on the narrator, in line with Morrison's assessment that "black people ignite critical moments of discovery or change or emphasis in literature not written by them" (*Playing* viii).[36] Indeed, a re-encounter with Omar leads Paul to leave his boardinghouse at the end of the novel.

While, like Guðmundsson's *Angels of the Universe*, Laxness's *Salka Valka* does not feature any non-White characters, I'd argue that coded language and racial stereotypes can be read in Steinþór Steinsson in a similar way to those associated with Omar the Black, adding problematic layers to his character. When *Salka Valka* was written in 1931, US-based racial stereotypes were already circulating in Icelandic culture, as demonstrated by the popularity of films like D. W. Griffith's *The Birth of a Nation* (1915), released in Iceland in 1920.[37] Aside from a priest with an interest in missionary work in China and India (324), Steinþór is the only character in the novel to refer to or likely to have interacted with people of color through his global journeys as a sailor. He states, for instance, that the life in Salka's face "has run through [his] blood in a hundred degrees of heat and fifty degrees of frost, both down south in Haiti and up north in Hudson Bay, among blacks, Indians, and Eskimos" (486), linking the north to the south through his interactions with people of color in both spaces.[38] Steinþór is introduced to the reader as "a big man . . . dark-haired, with a pockmarked, copper-colored face," with features that are "regular and strong, but a fire burned in his rust-colored eyes, dissolute, unrestrained, and wild" and a voice that is "strong and deep, yet with nuances that occasionally boarded on the lyrical" (15).[39] With his dark hair, copper face, and deep voice, Steinþór is coded as Black; the association of Blackness

106 CHAPTER 3

Figure 3.1 An advertisement for a screening of *The Birth of a Nation* in an Icelandic paper dated January 20, 1920. *Morgunblaðið*, Issue 61, p. 1, Timarit.is, National and University Library of Iceland, timarit.is/page/1205004

with "wildness" is also underscored by the description. This imagery appears again toward the end of the novel—when he is described as "copper-colored, black-maned" (492)—and he is repeatedly referred to as "pockmarked" (60), "the man with the burned head" (71), or simply as a "beast" (76), in line with racialized animalistic stereotypes.[40] And along similar lines, Hallberg Hallmundsson describes him as "a hard-drinking *gorilla* of a fisherman, full of swagger and animal magnetism" (42, emphasis mine). While Hallmundsson's term "gorilla" has racialized connotations, his description also emphasizes the layers to Steinþór's character. He isn't without charm, as depicted through his hold over Sigurlína and the fact that Salka simultaneously despises and is drawn to him—often as a result of his manipulations.[41]

As a sailor, he has seen more of the world than the majority of the inhabitants of Salka's secluded Icelandic town, and he speaks disparagingly of the people of color with whom he has interacted. He complains that he had to "shovel coals in a ship's hold in the company of black men and criminals" (Laxness, *Salka Valka* 229)—again highlighting this stereotypical connection—as well as "associate with both negroes and sodomites" (255). While the language in the latter example is outdated and offensive, it demonstrates the link between racial and sexual otherness in literary representations.[42] His existence as a sexual threat to Salka puts him in conversation with the US-grounded myth of the Black rapist, as highlighted through his description when he reappears later in the novel: his face "was bronze-colored and coarse, with huge jaws, chiseled features, thick lips but a regular mouth, bristly hair that stuck out in every direction, and eyes that glowed like hot copper. . . . Her face whitened and she momentarily lost her breath" (223). Straight out of a scene from *The Birth of a Nation*, Salka's face blanches as she loses her breath before the "beast rapist" stereotype, whose description here, complete with thick lips and bristly hair, is in line with minstrel imagery, first invented in the US in the 1800s.[43] Laxness's complicated depiction of Steinþór as a layered character challenges the lack of development common to sketchily outlined Black rapist types, even as he capitalizes on this racially charged imagery to amplify Steinþór's presence as a sexual threat, which I revisit below.

Building on this concept of coded or veiled Black presences, according to Abate, literary tomboys themselves were historically coded as Black, exposing the reliance on stereotypes and the exploitation of non-White peoples and cultures in the US-based liberatory narratives of White tomboys.[44] Abate has connected gender convincingly to race through the liminality of this border figure, straddling Whiteness and Blackness, with tomboyishness and Blackness "mutually construct[ing] or at least reinforc[ing] each other throughout these periods" (xiii). For instance, although Frankie is blonde like Mick and Salka, Abate notes that her face is referred to as "a dark ugly mug" (McCullers, *Member* 40), and her association with the term "freak" aligns her with Blackness and difference over Whiteness and "normality" (Abate 159). The use of coded Blackness is another aesthetic connection linking the novels: a poetics emphasizing the peripheralization of certain characters in already liminal spaces, building from Hosam Aboul-Ela's poetics of peripheralization, examined most expansively in chapter 4.

Pushing this association between literary tomboys and Blackness even further, Lisa Selin Davis asserts that "tomboyism in America is firmly rooted in racism," differentiating between the White, wealthy, urban tomboys playing outside in the nineteenth century and the enslaved rural girls, who wouldn't have been considered tomboys for engaging in masculine behaviors like physical labor. This distinction calls to mind Hortense J. Spillers's discussion of the ungendering of enslaved women. The system of slavery warped traditional understandings of gender roles for enslaved human beings, considered to be property rather than people. In reference to the endemic sexual exploitation of enslaved women, Spillers states that while "the gendered female *exists* for the male, we might suggest that the ungendered female—in an amazing stroke of pansexual potential—might be invaded/raided by another woman or man" (77). In analyzing these figures, it is important to be aware of the coded implications of these narratives and the contexts and histories out of which they arose, as well as to recognize the White literary tomboy as a racially privileged category in US culture and history (also in terms of gender with her masculine characteristics, though not always of an elevated class position). Through an intersectional lens, the colonial hierarchies of race, gender, class, and sexuality converge upon the bodies of the young protagonists of Laxness's and McCullers's novels.

DEPICTIONS OF SEXUAL VIOLENCE TOWARD YOUNG GIRLS IN THE NOVELS

With this in mind, I'd like to extend the exploration of the experiences of young, gendered characters in peripheralized societies by examining the depictions of sexual violence in the novels. I'll begin by observing that the most overt instance of sexual violence occurs toward a Black girl in *The Heart Is a Lonely Hunter*. Dr. Copeland awards his annual essay prize to Lancy Davis, whose older sister "had gone out to work as a servant when she was eleven years old and she had been raped by her employer, a white man past middle age" (McCullers, *Heart* 184). Lancy has struggled with his mental health since this incident. While the White tomboys encounter thwarted attempts at rape, importantly, the only rape victim across the three novels is a young Black girl, elucidating the interacting hierarchies of race, gender, and class in the novels. Lancy's sister's story, even her name, is not provided space beyond the basic facts of her experience, as well as the heavy impact of this violence on her brother.[45] The girl was just eleven years old at the time of the attack; Salka is the same age when Steinþór's assaults begin, and Frankie is twelve at the time of her assault. These instances of violence and their lasting effects also highlight the problematic positioning of children as sexualized beings by the men who attack them.[46] Both Graham-Bertolini and Perry emphasize "the devastating moments of sexual violence experienced or witnessed by [McCullers's] adolescent characters that shape how they inhabit their gendered sexuality" (Graham-Bertolini 2–3), connecting these moments of sexual violence to the young characters' understandings of themselves as gendered and sexual beings.

Frankie, in her naivete, mistakes her family's tenants having sex for Mr. Marlowe having a fit (McCullers, *Member* 40), and thus, she misses the nuances to her interactions with the red-haired solider who makes a date with her when she is dressed as F. Jasmine. While I acknowledge that he is drunk, I find it unbelievable that the soldier truly mistakes a twelve-year-old in a dress for a viable sexual partner and read him as more predatory than some scholars, underscoring the issue of the sexualization of children linking these novels.[47] Frankie meets the soldier again, and "their two conversations would not join together, and underneath there was a layer of queerness she could not place and understand" (133). He invites her upstairs and his behavior escalates until he grabs her as she tries to head for the door: "he grasped her skirt and, limpened by fright, she was pulled down beside him on the bed" (136). She narrowly avoids assault by biting his tongue and hitting him over the head with a glass pitcher (136). His aggression and irritation— "Come on, Jasmine. . . . Let's quit this stalling" (136)—would be abusive treatment of an adult woman but are even more absurd given Frankie's young age. She leaves him with an "amazed expression on his freckled face that was now pale, and a froth of blood [that] showed on his mouth" (137); Frankie and the reader never learn if he is dead or not. However, more importantly, Frankie safely makes her way out of the room, back to her street and to her cousin John Henry West. Significantly, the only rapists in McCullers's two novels are White men. In this way, she is seen as rejecting or writing back to the myth of the Black rapist, still widespread in the early twentieth-century US as an excuse for lynching and racial violence, as described in chapter 2.

Repeating the predatory dynamic of a man preying on a child, in Salka's case, her harasser is also her pseudo-stepfather Steinþór. Again, coded as Black and echoing the US-based Black rapist stereotype also present in Icelandic culture—one of his many layers—Steinþór assaults Sigurlína the first time readers encounter him, embracing her without consent and kissing her on the lips (Laxness, *Salka Valka* 18).[48] Shortly after the homeless mother and daughter are brought to stay with Steinþór's parents, he also molests eleven-year-old Salka. She states that he gropes her, "just like when lechers grope grownup girls. He groped me here and here and here and spoke some nonsense in my ear" (72). Sigurlína dismisses the abuse—"But he was probably just having fun with you" (72)—foreshadowing their problematic dynamic, with Sigurlína soon jealously regarding her eleven-year-old daughter as a rival for Steinþór's affection (unfortunately with cause).[49] The narrative voices emphasize the power and age differences between the two when Steinþór first tells young Salka of his pedophiliac romantic feelings for her: "*the child*, trembling, looked at *the man* with her troubled, terrified eyes" (135, emphasis mine). Couching this threat within a family dynamic, Laxness's novel perhaps intentionally connects these relationships to the reality of sexual abuse in Iceland. In her essay "*Litlar stelpur*," Kristjánsdóttir argues that Laxness was the first Icelandic writer to expose the ways young girls, including Salka, are groomed by older men and the damage that this sexual abuse causes children, another social issue critiqued by the novel and also revisited in chapter 4.

In a scene mirroring Frankie and the soldier, Steinþór grabs Salka and forces her down on the bed to prevent her from leaving while her mother brings him food from the kitchen before she is thrown from the room—seemingly still competing with her daughter. Positioning her as prey or a "little seal pup," whose blood he has smelled all winter, Steinþór declares that because of her, "the fire of life burns in my mortal bones, which I will hate until the lime in them has become dust at the bottom of the sea. Now the day of love has dawned in all its glory" (Laxness, *Salka Valka* 145). Echoing Frankie and the soldier's struggle in terms of the uncertainty of the outcome, the rest of the scene is ambiguous and cuts from Steinþór stepping toward Salka to Sigurlína and others bursting in to find Salka, described again as "the child," unconscious on the bed. The narrator ends the scene with the sentence "Such was Salka Valka's first personal experience of love" (145). As nothing in the scene portrays love, this would seem to be code for sex—if not pure sarcasm—implying Salka's rape. The fact that Steinþór did not rape her, if we take him at his word, is held back from both Salka and the readers until the end of the novel in the structure of deferred revelation, a tactic likewise favored by Faulkner.[50] In this revelatory scene, Steinþór voices his regret to Salka—"Unfortunately, I didn't succeed in doing so the other year. . . . It caused me immense regret for a thousand nights in cold and warm parts of the world. . . . [I vowed to do so] because you were the part of your mother that I most desired" (498)—before the encounter devolves into animalistic and sexualized physical fighting.[51] Regardless of the fact that these attacks were ultimately thwarted, all three novels call attention to sexual violence toward children through these ambiguously narrated scenes of aggression, as well as the attempts to normalize viewing young girls as sexual beings and the failure of their communities (often idealized, particularly in US southern literature) to protect them.[52]

The focus on Salka's early physical development provides another layer to this issue of the sexualization of children in the novel.[53] The narrator is omniscient though not static, shifting to different characters' viewpoints while resting primarily with Salka's. As in the descriptions of Gústa's body from Salka's perspective, "Laxness uses this freedom in many ways, sometimes describing events from above and outside as if seen through a camera lens, at other times using various characters as focus points" (Jóhannsson 384). He uses this "freedom" to emphasize Salka's maturing body. The narration of these sections remains primarily within her perspective, as she observes the growth of her breasts with horror: "They even seemed to become larger by the day, and were as sensitive as blossoms" (Laxness, *Salka Valka* 153). However, male characters also sexualize Salka's body: Angantýr cannot help noticing Salka's "swelling bosom, robust loins" (359), and Bogesen's less lecherous eye does not fail to detect "her bosom curvy beneath her woolen sweater" (334). In contrast, McCullers's novels are narrated by more stable omniscient third-person narrative voices that follow the main characters in *The Heart Is a Lonely Hunter* and primarily Frankie in *The Member of the Wedding*. Aside from their introductions or the descriptions in the scenes when Mick and Frankie uncharacteristically dress up, the narrators of McCullers's novels do not linger on the physical bodies of the young female characters—a difference that perhaps stems from the subject positions of the writers.

Concluding with this multifaceted examination of the sexualization of young girls forces us to double back around to the political aspects of the novels as filtered through the experiences of individual characters. Tomboy identities, embracing characteristics branded by society as more masculine, do not protect these characters from the threat of sexual violation and the positioning of children of any gender as sexual prey, which clearly marks the limits of their agency and the power of their disidentifications. A focus on sexual violence toward young girls runs through each novel, although to varying degrees of centrality: all three share an approach to this large-scale issue through the personal experiences of characters. Again, though not necessarily foregrounded overtly in each text, this emphasis comes to the fore when the three novels are read together with attention to gender, sexuality, and the complex colonial histories of the US South and Iceland.

The fact that these themes have been explored frequently in the scholarship on the novels of McCullers, a queer southern woman, whereas critical discussions of the work of Laxness, an Icelandic man assumed to be straight, have focused primarily on politics may connect to the identities of the authors, raising questions about the extent to which the subject positions of the writers impact our perceptions of the texts and what is centered in analyses of them. This suggests not only the blind spots or obstructed views of the authors, as mentioned above in terms of Laxness's knowledge of female sexuality, but also the obstructed views of readers and critics and the assumptions they place on texts.

Nevertheless, with attention to the experiences of these cross-cultural literary tomboys, we celebrate their individuality at the same we ensure that the threats to their safety and the vibrancy of their identities are not overlooked by society. Exploring the experiences of Salka, Mick, and Frankie together deepens our understandings of the multiplicitous ways twentieth-century Icelandic and US southern societies remain impacted by their colonial histories and the lingering hierarchical dynamics that accompany them. Such a comparative analysis expands beyond an emphasis on the overvaluation of Whiteness and forms of racial violence—whether physical, sexual, or linguistic—as exclusion, explored in the first two chapters, to reveal the intricacies and patterns relating to gender and sexuality in both societies and to validate the shades of resistance to cishetereopatriarchy located in these characters' defiant gender nonconformity. In this way, the liminal figure of the tomboy, connecting these diverse spaces, helps to elucidate other forms of liminality depicted in the novels. At the same time, these novels encourage us to read gender and sexuality as representative of broader postcolonial dynamics, with these hierarchical relationships holding more expansive significance beyond their individual specificity, as elucidated in the next chapter.

Chapter 4

"A WOMAN'S WILDNESS"

Power, Magic, and Intergenerational Ties in
Tiphanie Yanique and Fríða Áslaug Sigurðardóttir

One more indirect effect of colonization is the way it links spaces with diverse histories and cultures across the globe from the arctic north to the tropical south. From the thirteenth to twentieth centuries, Denmark's empire extended from parts of present-day Estonia and forts on the east coast of India to the Gold Coast of Africa (Ghana) and Norway, Greenland, the Faroe Islands, Orkney, Shetland, and Iceland in the north (Blaagaard and Andreassen 83). By merging with Norway in 1381, Denmark had acquired Iceland, which had been incorporated into Norway in the late thirteenth century (S. G. Magnússon 19). Although late to the position of colonial power, Denmark also colonized St. Thomas in 1671, St. John in 1717, and in 1733 purchased St. Croix from France (Loftsdóttir and Pálsson 41). However, the positionings of each space were not equal: "Iceland's status in this complex and heterogeneous state was that of a dependency ('biland' in Danish), which gave it a certain preferential status to the Danish colonies (such as Greenland and the Virgin Islands)" (Hálfdanarson, "Iceland: A Peaceful Secession" 88).[1] Nevertheless, as Kristín Loftsdóttir and Gísli Pálsson assert in their article about Hans Jónatan, a man born into slavery in St. Croix who was transferred to Copenhagen and later escaped to Iceland to avoid being sent back to St. Croix, "colonialism linked parts of the world that previously had little or no connection to each other" (38)—here St. Thomas and Iceland.

In this chapter I will analyze intergenerational family dynamics; women's experiences; and the relationship between power, magic, and history, primarily examining two novels from nations formerly controlled by Denmark—Tiphanie Yanique's *Land of Love and Drowning* (2014), which takes place on St. Thomas in the US Virgin Islands, and Fríða Áslaug Sigurðardóttir's *Night Watch* (1995; *Meðan nóttin líður*, 1990), set in rural Iceland—with connections also drawn to Gayl Jones's US southern geographies in *Corregidora* (1975). These books are revealing in terms of the stories that elude broader historical accounts: How are we remembered? What survives us for future generations? They both explore intergenerational ties between women, the multiplicity of truth, and the shifting, inaccessible nature of history, and when read together they expand the focus of this book outward beyond the overlapping nodes of the US South and Iceland that have served as the primary emphasis thus far.[2]

THE SPECTRAL AND ALLEGORICAL PRESENCE OF DANISH COLONIALISM AND US NEOCOLONIALISM

Danish colonialism is not central to either novel—instead acting as an absent presence that itself can be seen as resistance to the all-encompassing nature of that history—and I do not intend to re-impose colonial history here but to consider the references present, both spectral and allegorical, before shifting to the interpersonal. Writing about Nella Larsen's *Quicksand*, Arne Lunde and Anna Westerstahl Stenport describe the "novel's silence (its present 'absence' if you will) about the Danish colonial legacy" as paralleling the Danish public silence concerning its colonial history when the novel was written (229). Shades of that silence can be found in Yanique's and Sigurðardóttir's novels; however, I argue that in these texts silence functions as a more active refusal to be defined solely by colonial and neocolonial dynamics—less an absence and more a latent presence. These dynamics are a reality but remain in the background, out of focus. While the novels in this chapter do not explicitly address colonial ties and histories, they gesture toward these legacies through the interconnection of related issues, such as gender, family, sexuality, and national identity, with gender politics standing allegorically for broader colonial dynamics. Looking at these spaces together with a focus on the experiences of women helps us to understand coloniality, its accompanying effects, and the true depths of their impacts on more individual scales: these histories are still with us.

While peripheral to events of each novel, Denmark is a point of connection linking St. Thomas and Iceland. *Land of Love and Drowning* focuses primarily on the experiences and voices of women; however, it begins with the perspective of the patriarch, Captain Owen Arthur Bradshaw, who can trace his lineage back to West Africans, Europeans, Asians, and the Caribs, who are indigenous to the islands. The novel opens at the home of Mr. Lovernkrandt, a Danish businessman who is not leaving the island despite the fact that "Denmark was giving up on the West Indies and America was buying in" (Yanique, *Land* 3), the language highlighting the financial nature of the transaction. A few pages later, the narrators, who function similarly to a Greek chorus and are positioned as "Old Wives" (alongside Eeona, Anette, and Jacob, who each narrate sections), describe Owen's untimely death as not of old age but of love. The Old Wives also link Owen's death to the historic moment: "The Danish West Indies will become the United States Virgin Islands and then this patriarch will die. And perhaps these things are the same" (5).[3] From the start, patriarchal and political powers are related, clearing space for the more subversive experiences and stories of the women in the Bradshaw family that will soon overtake the text and situating the story in the realm of the interpersonal, as opposed to the overtly political.

The direct involvement of Nordic countries in colonialism combats the silences found in Danish national memory. The region economically benefited from slavery and colonialism, with plantations operating in both the Swedish and Danish colonies in the West Indies (Palmberg 40–41). The first slave ship landed on St. Thomas in 1673 (Palmberg 45), demonstrating the entwinement of slavery and colonialism in the Danish Caribbean. St. Thomas remained under Danish colonial rule until 1917 when the Danish West Indies were transferred to US control, primarily as a result of their strategic position in the passage to the Panama Canal. US citizenship was granted to inhabitants of the Virgin Islands (USVI) in 1927, and while they have sent a member to the US House of Representatives since 1973, that member does not have a vote, limiting the impact of the USVI on US politics. With this historical context in the background, Yanique's novel primarily focuses on the children of Owen and his wife Antoinette, Eeona and Anette, as well as Anette's children, Ronalda, Youme, and Frank, and their experiences in the period following the transfer of the Danish West Indies. With the knowledge that the transfer occurred in 1917, described by Anette as "Transfer Day," it is possible to piece together a chronology for the novel (Yanique, *Land* 11). However, time and its passage are not clearly conveyed, and it is challenging to summarize the events of the plot aside from these broad strokes. The difficulty in doing so embodies Hosam Aboul-Ela's concept of the poetics of peripheralization, or the ways in which the aesthetics reflect the "historiography of the periphery" (*Other South* 136), which may take a different form from that of the core—in this case, with a nebulous sense of time's passing in the novel. The historical events referenced collide with the folkloric feel to various episodes, revealing a feminist resistance to Eurocentric linear narrations and a rejection of colonial cishetereopatriarchy. References to time are present but rarely straightforward.

In another example of this textual resistance, the family dynamics deemphasize the patriarchs in favor of a matriarchal lineage. Anette is the lifeblood connecting her family. Her children's names divulge their secondary parentage or fathers: Ronalda's father is Ronald Smalls, and Frank's is Franky Joseph. Anette and her half brother Jacob Esau McKenzie, who (although they are both unaware) is not a McKenzie but also a Bradshaw, together create Eve Youme, nicknamed "Me" for a reflexive touch. The name she uses, Youme, emphasizes the fused bloodlines, and her first name, Eve, reflects Jacob's fallacious belief that she is the first female McKenzie (225). Eeona's name, according to the family's former caretaker Hippolyte Lammartine (potentially one of the "Old Wives"), comes from "He Own Her" (343), representing her problematic entangled familial, romantic, and likely sexual connection to her father Owen, with his name resembling the verb "own." Anette's name seems to stem from her mother's, Antoinette, with both also echoing characters in Jean Rhys's famous novel about gender, power, and "madness," *Wide Sargasso Sea.*[4] Moreover, Antoinette's family name, Stemme, resonates with the Danish word *stem*, or to vote, underscoring the "transfer" to US citizenship but without voting rights or any say in the governing systems.[5]

Transfer Day is narrated by Anette, who positions herself as "the historian in this family," with history presented in a particular way, introducing us to the magical thread and connection to folklore running throughout the novel: "Nowadays people think historians are stuffy types, but history is a kind of magic I doing here" (Yanique, *Land* 10). Madison Smartt Bell notes that, born on the cusp of her family's downfall, "Anette has a saltier sensibility, expressed in a bawdy West Indian patois." Although I would not agree with the choice of demeaning descriptor, Anette's more colloquial voice stands out among the other narrators. Anette describes the transfer of the three islands and their lack of agency: "Denmark decide it don't want we. America decide it do. One find we unnecessary because they way up in Europe. The next find we absolutely necessary because they backside sitting on the Caribbean. Just so we get pass from hand to hand" (Yanique, *Land* 10–11). She describes how everyone went to "the military Barracks and wave toonchy American flags" and wondered about statehood (11). There were protesters wearing yellow, "the color of we islands" (12), instead of red, white, and blue. Anette details the playing of the Danish national anthem and the lowering of the Danish flag before the raising of the US flag, which Antoinette tells Eeona is freedom

Figure 4.1 Transfer of the Danish West Indies to US control on March 31, 1917, with the lowering of the Danish flag to Denmark's national anthem. Photograph by John Lee, National Museum of Denmark.

Figure 4.2 Transfer ceremony on March 31, 1917. The US flag is raised while a military band plays the US national anthem. Photograph by John Lee, National Museum of Denmark.

(14). Anette ends with "And just so, we go from Danish to American like it ain nothing. Like it ain everything" (14). The colonial connection to Denmark is submerged beneath the weight of the US's strong presence and influence but continues to haunt the novel—a latent presence—in a similar manner to Owen's lingering impact after his death, which is given emphasis through the novel's focus on the individual scale of the Bradshaws, the McKenzies, and their experiences and relationships.

Demonstrated by way of the shadow left by Owen's death and financial ruin in the text, Denmark's presence remains palpable, though spectral, even after St. Thomas, St. John, and St. Croix no longer have official ties to Denmark. Passing references are made to Denmark and the Danish; for instance, loud, drunk American tourists are juxtaposed with other White people in St. Thomas, such as "old Danes who hadn't quit" (Yanique, *Land* 235), and the US-owned Hilton hotel is contrasted with the "Grand Hotel with the austere Danish architecture" (245). Toward the end of the novel, the Beach Occupation Movement and Bacchanal (BOMB) protesters advocating for open beach access for the residents of the islands are held on Coast Guard ships. Youme notes, "We all chatted like it was Food Fair Day, just with no food, or like on Transfer Day so many years ago, which most of us could not recall because we'd not yet been born then" (359), seemingly coming full circle from the novel's opening, in which Anette, who also hadn't been born, narrates the Transfer Day. However, unlike the receding Danish colonial control on Transfer Day, the US influence remains more pronounced after the BOMB protests conclude. Despite this victory regarding control over the beaches, the neocolonial ties between the US and the Virgin Islands remain strong into the contemporary period.

Iceland, across the North Atlantic Ocean from St. Thomas, is another space with lingering colonial ties to Denmark, in addition to a more persistent US neocolonial presence. As outlined in the previous chapters, Iceland became a sovereign state in a personal union with Denmark in 1918—a year after the transfer of the Danish West Indies to the US—before acquiring full independence in 1944. However, Iceland also endured a US military presence effectively from 1941 to 2006 (Hall 22). The presence of the US military base at Keflavík was a central political issue in the second half of the twentieth century, continuing for several decades. Those against the base cited the protection of national sovereignty as a primary objection (S. G. Magnússon 247), with the US base also complicating Iceland's history of neutrality and pacifism. Parallels can be made to the lack of national self-determination accompanying the transfer of the Danish West Indies to US control. While the political issue of the military presence appears briefly in the novel, Sigurðardóttir's *Night Watch* focuses primarily on the experiences of an individual family, grounded in the viewpoint of successful advertising executive Nina, who returns to the area of Hornstrandir in the Northwest where she was raised in order to sit beside Thordis, her dying mother. A writer, Nina is overwhelmed by the stories of her female predecessors, compulsively remembering and recording the segments of their stories that have been passed down to her. Over her three days of vigil, Nina reflects on the gaps between the farming society of yesterday and her modern lifestyle. Nina is a member of a higher class than the rest of her family, a point underscored by her references to her "dark blue, gleaming Jaguar," her Armani suit, and her wearing "a fur coat at an anti-base demonstration," a protest against the US military presence—a cause to which she doesn't seem particularly committed (Sigurðardóttir 109, 136).[6] Indeed, Nina portrays herself as feeling "rootless, foreign, lost. She looks back in her search for meaningful values which can serve for modern life. This cavalcade of memories is thus filled with soul-searching flashbacks" (Rosenblad and Sigurðardóttir-Rosenblad 168). Nina, who has built a life around distinguishing herself from her ancestors' primarily domestic experiences, reflects on where she comes from and struggles internally with the extent to which the experiences we survive and the memories we knit together hold any meaning that outlasts us.

The novel highlights the murky line between what happened in the past and what is invented or layered onto it. Nina sees in death "the teeming writhing worms," while her daughter Sarah sees "metamorphosis, conception, restoration" (Sigurðardóttir 120). Nina equates this more optimistic worldview with her daughter being "totally blind to reality" (121), stating her version in stark terms: "Reality: Thordis, born in a turf cottage, just before the turn of the century, in a narrow isolated inlet. Twenty-four or -five years old, she married her childhood sweetheart, Olafur, and had eight children by him, five of whom are alive," ending with a description of how she now lies, "a mute heap of flesh, connected to bags of intravenous infusion and a urine receptacle, a sign of life, her last: urine that flows into a transparent bag attached to a white bed" (121). This moment with her mother's physical body, a "mute heap of flesh," is what Nina embraces as reality—all the other interpretations are positioned as versions of the truth layered upon it.

Unlike *Land of Love and Drowning*, which is narrated not only by the Old Wives but also directly by Anette and Eeona with two sections granted to Jacob's deferential, interrupting voice, everything the reader has access to in *Night Watch* is filtered through Nina, who switches between first- and third-person narration. Although rejecting an easily definable plot, *Land of Love and Drowning* progresses primarily in a chronological fashion through the lives of the Bradshaw family with antilinear flashes backward and forward. For instance, the Old Wives hint even before Anette is born that she would become the "redhead woman who would stain Rebekah's son's soul" (Yanique, *Land* 41), that of her half brother Jacob. In contrast, less happens in the present of *Night Watch*. As Nina sits with her mother and has conversations with other visitors, flashbacks to previous generations take over the narrative and provide more of the action, though still narrated by Nina. While these begin with Sunneva, the earliest of her "ancestral women" (Sigurðardóttir 122), they are not confined to chronological order, instead incorporating Nina's own memories aside her reconstructions of Thordis's and her sister Maria's recollections. *Night Watch* similarly employs a non-linear structure that we might associate with a poetics of peripheralization: an anticolonial, feminist resistance to Eurocentric linear narratives. The folkloric references and magical realist aspects common to both texts represent alternative or subaltern forms of knowledge from outside society's hierarchies and power structures. As in Yanique's novel, political, and in this context more masculine, references—for instance, Iceland's relation to both Denmark and the US—are also present in *Night Watch*, yet more subtle and submerged due to the surreal style of Sigurðardóttir's text. One needs to read between the lines of Nina's depictions.

More specifically, Copenhagen is positioned as the metropole in this novel, although the depiction of the colonial dynamics between Iceland and Denmark is understated and given even less space than in Yanique's. Thordis's sister Maria has spent much of her life abroad—living in Copenhagen and striving to escape her class position. She is a parallel to Eeona in *Land of Love and Drowning* as a strong, unmarried aunt figure who leaves home and who also covets membership (or, for Eeona, the reinstatement of membership) in a higher class. I will return shortly to the materiality and what is physically passed down between the generations, but one item is a letter from Katherine to Maria received when the latter lived in Copenhagen. The letter is "quite yellow with age" with "no grand tidings, no pieces of advice, wisdom—nothing but an ordinary letter from an old woman in the provinces to her daughter in a far-off country" (Sigurðardóttir 67), emphasizing the distance between here and there. Nina discovers that Maria may have gone abroad to learn to paint (70)—the metropole being associated with art and culture—but she is limited in that dream (by gender? by class? by her appearance?) and does not advance "past the stage of being a model at that academy of theirs" (71). According to Maria, there is no future in the peripheries, and she implores Thordis to join her abroad—"come with me, let's go abroad, no future here . . . then there is the ball next weekend and the play they will be putting on, you just can't miss that, oh" (86). For Maria, life happens in the metropole.

Maria narrates to Nina vague flashbacks to her life in the metropole. Thordis visits, and the girls are allowed to alter the mistress of the house's cast-off garments to fit themselves, performing membership in a higher class. Although the city is not named in this section as Copenhagen, this is the likely setting, given the thirty years that Maria lived there "from just after the First World War to sometime after the Second" and their role at the consulate (Sigurðardóttir 81), with the Icelandic embassy in Denmark having opened in 1920 ("Embassy"). While Copenhagen is portrayed as full of life and culture, particularly in comparison with rural turn-of-the-century Iceland, the wealth and splendor were derived from its colonial holdings and role in the slave trade: "In the list of countries with the dubious distinction of being the world's leading slave-trading nations, Denmark lies seventh, one place behind the United States" (Bone 64). This exploitative history and the treatment of women, and particularly women of color, under the colonial system isn't fully masked—even in Maria's telling.

Maria casts her story as "the intelligent maid and the young master, the consul's son" or, to Nina's mind, "Cinderella: stupid women's everlasting daydream" (Sigurðardóttir 88); indeed, both Nina and the readers recognize the exploitative dynamics involved. The scene is set with Maria serving coffee and cognac to a group of men reading a letter

> from a newly appointed governor in distant parts, containing a description of local women, followed by an enumeration that Maria can still recall, word for word, after all these years: the merchant's daughter, the vicar's daughter, the doctor's daughter, the daughters of the nobility—they all get their due. The men writhe with laughter, not least the young man by the window [Maria's implied lover], and, as soon as she proceeds with her story, Maria's voice grows hard. (89)[7]

In this atmosphere one of the men assaults Maria, his hand "gliding down her buttock, her thigh, to grasp her from below" (89). She is "transfixed, surrounded by uproarious laughter; howling, laughing masks, predator's eyes everywhere" until the "master himself" (89), presumably the consul, "pluck[s] the assailant away" (90)—the verb here underscoring the grasp. Maria's sexual assault in this scene is narrated alongside the exploitation of "local women" by a colonial governor in "distant parts," the novel's only direct reference to Denmark's other global colonies and seemingly the exploitation of women across lines of race, color, and class, with everyone from the merchant's daughter to the daughters of the nobility "get[ting] their due." Here, Maria's exploitation as a rural, working-class White woman from Iceland serving as a "maid . . . never the housekeeper, doesn't use that title" to the consul in Copenhagen is related to other women's experiences of exploitation under a colonial system, recognizing the limits to this comparison to avoid the conflation of experiences across racial lines (90). The novels are both invested in an exploration of gender and class dynamics, yet race and color play a much larger role in Yanique's novel. These identities constitute more of a latent presence in Sigurðardóttir's narrative, where colonial legacies remain significant even when their impacts are less visible.

While Iceland was still ethnically homogeneous during the early twentieth-century period focused on in Sigurðardóttir's novel, in recent years the country has become more international, with 14.5 percent of the population identifying as foreign citizens in 2021 (Fontaine, "Foreign Nationals"). Given this history, racial, ethnic, and national differences are not central to the dynamics of *Night Watch*. As emphasized throughout this book, Iceland's experience as a dependency of Denmark differs from the horrors of plantation slavery and the experiences of other colonies in the Global South, a difference that can be linked to racial similarities, but likely also the shared history, language, and culture between Denmark and Iceland. Loftsdóttir argues that commercial agencies, the government, and the tourism industry emphasize Iceland as "exotic"—an association Icelanders tried to bury for centuries ("The Exotic North" 253)—while it remains "firmly located within the safety of the first world, offering all the necessary infrastructure and luxuries" (*Crisis and Coloniality* 153). Loftsdóttir goes on to note that if Whiteness draws power from the fact that White individuals do not have to define themselves in racialized terms, then in Iceland "while experiencing wild nature and natives, tourists that would be socially classified as white would generally not have to recognize themselves as racialized" (155).[8] In this way, travelers in Iceland are not "reminded of the contemporary conditions of insecurity and inequality which characterize the lives of many people in the global south," and the "exotic can be experienced, touched and observed without any of the unpleasant messiness of the present" (155). However, this is not an option for many former colonies in the Global South, including another popular destination for tourists: the Caribbean. The USVI provide a direct contrast to Iceland here, amplified by the shifting racial categorization from a more fluid understanding in the West Indies under Danish colonialism to the binary system of race promoted by US neocolonialism, which Jacob McKenzie experiences directly during his time in New Orleans, described below.[9]

Yanique dramatizes the insider-outsider status of the Virgin Islanders vis-à-vis US nationhood and citizenship. As Jennifer Donahue asserts, "the conception of the Caribbean as an exotic, resource-filled region is grossly inaccurate and has fueled a culture of exploitation" (108). Racial dynamics and the exploitative relationships between not only the US and St. Thomas but also tourists and locals are central to Yanique's novel. She depicts the way tourists from the mainland US hold a higher status in the USVI than the inhabitants, culminating in the BOMB movement. For instance, mainland tourists are given access to the shore, and islanders are denied this right. Anette and her family push for beach access for everyone, which the narrators position alongside other national and global movements, from the Weathermen and the Black Panthers to the Vietnam War: "John F. Kennedy died. Che Guevara died. Martin Luther King, Jr., died. And in the Virgin Islands we had the BOMB. We were marching on the sand and doing wade-ins and soak-ins and—for those who could—swim-ins. Running to the beaches in the middle of the night, past the guards and the dogs" (Yanique, *Land* 349). As Yanique describes in her author's note, the fictionalized success of this campaign is based on the real-world Positive Action Movement that resulted in the Virgin Islands Open Shorelines Act (395).

While the US can be seen as supplanting Denmark in terms of colonial dynamics in both the USVI (through the transfer) and Iceland (through the extended US military presence), this history is approached more directly in *Land of Love and Drowning*. A separate chapter would be needed to fully analyze Yanique's approaches to critiquing US power and influence in the region in both direct and nuanced ways. While some of the residents of St. Thomas were optimistic about the weight of their new American identities on Transfer Day, Yanique lays bare the distinctions between citizens of the mainland US and the islanders in the wake of the hurricane toward the end of the novel: "Many Americans on the island had been cradled off to civilization on the mainland by the federal government. It didn't matter that the native islanders were also Americans—no islanders were welcomed on those flights out" (318).[10] Further, the descriptions of Jacob's experiences while stationed in the US, which fellow serviceman Spice from Grenada terms "Naziland, U.S.A." (134), critique racial dynamics in the country. His time in New Orleans showcases the binary approach to race—"How mulatto Caribbean men like he was, who were educated and high-bred, could go to American colleges and become Negro overnight" (131)—alongside entrenched racial prejudices, such as the use of the n-word in reference to Jacob and his friends.[11] Through this example and later references to the "brewing" of "another American war . . . this time in Korea" (226), Yanique demonstrates the impact of US foreign policy and military conflicts on the islands. However, during Anette's family's confrontation with a man "from another Caribbean island, one far down the chain" (334), sent by the American woman who owns the land to remove them from her beachfront property, the man views them all as Americans: "*Why the hell did I leave Antigua? To come here and be in the middle of these blasted Americans?*" (335).

This moment adds complexity in terms of national identification based on one's perspective, recalling the distinctions between how you identify and how others identify you that I discussed in chapter 1.

Relatedly, an invasive American presence is subtly depicted in *Night Watch*. Aside from Nina's passing reference to wearing "her sealskin coat when she offered her support to the sweater gang against the US base in our country" (Sigurðardóttir 136), the US's intrusion in Iceland appears primarily through a protest Martha recounts for Nina. While the subject of the protest is not explicit to readers unknowledgeable about Icelandic history—the lack of specificity perhaps also representing Martha's imperfect memory or Nina's low level of investment in the political causes of her community—Martha describes the country as "a target, an atomic station" (133). This is a reference to the political situation of the US pushing for a military base in Iceland, explored through Halldór Laxness's *The Atom Station*, analyzed in chapter 1. While the US is never named directly in this scene, the repetition of another key phrase, "sell[ing] the country" (133), which also appears throughout Laxness's novel, helps to solidify the connection to this transatlantic historical episode. Martha recalls protesting "outside of the house that belonged to the people who might sell the country" (133), as well as the grasping hands when the man did appear, "wanting to kill him, murder him, the traitor who believed he could sell our country" (134). Thus, the discontent with the US military's intrusive power is represented in the novel through recollections of anger toward the Icelandic politicians opening up the country in this way—several layers removed from a direct critique of US neoimperial power.

WHAT IS PASSED DOWN: INTERGENERATIONAL FAMILY CONNECTIONS

The spatial relations of *Night Watch* and *Land of Love and Drowning*—connecting a nation considered part of the Far North to one considered part of the Global South through their former dependence on Denmark and present shouldering (to different degrees) of an intrusive US presence—exist alongside comparable temporal dynamics. Intergenerational family connections are at the heart of both works. The family histories are filtered through Nina the writer and Anette the historian (along with her sister and the Old Wives). Nina and Anette each play a direct role in some of the events related and recount their ancestors' experiences at other times, preserving the complexity of these intimate relationships. For instance, the women in Nina's family are connected in natural and supernatural ways, such as the moment when

Nina laughs in Katherine's dream—"She is Nemesis in a dream about a dream and discharges icy showers of laughter and words" (Sigurðardóttir 55)—or when, sitting next to her mother's body, she feels herself merged with her ancestors—"Here I sit: Nina, Katherine, Sunneva. A pillar of salt" (164). This reference to the biblical story of Lot's wife, turned into a pillar of salt for disobeying God's order not to glance back at the burning city of Sodom, both emphasizes Nina's underlying desire to break out of the trope of the good, obedient wife and also has implications for her backward-looking glance at her family's histories.[12] Through this looking back, Nina's identity fuses with those of the women who came before her: she is simultaneously herself, Katherine, and Sunneva.

Similarly, the women in the Bradshaw family share natural and supernatural bonds, including a degree of control over events and occurrences. For example, Anette believes that she brought herself to the point of death and back again to prevent Eeona from sending her off to St. Croix (Yanique, *Land* 97). In addition, women of the Stemme family are linked to the mermaid-like Duene of Anegada, who are known for living in the sea, having long hair, and walking backward (83). While Eeona's hair displays other worldly powers when unleashed, it is Youme whose feet are facing in the wrong direction and who dramatically charges into the sea during the final BOMB protest. According to Cherene Sherrard-Johnson, "Yanique's Duene merge Danish mariners' lore with West African deities associated with water and miscegenation. Her Virgin Island mermaids evince an atavistic 'wildness' passed down through oral history and incest" (108), which she relates to Hans Christian Andersen's *The Little Mermaid* (1837), the title character of which, like "rum, sugarcane, and chattel," also traversed Atlantic routes (108). This association connects the women in Youme's family not only to each other, but also to their transatlantic histories and cultural fusions.

Writing back to historical impulses to define women in relation to men, these two novels position men's experiences and voices as secondary to women's in terms of both the content and the structure of the novels, which relates back to these texts' poetics of peripheralization and their deemphasis of Eurocentric linear plot conventions. Anette's life can be broken into three phases in *Land of Love and Drowning*, organized around relationships, yet the emphasis remains on herself and her development as a character.[13] Anette's first husband is Ronald, with whom she never gets "the chance to figure out the love thing" (Yanique, *Land* 145). She next falls deeply for her half brother Jacob Esau McKenzie, thinking "This too wild and fast to be love. But it is. Like in the movies, only for real" (170). Finally, she raises her daughters and son Frank with her husband Franky Joseph, who has been in love with her since childhood and provides a more stable position in the community—although her affair with Jacob continues to the end of the novel.[14] While structured by these relationships, the focus of the narration remains on Anette's development as a woman, sister, and mother against the background of her shifting class position and uncertain national identity following the transfer. The primary emphasis on Anette demonstrates the narrative's relative disinterest in men, also a feature of *Night Watch*, in which Nina and the women of her family are the focus. The romance plots call attention to both societies' obsessions with nuclear family structures, patriarchal lineage, and nationhood—the patriarchal and the national are linked through strategies of containment and regulating behavior. These are subverted in the novels by Anette's expansive family, swelling beyond the nuclear to encompass three different fathers, as well as Nina's seeming indifference toward marriage and motherhood, women's responsibilities that are commonly positioned as foundational to the nation.

Nina's story is similarly structured, flashing between her three relationships. With her first love Arnar, Nina writes and he paints, but after a while, he doesn't have time to listen to what she has written, and she pretends not to notice his new paintings (Sigurðardóttir 42). As the woman in the relationship, Nina is expected to handle the domestic responsibilities: "No clean socks, Nina, yet you are writing again, so how am I to get to my exhibition . . . haddock again, haddock, always haddock, don't you know how to cook anything else. And slammed doors" (72). She leaves Arnar for Gudjon, a lawyer who lauds the bohemians with whom he never fully fits. Although she marries and has Sarah with Gudjon, it is clear even to her daughter that she has never loved him. Finally, Andreas lingers in the background of the present period. He wants to be there for Nina during her mother's last days, believing the two to be in a relationship, whereas Nina sees him as her "bedfellow who has got his lines confused and is starting to worry, wants to help, feels miserable" (163). Each of these relationships reveal much about Nina as a character—what she wants and values in her life, such as her independence and ability to write, as well as her disinterest in connecting with men on a deeper level. This disinterest is perhaps a lingering effect from the deterioration of her first relationship with Arnar and her unexamined guilt and trauma surrounding his death or simply a lifestyle choice. In this way, the descriptions of her relationships and how she relates them present readers with a more layered view of her character than just accepting her self-depictions (or even self-deceptions) at face value. The ability to see behind Nina's mask allows us to view her more accurately, highlighting the details of her life—such as her rejection of gender roles and the accompanying domesticity—beyond her function as a conduit for the stories of her ancestors.

While relationships help to structure the lives of protagonists in each novel, women remain at the center, pushing men, their voices, and their experiences into the background. Nina in *Night Watch* and Eeona and Anette in *Land of Love and Drowning* all break out of societal expectations for women's lives. Nina does this through her career and her writing, asserting that "I was writing. I was *not* the painter's wife. Never would be" (Sigurðardóttir 44). Her portrayal of her sexuality as uncoupled from marriage and reproduction also runs counter to societal conventions: "That painful craving. . . . Sexuality that's all. Hormones rebel against the very concept of annihilation" (38). Eeona's sexuality is likewise primarily divorced from marriage and motherhood and, additionally, repressed by her respectability politics and the value she places in her formerly elevated class position. While she raised Anette following her mother's death and gives birth to a stillborn child with Kweku Prideux, the Anancy figure—a spider who is a "quintessential hero of traditional creole folklore" and "masterful trickster" (De Souza 339, 340)—motherhood is otherwise not part of Eeona's story.[15] A snippet from the community's talk emphasizes the ways in which the Bradshaw women operate outside of society's norms:

> *Them poor Bradshaw sisters. . . . The elder daughter used to be so pretty but then she disappear and return a old maid. And that Anette one—a divorcée! Gone and had a second child with piano-playing-war-hero Jacob McKenzie—so she say. He gone and left she and the child. Gone a whole year almost. Now look how she jump on the first green-eye man that come along!* (Yanique, *Land* 250)

Beauty not tied to attracting a husband; sexuality not always bound to childbirth; divorce; relationships with multiple men; children outside of marriage: Eeona and Anette's life choices fly in the face of their community's conventions, as captured through the ways in which they are discussed and remembered.

While motherhood is central to the experience of being a woman for Anette, who gives birth to her first child in her teens, Yanique's novel does not depict it as the essence of womanhood; for instance, it has a minimal role in Eeona's experiences. Similar to *Night Watch*—where Nina's daughter, Sarah, is the more maternal figure—*Land of Love and Drowning* demonstrates the messiness of mother/daughter dynamics, an aspect of the texts brought to light by this comparative focus.[16] Yanique does not idealize motherhood but holds space for complexity—such as matriarch Antoinette's jealousy of Eeona's relationship with her father, her likely knowledge of her husband's sexual abuse, and her attempts to abort Anette. If we trust Eeona's narration, then Antoinette was "jealous of [her]," due in part to her beauty: "She peered from my face to her own as if searching my face for a history of herself" (Yanique, *Land* 26). She finds a "history of herself" in Anette's red hair, "a trait from Antoinette's line" (48), something else passed down to Antoinette's "little Duene daughter" (49). However, Antoinette attempts to abort Anette, with help from her husband's mistress Rebekah McKenzie, Jacob's mother, positioned as the "witch, that obeah woman" (35), "Owen's witch woman" (36), and "a woman who managed to do as she pleased" (38). When all her remedies fail, Rebekah concludes, "This child will kill you before you kill her" (42), seemingly bestowing an otherworldly strength or power upon unborn Anette. Illustrating the multilayered family dynamics and alternative family structures, Rebekah also reveals that Antoinette "won't be mother to this one" and, in fact, that role falls to her older sister Eeona (42).

Next, I'd like to incorporate Gayl Jones's novel *Corregidora* into this discussion of the complexity of motherhood and what is passed down between generations. This novel illustrates two inheritances from slavery and colonialism: intergenerational trauma and the sexualization of young girls. Jones's novel opens with blues singer Ursa Corregidora—another female creator, alongside writer Nina and historian Anette, creating her own "new world song" (Jones 59)—who has just lost her ability to reproduce after her partner Mutt, in a fit of jealous possession, pushes her down the stairs. Ursa has a complicated family history and a visceral relationship with the forms of sexual violence institutionalized by slavery. Her name comes to her from "Old man Corregidora, the Portuguese slave breeder" by way of her great-grandmother, grandmother, and mother—the latter two women were both fathered by Corregidora (8–9). Like the name itself, stories of sexual violence were passed down through the generations of women in Ursa's family: "We were supposed to pass it down like that from generation to generation so we'd never forget. Even though they'd burned everything to play like it didn't never happen" (9). The violence is positioned as something that happened "down there" (9), yet it remains present with Ursa as she moves spatially through the novel. Indeed, visiting the past also involves geographic and cultural shifts. Brazil, the space where the plantation violence transpired, is never directly named, but the novel offers enough hints to trace the Corregidora women's move slowly north from Brazil to Louisiana to Kentucky (Sharpe 322). This is not simply a story of African American slavery but instead connects to a hemispheric history.[17] While the official records of Brazilian slavery were destroyed, Ursa's family attempts to keep evidence of their experiences alive through "*making generations*" and the oral transmission of trauma (22), and thus, her inability to create children is a particularly layered loss. This novel elucidates well the blurred line between preserving family histories and reproducing trauma across generations.

Illustrating once again the poetics of peripheralization, the aesthetics of Jones's novel amplify the content, centering the intergenerational familial trauma from the system of slavery. More specifically, the collective experiences of violence shared by the Corregidora women rupture the presentation of time in the novel, resulting in shifts from linear conceptions of time to circular repetitive structures that highlight what is passed down from one generation to the next. The boundaries of the past, present, and future blur within Ursa: she physically feels this blurring in her body, as demonstrated by the range of metaphors she uses in attempts to capture it, such as "Stained with another's past as well as our own. Their past in my blood" (Jones 45), "I have a birthmark between my legs" (45), "My veins are centuries meeting" (46), and "*I have tears for eyes. I was made to touch my past at an early age*" (77). History runs through her very veins and mixes with the blood that sustains her body, encapsulating this merging of past and present into one. Similarly, Ursa and her relatives do not simply listen or relate to each other's stories but experience them, becoming one another—like Nina fusing with Katherine and Sunneva. For instance, Ursa describes her mother telling one of Great Gram's stories, stating, "I stared at her because she wasn't Mama now, she was Great Gram talking" (124).[18] Another time, Ursa describes a conversation with her mother: "I said nothing. She was telling me she knew about my own private memory" (122). The borders between selves and previous generations prove permeable, and Ursa becomes Great Gram by the novel's end—if only within herself, as when she reflects, "It was like I didn't know how much was me and Mutt and how much was Great Gram and Corregidora" (184). As often as Mutt tells Ursa "we ain't them" (151), she feels this connection in her body, and a sexual act—as opposed to an emotional link—causes her to become Great Gram. The novel asks us to suspend our disbelief and accept that the identities of these women merge, granting them access to memories that are not their own and have never been spoken out loud. *Corregidora* provides an extreme example of both the merging of identities across generations of women and the complexity of what is transmitted between them, which helps to illuminate these features of *Night Watch* and *The Land of Love and Drowning*. The bonds between women in these families, forged through difficult circumstances, defy our expectations of reality.

Furthermore, the sexualization of young girls, explored in chapter 3, spans all three novels. It is least central to *Night Watch*, where it appears in flashbacks to interactions between Nina as a young girl and her older sister Martha's husband, Gustav. Nina describes herself repeatedly in the third person in this section as "the little girl Nina," perhaps to underscore her vulnerability as opposed to culpability, alongside her arousal: "She remembers the coarse stubble, the soft mouth and the tongue that parted the little girl's lips, the hot, devouring numbness flowing through her body" (Sigurðardóttir 138). Martha holds her responsible despite her age: "Don't you think I remember how you behaved with him when you were a little girl" (138).[19] Nina's recollections of her later flirtatious behavior with Gustav, her husband Gudjon, and her brother Helgi are one of the few places where incest enters the novel: "Nina, the centre of attention, would flirt with them all—with her brother-in-law, her brother, and her husband" (143). The structure of the sentence positions agency with Nina. Eventually this dynamic ends in violence, with Helgi beating Gustav and saying, "Two aren't enough for you, take the third as well" (143)—a reference to Gustav's relationship with the third sister, Rachel, that predated his romance with Martha. It is unclear if Helgi's motivation here is jealousy, resulting from Nina's flirtations with other men, or purely a protective impulse in reaction to Gustav's behavior.

Similarly, the sexualization of young girls is often entangled with incest in *Land of Love and Drowning*, appearing foremost in the depiction of Eeona's complex feelings for and relationship with her father, which I follow scholars like Rebecca Romdhani and Donahue in reading as abusive.[20] According to Romdhani, the pedophiliac and incestuous connection between Eeona and Owen purposely provokes "the response of disgust in the reader in order to compel her to critically reflect on the ways that stories violate girls and women, and on the real-world implication of this symbolic violence," with that disgust intended as critique (79).[21] Donahue positions Eeona's "romantic feelings for her father, admittedly outside the bounds of social norms," as "a result of the grooming process," situating Owen as a predator who "preys on Eeona's need for validation" (110). In terms of the mother's culpability, Donahue argues that Antoinette attempts to regulate her daughter's sexuality by teaching her to suppress its expression (109), whereas Romdhani calls out Antoinette's role in ignoring the abuse more directly. The father-daughter relationship is ambiguous and differs across accounts. Eeona does not mention a sexual relationship—although she does mention "the special truth: Louis Moreau would not be the first man whom I kissed" (47). On the other hand, the Old Wives imply that Eeona's pubic hair is silver or gray as a result of her relationship with Owen, and according to them, "only her father had ever touched her there" (23). The reality of what happened between father and daughter falls into the novel's gaps. Yet, given both the Old Wives' statements and the implications of what Eeona herself narrates, I'd argue that it is more likely than not that abuse occurred, which positions Owen as a predator and implicates Antoinette for failing to protect her daughter.

This theme is also very present in *Corregidora*, although decoupled from incest.[22] Ursa's husband, Tadpole, hires young Vivian to sing at his club, and she also ends up in his bed. When Ursa finally sees her, she describes her as looking "fifteen and older than fifteen" (Jones 86). Her difficult life and portrayal as a "vixen," an association reflected in her name, does not undercut the text's sexualization of young Vivian. Ursa also describes her own experience with an older man sexualizing her as a young girl, reaching between her legs and saying, "Gimme what you got" (95). Moreover, fourteen-year-old Jeffy touches Ursa's breasts in the night at Cat's house (39), and it is later revealed through an overheard conversation that Jeffy and Cat are lovers despite Jeffy's young age (47). In various ways, then, all three novels attempt to mask the sexualization and abuse of young girls—through the portrayal of Nina's agency and arousal, Eeona's belief that she has romantic feelings for her father, and Vivian's portrayal as older than her age—yet these attempts do not hold. Whether intentionally or not, all three novels spotlight the sexualization of young girls alongside the inheritance of intergenerational family trauma. Motherhood is complex in the novels, and children are not spared from the transmission of traumatic histories. However, while the portrayals are layered and multifaceted, all three novels depict the reality of the treatment of young girls as sexually available beings grounded in the transatlantic experiences of the cisheteropatriarchal systems of slavery and colonialism. In this way, they gesture back once more to the looming impacts of Denmark (or Portugal in Jones's novel) and the hierarchical and exploitative dynamics that accompany these histories.[23]

In addition to the histories of trauma and experiences of previous generations, *Corregidora* demonstrates that something intangible is passed down through the body, which Ursa catches a glimpse of in a photograph of herself: "I'd always thought I was different. *Their* daughter, but somehow different. Maybe less Corregidora. I don't know. But when I saw that picture, I knew I had it. What my mother and my mother's mother before her had" (Jones 60).[24] Like Anette's red hair and Eeona's Duene-like beauty, physical traits and memories provide a direct link with previous generations, in addition to material objects that retain a connection to familial histories and experiences. In *Corregidora* this manifests in a photograph of the abusive patriarch Corregidora: "The photograph's in that brown envelope," Ursa says to Tadpole

(12). He responds that Corregidora looks like how she described him and questions how she was "*really* taught to feel about him" (13). This question probes the murky effects of the transmission of trauma across generations and how mothers may contribute to this process, further complicating the depictions of motherhood in this novel in line with the discussion above.

Along with experiences, memories, and otherworldly qualities, from mermaid-like Youme to dream-walking Nina, material objects are passed down from one generation to the next in Youme's and Nina's families, which helps to provide an anchor to the physical world. In *Land of Love and Drowning*, Owen's death results in economic ruin for the family, who must sell Villa by the Sea, their furniture, and other belongings; however, portraits help to keep the family's history alive and play a key role in a major moment of revelation in the text. When visiting the fancy Hibiscus Hotel—an exoticized name that Anette deems nonsensical, asking, "Who want a hotel that sound like it fill with hibiscus?" (Jones 337)—Anette re-encounters Hippolyte and discovers that the hotel was her family's former home, Villa by the Sea. However, it is not only Hippolyte's claims that lead to this revelatory moment but a painting of the home's former owner, her mother Antoinette Stemme Bradshaw, that also depicts herself and Eeona: "She the milky picture Eeona insist I hang up in my living room. . . . But the picture I seeing here is of a woman a little older. Standing next to she is a girl so beautiful that even I know she must be a soucouyant. In this Antoinette lap is a baby, sitting like a little ugly dollie" (342). Anette not only sees the likeness of her mother in the canvas, but herself as a baby and her mythically beautiful sister. This material object survives through multiple generations to reveal the family's history, along with Hippolyte's recounting of his version, including the buried stories of incest and infidelity that resulted in their half brother and Anette's lover Jacob.

Together with Katherine's letter to Maria, mysterious matriarch Sunneva's shawl is passed between the generations in *Night Watch*, ending up with Nina, who brings it to Thordis's bedside. The shawl's original owner Sunneva has unknown and perhaps even otherworldly origins—"Some say from the north, from the east or even the south. Others whisper about faraway lands and elfin parts" (Sigurðardóttir 11–12)—adding to the mystery surrounding this object, a tangible link between so many generations. For instance, the shawl arrives "by some mysterious route" at the home of Jacob, Sunneva's implied lover and her husband's pseudo-son who seemingly takes his own life (29). Then, Sunneva gives the shawl to her daughter Solveig on the eve of sending her away to "learn more so she could improve her circumstances" (58). Solveig comes back "altered" and pregnant (58), ending her life by

Witch's Cliff, an aptly named "solitary rock high up in the mountains, a gigantic female shape in the early morning mist, a stone witch" (59). On the eve of Solveig's death, Sunneva passes the item to Solveig's daughter-in-law Katherine: "Now she is the one to carry her shawl, Sunneva's shawl" (59). The shawl appears in key moments, typically around a death, linking the women of the family together.[25] However, the shawl and its bequeathal cause conflict between pairs of sisters as well. Katherine intended for the shawl to go to her older daughter, Maria; however, Sunneva appears in Katherine's dream instructing her to send it to Thordis. Maria holds onto the fact that she "was supposed to have it, not her—" (106). This dynamic is echoed in the relationship between Martha and Nina (with the eldest Rachel left out entirely). Although Martha is the older sister, Nina is given the shawl, which exacerbates Martha's existing resentment toward Nina for having access to things that she didn't due to the sacrifices of the other family members, viewing her as "an alien Nina . . . an educated, treacherous Nina" (124).[26] Although Nina, with her Jaguar and Armani suit, would seem to have little in common with her family, her inner turmoil, reflections, and musings reveal the extent to which she has never forgotten where she came from.

While Nina eventually accepts the shawl as an "unwelcome" gift (Sigurðardóttir 102), she initially did not want it. Narrating her previous self in the third person, Nina demonstrates her distance from her predecessors: "She belonged to the age of the bomb, did Nina, to a world ruled by titans who left no room for shabby trash, for relics. . . . So she jeered at an old shawl, shoved it away. She belonged neither to the world of green grass, nor that of ancestral women who submitted to their fates" (122). Nina views herself apart from the "ancestral women," as both modern and free from history.[27] She believes her mother wants to "shackle her" and "attach her to history, to a long since extinct story reeking with the stench of old blood, earth and decay" (122). Though coded, the "trap" Nina describes contains shades of motherhood: the shawl reminds her of "the most primordial of all traps laid by life: a single instant when everything changes—nine months here, years there, the rest of your life. Don't delude yourself into thinking you are free, for your abdomen holds the magic key to life itself" (122). Through the references to "nine months" and her "abdomen hold[ing] the magic key to life itself," Nina would seem to want to avoid the family life and domestic responsibilities her predecessors experienced. Her earlier reflection—"Don't want to think about the innumerable, forever pregnant bodies that sustain life, century after century. I can't bear it" (49)—supports this sentiment. While she breaks out of the domestic life of her ancestors to an extent, she does not ultimately avoid motherhood herself. It is fitting that the final time

134 CHAPTER 4

the shawl is referenced in the novel is in relation to Nina's daughter, Sarah, and the care she shows her mother: "[Sarah] starts to talk about the shawl, wants to know what Sunneva's old shawl is doing on the coverlet" (161), before wrapping it around her mother's shoulders, saying, "It'll warm you" (162). In addition to showcasing sibling tensions, the shawl ultimately connects the generations of women in Nina's family together, binding them to each other and to their histories.

In addition to physical traits and material objects, names are passed down from one generation to the next. For instance, in *Corregidora*, Ursa never took her husband's name when they were married and recalls in Mutt's imagined or reconstructed voice, "*Ain't even took my name. You Corregidora's, ain't you? Ain't even took my name. You ain't my woman*" (Jones 61), with naming reflecting possession. In *Night Watch* none of the first names are repeated in Nina's family, as is often the case in Icelandic families, and patronymic (or, less frequently, matronymic) names are used instead of surnames. The weighty absence around patronymics in the novel links back to the latent presence of colonial politics or a sublimated focus on more masculine, national power dynamics. Icelandic naming conventions put less emphasis on last names, and as a result, this family could stand in for multiple others. In contrast, naming is central to *Land of Love and Drowning* and is associated with power and magic, as Anette demonstrates when she claims that "naming is a voodoo all parents do" (225). This echoes her mom's decision to name her Anette after herself with her maiden name Stemme on the birth certificate in the place of a middle name. The baby's redness or "lobsterness" reminded Antoinette of Anegada, and "Naming is a parent's first sorcery" (45). Deciding to bestow a nickname also demonstrates power, as no one calls Anette "Nettie" aside from Jacob: "Is a kind of voodoo he putting on me and I don't have strength to do magic back on him" (340). However, what one is called can also influence one's lifepath. Anette was told to avoid a boy named Esau, not Jacob; one wonders how the events of the story would have played out had he been called by his second name.

BEYOND REALISM:
MAGIC, BEAUTY, POWER, AND DANGER

Yanique's positioning of naming as a sorcery of parents highlights the features of *Land of Love and Drowning* and *Night Watch* that exist beyond the limits of accepted "reality." Reality, however, may be constructed differently in various geographies and cultures. Daisy L. Neijmann states that "Iceland is full of ghosts" that are a "part of the traditional Icelandic perception of what constitutes reality"; she connects this trope to the interest in magical realism in Iceland, though it is important to note that definitions of magical realism depend on an individual's or culture's conception of reality ("'Girl Interrupting'" 58).[28] According to writer Svava Jakobsdóttir, the saga realism that has influenced Icelandic literature to this day differs from that of the nineteenth-century bourgeois novel, and Neijmann describes this saga realism as "a realism that allows for a deeper, wider understanding and perception of what is 'real'" ("'Girl Interrupting'" 58).[29] Once again the form of a text, here saga realism or magical realism, can offer alternatives to conventional European literary realism—further shades of the poetics of peripheralization. While not expressly magical realism, *Night Watch* leaves openings for alternative conceptions of reality, such as Nina's grandmother's: "My grandmother Katherine believed in dreams and visions and fairies. She believed in invisible people, hobgoblins, and phantoms, in right and wrong, the one and only truth, salvation, even in Yaveh and his gang. All this she easily packed into reality, without batting an eyelid" (Sigurðardóttir 67). By connecting fairies, hobgoblins, and phantoms to religious references like Yaveh, the one truth, and salvation, Nina positions her grandmother's magical reality as another way of interacting with the world alongside other more widely accepted belief systems.

Like the powerful folktales in Yanique's novel, stories themselves and words more generally have magic and power in *Night Watch*, with storytelling positioned as a gendered phenomenon in Nina's family. Nina inherits the interest in family stories from her aunt, fiercely recording them in her mother's room. While she claims to be only killing time with "old tales, reminiscences" (Sigurðardóttir 47), even she herself knows that this is a half-truth: "Words are magic. They try to get the better of me, materializing as images, episodes, people, whole arrays of squirming, mesmerizing, menacing words everywhere I turn" (47). She tries to wriggle away from them just as she avoids looking at her mother's bed, deep down knowing the two are "interrelated, always, that written words are senseless, false, unless a force grinds them together, pressing all the juice out of them, until fusion is achieved, indefinable fusion that remoulds everything" (47).[30] Her words and their magic are entwined with the family histories and matriarchal lineages they recount, as well as her feelings about her dying mother lying in the room with her. The balance between art or poetic expression and stark, embodied reality is one that Nina struggles with throughout the novel. At times, she expresses discomfort with forms of poetic expression, yet they survive the latter, embodied reality, alongside the family stories connecting generations of women.

136 CHAPTER 4

Stories and mythologies similarly abound in *Land of Love and Drowning*, grounded in Caribbean geographies and transatlantic histories. Yanique's novel depicts, in Cherene Sherrard-Johnson's terms, the "complex displacement resulting from the politics of Transfer [that] enables [her] particular manifestation of archipelagic diaspora: one that reveals the submerged history of Atlantic slavery in Denmark and the resulting circulation of mythic figures that surface from colonial encounters" (95). According to Sherrard-Johnson, Yanique draws on the diverse cultural influences of the Virgin Islands that include West African mythologies, European maritime culture from the latent presence of Danish colonialism, and resistant ecologies to create a magical realist setting specific to the Virgin Islands (95), including "mermaids, iterations of Anancy, the trickster who can be found in West African, Caribbean, and African American folklore, and Pan-Caribbean figures like *la diablesse* (also known as the cowfoot woman)" (108). While many of the magical aspects of the novel are associated with the Bradshaw women and their Duene heritage, Owen's lover Rebekah is linked to La Diablesse through her status as an obeah women with one hoofed foot, and her husband and Eeona's lover, Benjamin McKenzie (also known as Kweku Prideux) is the novel's Anancy figure.[31] Although Eeona and her sister are both associated with the Duene from their ancestral home of Anegada, the former's beauty also positions her with another folktale as a "soucouyant" or an "ugly witch living in a beautiful woman skin" (Yanique, *Land* 222), first identified as such by Jacob and later by Anette in front of the family portrait (342). Hippolyte likewise avers that Eeona "turn out witchy" (343), saying that "she a witch already" before adding, "Even she red baby sister is something" (344). The Bradshaw women exemplify the diverse power found in women, which encompasses wildness, witchiness, beauty, and perhaps even a little danger.

Relatedly, many of the otherworldly aspects of *Night Watch* are associated with the wild, witchy, and beautiful matriarch Sunneva, positioned as a mysterious outsider like Antoinette from Anegada yet with unknown origins. Farmer Stefan, a widower in his fifties, returns "with a very young girl by his side, his wife-to-be. A quiet girl, fair with singularly inscrutable eyes that troubled those who stared too boldly into them. . . . Sunneva—a heathen, alien name. . . . You never saw a wrinkle in her clothes and they said that her neatness must be supernatural. . . . She certainly was different, that much was obvious" (Sigurðardóttir 11–12).[32] The complex power dynamics in their relationship are revealed in this section: Sunneva is much younger, yet her eyes are capable of troubling the too bold gazer. Given the domestic and familial roles associated with Icelandic women during the period, it seems appropriate that Sunneva's supernatural power in this context is her neatness. Her depiction reveals much about the close-knit community through their view of her as a threat from the outside and their interactions with her.

As they are to Antoinette and Eeona's witchiness in *Land of Love and Drowning*, mobility and folk knowledge are central to Sunneva's wildness: "She would laugh when nobody saw any reason to and at times she would take off in the evenings, when all good Christians had gone to bed. Never said much about what she had been doing. Probably collecting herbs. Most likely she knew how to use them, too" (Sigurðardóttir 12). Sunneva's witchy powers are not only revealed by her subaltern knowledge of herbs, but also her beauty, sexuality, and impact on men, such as her alleged lover Jacob, who "is not bothered by evil spirits, only by his own fear. . . . After all, it is said that he has made the mistake of gazing too boldly into the young mistress's bright eyes" (13). Sunneva is described as capable of "tackling these dark-browed men who apparently appreciate her strange dances, when she flits from one partner to another. Fingers stroke her fair plaits or reach around her waist, probe for her breasts encased by a dark bodice, but then all is gone—a mirage drifting away—while a bewitching laughter resounds under the rafters" (13). This description centers her otherness with her "strange dances" and "bewitching laughter." In another ambiguous scene illustrating her mysterious otherness, Fridmey, who also loved Jacob, sees Sunneva, described here as an "unknown woman," her face "limp and heavy with some kind of craving, a dull glow, her lips swollen, her eyes hazy" and "a secretive smile on an unfamiliar face"(19). She waves to an unknown man in black, an implied satanic figure given his impact on witchy Sunneva (19), whose smile Stefan describes as having "cast a spell upon him" (32). Fridmey wants to "grab the raised hand and say: Don't! Don't wave! Can't you see who this is? But she says nothing, does nothing to challenge the black magic in the air" (19). The vague, otherworldly depictions of Sunneva and others' encounters with her position her as a source of unknown feminine power and subaltern knowledges, with her character melding wildness, witchiness, and beauty.

The beauty of the Bradshaw women also connects to wildness, as well as to Anegada and the magical power of the Duene. Owen reprimands Antoinette, "You speak of our child, but your influence is causing her to have your same wildness. She is becoming bold, going beyond herself" (Yanique, *Land* 16). To Owen, and society more generally, a daughter becoming bold is seen as negative and associated with wildness. Antoinette introduces Eeona to the Duene, the Anancy, and the other folk stories, which she interiorizes and becomes the source of for her family; the tales form a link between the women, echoing Sigurðardóttir's use of family stories. Whether sharing them in whispers with the children, recording them in Kweku Prideux's house for him to feed off, or scrawling them on the walls of her chambers at the inn, Eeona is deeply connected to this folk history. She learned early that the Duene of Anegada "protect the wild things from our destruction" and do not love humans: "They love only themselves and the wildness, Mama said" (28). She defines "the wildness" as "many things besides a gathering of trees or a pooling of water" (28). Eeona reflects on the stories and her relationship to them: "I came to understand that the wildness could be inside of me" (28). Toward the end of the novel Eeona disappears for a period, leaving a note that says, "I am more wild than Mama" (347), connecting her witchy and wild power back once more to Antoinette and Anegada. In addition to being a source of wildness herself, Eeona is able to identify it in others, including her mother and sister: "Mama had wild and wandering tendencies. I always knew I had the same" (27), and "I would miss wild Anette who could climb trees and manage other unladylike things" (53).[33] The Old Wives also position the Bradshaw women, including Antoinette and Youme, as wild. Throughout both novels, the association of wildness with boldness, mobility, and nature renders it a form of feminist and anticolonial resistance to societal expectations defined by normative masculine and national structures: these characters cannot be contained in univocal, linear narratives. Like *Night Watch*'s Sunneva, Eeona's wildness is also linked to beauty and witchiness, connecting her to the other women in her family. The St. Thomas society in the novel does not seem to know what to do with Eeona's wild power, including her unearthly beauty, which she tones down by frequently wearing her hair up and dressing in blue, the color of the Virgin Mary. Eeona is positioned by characters and narrators alike as a source of witchiness in the novel. The Old Wives describe her as flying "like a witch" when she swims near her father's sunken ship toward the novel's end (Yanique, *Land* 383). When Eeona wants to sell the inn, Anette's reaction frames her in these terms: "*Crazy witch*, she wanted to say to her sister" (386). Likewise, this language is found in her favorite niece Youme's claim that "Auntie Eeona, you'll be like a witch flying in the night" (281).[34] In *Caliban and the Witch*, Silvia Federici asserts that the witch in the sixteenth- and seventeenth-century European witch hunts was not only the midwife and the beggar who stole to survive, but also the woman who avoided maternity and the "loose, promiscuous woman" who "exercised her sexuality outside the bonds of marriage and procreation" (184).[35] Thus, Eeona's lifestyle choices, which fly in the face of conventional marriage and motherhood, help solidify her position as the novel's central witch.

However, witchiness as power also links Eeona to both Youme and Anette. Eeona senses these possibilities in her niece and responds using Youme's nickname, "Me, we are witches" (Yanique, *Land* 281). Anette admits as much about herself when describing how wearing red makes her feel strong around Jacob: "Is true that I want Jacob to desire me, but is really that I want to be toughlike and in control. Is a witch thing" (337). Witches are cross-cultural figures of strong women who are feared as a result of their shirking of societal conventions, as well as access to folk medicine and knowledges. They are mythical beings whose power is not necessarily granted by the society's power structures or linked to their sexuality or relationships with men but something inherent within themselves. In the end, Eeona and Youme move to their ancestral Duene land of Anegada.[36] Anette divulges that Youme is "sick" or "has that thing . . . that obeah thing. The magic thing" (388), which she has known since Youme read her mind during the hurricane (308).[37] Eeona pacifies her sister by explaining that there are others like Youme on Anegada, and she can come to understand herself there. According to Sherrard-Johnson, Eve Youme surpasses Eeona as "a resistant and agented water woman" who "galvanizes her otherness, her 'wildness,' to resist the privatization of beaches and argues for the full American citizenship of Virgin Islanders through her participation in the BOMB movement" (108), manipulating the family's wild power for broader social good. Not only does Anette recognize her sister Eeona as "a woman who was fierce and elegant and the queen of somewhere" in this final interaction (Yanique, *Land* 388), but she also accepts that "she had that in her, too" (389). Youme's strength connects her to both her aunt and mother.

In line with many historical attempts to discredit feminine forms of power, wildness is associated with madness throughout Yanique's novel. Jacob, impervious to Eeona's beauty in the face of his love for Anette, voices society's rumors, saying, "I heard that she a little wild. . . . I've heard that she does get a little twist in the head. Go wandering when she get ready" (Yanique, *Land* 220). Eeona's wandering is a version of mobility associated with feminine wildness: "She would walk to the sea. She would walk to the mountains. She would return home and it would start again" (123). Indeed, Eeona's power exceeds societal norms and her community's capacity for understanding. She is associated with having "episodes" throughout, another link to her wandering Anegadan mother. Antoinette's episodes are described as "a state where she wanted and hungered and that took many slights of magic to calm. The doctor said it was nervousness brought on by the pregnancies and miscarriages. A woman's wildness" (17).[38] Here, the episodes are positioned as the desire for more and associated not only with a need for magic but with the gendered experiences of pregnancies and miscarriages—specifically a "woman's wildness."

The episodes are also linked to the Duene and a societal need for women to be contained or, in the language of the novel, "self-possessed." Eeona states that "The story of the Duene was used to warn me. If a woman was not self-possessed, she was in danger of wildness. I knew my mother suffered from this. Episodes, we called them. Papa described the episodes as a bit of rebellion and impetuousness" (Yanique, *Land* 26–27).[39] Similar to the framing of her mother's rebelliousness as "episodes," positioning the unexplainable in Eeona as "episodes" is a way for society to attempt to understand, dismiss, and even control her. For Donahue, the power to be found in wildness in the novel "is mediated by external sources, be it developers or patriarchal influence. In evoking questions of ownership and possession, the author highlights the precarious nature of female agency" (115), with Eeona craving to be "owned" (114)—a term that takes on problematic resonances given the histories of colonialism in the novel and its attempts to control, contain, and exploit wildness. There are also reverberations of her problematic relationship with her father Owen, who wants to "own" her, and his status as a patriarchal, colonial figure—gender politics and abusive family dynamics reflecting broader colonial relations. While I agree that the agency found in wildness is not unlimited, I'd add that the path Eeona's life takes despite her own desires for it highlight the power within the precarity.

Donahue goes on to say that "Eeona's demeanor points to the tendency to pathologize women who defy social norms. Importantly, such logistical leaps reify the link between hysteria and women. In *Land of Love and Drowning*, Yanique explores the consequences of what society deems 'unnatural'" (115). Eeona is pathologized by the community, and even her family, for living outside of societal expectations in many ways. More specifically, Anette wonders if her sister is "having an episode" when she disappears from the inn and is seen "wandering the roads at night like a ghost" (Yanique, *Land* 372). When one of the officers searching for her puts his finger to his temple, twirls it, and asks if Eeona is "crazy," Anette considers that "Maybe sister Eeona had finally gone crazy. No children. No husband. And all that nastiness Mr. Lyte had talked about" (372). Through references to her lifestyle choices, the lack of a child or husband, Anette connects the episodes to her sister's living outside of the community's heteronormative expectations for her—at one point, Franky wonders if "she was one of those women who preferred women" (283). However, Eeona's status as some type of queer role model is tempered by the judgmental, classist aspects of her character. A parallel can be drawn to Nina's rejection of heteronormative expectations for her life and her disinterest in motherhood, although she also seemingly prefers men. There is a power in Eeona that, despite her own wishes for herself, comes from her defiance of society's expectations for the shape of her life—something wild and possibly even dangerous that her polite social polish cannot effectively mask or contain. The Old Wives underscore this connection as well: when Eeona is on the brink of thirty, she is neither desperate nor resigned like many women in her community, and they add that "an old maid and a free woman might be the same dangerous witchlike thing" (117). During this search for Eeona, Anette feels some of her own wild power when the police drive her back to Eeona's inn: "With the bars between her and the men, she felt like something dangerous" (372).[40]

This is not the first time Anette feels dangerous, a sensation that serves as another link between the sisters and their power. She also admits to feeling this way after meeting Jacob, saying, "I can't lie. I know the power I had. I know I dangerous" (Yanique, *Land* 166); she describes what was happening between them as "magical and dangerous and not just the timing" (168).[41] Toward the end of the novel, Jacob reflects on his decision to let Youme and her backward feet be, stating, "I remember that beauty can be dangerous . . . I don't know . . . perhaps even that danger is worth it" (367). This statement links the Bradshaw women's beauty directly to danger, which in turn connects Youme to Anette, Eeona, and Antoinette before her. Yet Eeona embodies a danger that extends beyond her beauty and her wildness to the family stories and folklore she inherits. Reflecting on the Duene story, so close to Eeona's heart, Rebekah ruminates, "It was meant to be a harmless story, but even stories that seem harmless are never without their danger" (83), and Anette wonders if "her sister was a kind of danger to her family, there whispering stories about their kingly history" (295). Anette muses on the impact of stories on behaviors and choices: Eeona's knowledge, not only of Anegadan mythology but also the family's histories, might affect those in the present, their understandings of the past, and their expectations for the future.

The women in *Night Watch* also hold a certain danger that connects them to nature; like Sunneva (and the Bradshaw women), nature is an entity containing beauty and danger simultaneously. Nature—its wildness, its perceived need to be tamed or contained—has certain associations with the exoticized peripheries of the colonial project, in addition to its link to women's bodies. Sigurðardóttir emphasizes the treachery of the Far North setting by describing a location where birds that have been knocked off cliffs with stones fall into "this vast complexity of fecundity and annihilation" (10).[42] This landscape facilitates the suicides of multiple men in the novel, which are also linked to the supposed treachery of women—a positioning we should question. Nina indicates that witchlike women like Sunneva hold a power that can bring

142   CHAPTER 4

men to their deaths, and though Jacob's death and its causes are hazy, Stefan seems to hold Sunneva responsible for it.[43] Further, Nina vividly remembers her "cliff dream" of having stood with her brother Helgi and boyfriend Arnar over a cliff, during which "Helgi shouted to be heard through the din of airplanes: 'That was [where] Jacob fell. And Halldor [who shot himself over a cliff].' Nina discerned fear in both their faces, fear and a tremulous yearning" (101). The circumstances of Arnar's death by train—"Fallen from the platform. Somewhere out there in the world" (103)—are key pieces of information that are deferred until two-thirds through the novel, cast in a certain light by Nina's representation of his death wish. Not named by Nina as suicide, but as "absolutely ludicrous; senseless coincidence" (103), readers at least cannot help considering his death in those terms, particularly alongside the other men's suicides throughout the novel. When she leaves a party with Gudjon after her years-long relationship with Arnar, Nina admits to seeing "only indifference, mockery and cruelty" in Arnar's smile: "She has no wish to see things differently" (102). Here, the novel makes possible multiple truths and draws attention to the admittedly biased perspective of the narrator, choosing to see things in a way that doesn't hold her cruelty responsible for her ex-boyfriend's possible suicide. And Sigurðardóttir defers the revelation of another death until the very end of the novel: Nina's father's death by drowning, seemingly leaving his family for the capital, or "Land of Plenty" (156). In a society with a strong connection to fishing and the sea, drowning, like a disappearance during a storm, is a reality in Icelandic literature and culture: walking into the sea is a common form of suicide, alongside those that incorporate the wild terrain, circling back to the linked beauty and danger found in nature.[44]

Drowning is also central to Yanique's novel, as indicated by its appearance in the title, and Owen's death is similarly left open to interpretation. Knowing his relationship with his daughter Eeona cannot continue, he arranges to have her marry Frenchman Louis Moreau, telling her, "There can be no more of this" (Yanique, *Land* 65). Eeona responds, "Then I wish you would die, Papa. I wish you would just die" (65). A telegram the following evening shares that "*Homecoming* wrecked on Anegada reef. Two survivors. Captain not among them" (65). Whether his death is read as suicide resulting from his decision to end the relationship with his daughter, which would never be socially acceptable, or the result of magical revenge or jealousy, continuing the trope of blaming women, is not clear to the readers or the community. It "was whispered that the murderess was a woman with backward-facing feet and hair like the sea [Duene imagery]. Perhaps it was the captain's witch mistress, who knew magic and knew love and knew they were one and the same, despite any sin" (67), a reference to Rebekah. Nevertheless, given her last words to him, Eeona, "who knew she could sink ships, could only blame herself" (67). Both novels are connected by this thread of ambiguous suicides resulting from problematic relationships where blame is situated with women and girls. Like the treacherous cliffs of Iceland, the sea of the Virgin Islands holds beauty but also power and danger. Each locale is depicted as closely connected to the natural spirit of the place. The beauty and danger of wild things are linked to the Duene and by extension to the Bradshaw women, as well as to Sunneva and her descendants.[45] In this way, women in both novels reclaim the feminine power of the natural, the wild, and even the magical in the face of the hierarchies and exoticized formulations of colonialism.

RECORDING MULTIPLE TRUTHS AND ALTERNATIVE HISTORIES

Finally, *Night Watch* and *Land of Love and Drowning* clear space for these subversive female characters in the family accounts and broader histories—emphasizing what is passed down between family members and the fallibility of memory, as well as making room for alternative stories in history's records. History's "truths" are never accessible to those in the present and are always changeable, leading us to question how accurate our family histories, and even our own memories, can be. The truth is always multiple in Sigurðardóttir's novel, which depicts Nina as inheriting versions of it through her ancestors' interpretations. This is showcased when she tries to understand her grandmother's motivations for inviting her husband's former lover, who bore him two children while working for the family, back to live with them: "Pity? Incredible! I raise my voice: 'Charity'—feeling my voice crack—'Are you sure it was charity? Couldn't it have been revenge?'" (Sigurðardóttir 56). Our knowledge of history depends on the interpretations of those who pass the stories down.

Similarly, as a young girl, Nina hears her mother and Maria arguing about whether Fridmey forgave Sunneva over the forty years they lived together after losing Jacob (whom they both loved), although neither has access to Fridmey's truth or interpretation of the events. Nina, however, develops her own truth: "But the little girl, Nina, Katherine Sunneva, knows in her heart that Fridmey never forgave Sunneva. She knows. She is eleven, almost twelve. She has read about the terrible forces of destiny and passion, and can hardly wait to be drawn into the swirl" (Sigurðardóttir 22). Thus, Nina has her own relationship to the family stories and holds a different truth or belief than her mother—although here the reality is inaccessible and even then possibly multiple given human complexity, with Fridmey showing herself capable of both forgiveness and its opposite depending on the day. Nina directly recognizes that the truths of others' experiences are never accessible, regardless of how much time has passed: "I watch the woman in the pantry, the man on the snowfield and realize abruptly that I shall never understand their lives, never understand what they shared" (76). Although distinctions of time and culture may exacerbate her separateness from them, even without such distance, the layers to their feelings would still be sheltered from her understanding—demonstrating that aspects of other people's memories, experiences, and histories (and perhaps even our own) remain out of reach.

In *Land of Love and Drowning*, Anette's and Eeona's relationships to the events that they narrate illustrate the inaccessible nature of shifting histories. Anette as narrator holds aspects of the story back from the other narrative voices, asserting, "I need to keep something to myself. Secret. In truth, I ain even telling you everything" (Yanique, *Land* 187). However, we learn that they already know: "What Anette is not telling, because she will never tell, was what happened only a week later between her and Jacob Esau" (187). Similarly, Eeona describes an experience leading up to when she leaves Kweku Prideux, declaring, "I never could bring myself to tell my sister the true story, but I shall deliver it here and now" (208). She then provides multiple versions of the truth, demonstrating her awareness of the ways in which we can lie even to ourselves. In the first version, she says she "swam naked in the ocean lights," and Prideux "will look at me as though I were some mythical creature who did what she wanted" (212). She interrupts herself, clarifying, "My dear. That is not what really happened. That was all just a story I told myself" (212). In version two, she is less defiant and doesn't go in the water: "I did not turn into a Duene or a soucouyant. . . . Still, I felt defiantly magical, like some creature who had seen a hint that she might do as she pleased" (213), followed by "Oh, dear. Please accept my apologies, for that, too, was a story" (213). She then states, "The very truth, my love, is that I did not even make it to the beach for the baptism I had planned. . . . I was not a shadow nor was I a bird nor was I a magical creature. Instead, I simply stood there and imagined myself going to the beach and swimming and then drowning or drowning myself" (213), before she walks through the rain and into their house. It is unclear who she is addressing as "my dear" and "my love" here, whether the Old Wives or another character with them listening in on the conversation. However, Eeona's first-person testimony underscores the unreliability of other similarly narrated accounts, as well as the multiplicity embedded even within a single viewpoint of events. Similar to the impact of structural features like nonlinear time and the multiplicity of history—upending Eurocentric literary forms and colonial accounts and records—magical connections, subaltern knowledges, and intergenerational bonds between women survive through time. Form and content align in this feminist, anticolonial resistance.

Moreover, histories change over time, and what we have access to may only bear a passing resemblance to truths as they were. The beach known as Flash of Beauty serves as a useful example of what is remembered and what becomes the truth: "Flash of Beauty had not been originally named after Eeona and Moreau, but that was the story told, and so now that was how it was" (Yanique, *Land* 381). The fact that this is not only what is remembered but becomes "how it was" illustrates memory's ability to alter past events in the novel. Additionally, after Eeona leaves and Anette's family no longer has access to her folktales, they invent their own versions:

> In young Frank's version Anancy always shared everything equally with everyone at the end. In our usual version Anancy is tricky— would never share a thing, not a piece of fruit, not the deed to his big house on a hill. Papa Franky told about the seductress with a hoof foot, who, so the myth went, could sing like a piano. They had forgotten exactly how the myths went, but they told them anyway. Was La Diablesse the same thing as a soucouyant? Was Anancy the spider man a Duene himself? (312–13)

The original folktales learned by Eeona are passed down through the family; however, they retain the marks of the different narrators through whom they pass, demonstrating the shifting nature of oral histories and, by extension, written ones. Anette admits as much in her section: "This ain true history. I just saying that given what we know about the place and about the time, my version seem to have a truth somewhere" (33). All histories are partial— someone's version—and seem to hold their own truths, underscoring the fluid nature of memories, folklore, and even histories more broadly.

In addition to its investment in the multiplicity of truth and the inaccessible nature of history, *Night Watch* explores questions of agency and the extent to which the events that happen to us are within our control. Nina describes her mother as a fatalist who doesn't believe in her ability to impact events: "But she turned her back on converging roads, roads that led elsewhere. She rejected options, possibilities, and returned to her inlet. Had no faith in choice. Saying, I guess we don't have any say in what happens to us. But we do decide what to do about it" (Sigurðardóttir 119).[46] Nina's memory of this statement, which would seem to reveal much about the speaker, is also inexact—"Or maybe that was somebody else. Maybe Susy, or Lawrence.

Maybe even Eric. Or Sarah?" (119)—throwing into question the extent to which it matters who thinks, says, or experiences what in the enmeshed and imperfect records of family histories. Nina struggles with what is passed down and why it matters when no one remembers accurately and everyone dies: "The girl in the picture, the one who is long gone, lost, gobbled up by avaricious time, like Sunneva, Jacob, Katherine, Maria, like we all are. We die again and again, all of us; before we turn into mute heaps of flesh in some bed, we die" (120).[47] Nina focuses on physical reality and expresses skepticism of anything beyond it, emphasizing her belief that what survives us—in addition to words and stories—are future generations, from Sunneva and Jacob to Katherine to Maria. One of the book's refrains inquires, "And who are your people?" (73). First asked by Olafur, cast as "a giant, terrible to behold" (73), the question is posed three times, in accordance with a fairy tale structure, before reality is unmasked: "An old hulk in far too large a robe, neither folklore nor fairy tale, just a confused old soul wandering through the corridors of a hospital. . . . A senile old chap, the man of the mountain, the fairy king, the Knight of the Lily, that's all" (73). While Olafur is the name of Nina's father, adding to the surreal mood of the scene, this refrain is spoken by another resident of the hospital, wandering the halls. Yet Nina repeats it again and again throughout the section, embedding it within the bones of her narration, a question she reveals she has previously made fun of with the straightforward response, "I am me, that's all" (74). However, the stories she furiously records are telling, and like the return of the repressed, she cannot escape her lineage nor her connection to the family legacies she inherits or the generations that will follow her.

Nina directly experiences the layering of histories, as she reflects on the stories of her ancestors in relation to herself. While passing references are made to broader historical events, such as the politicians "sell[ing] the country" to the US (Sigurðardóttir 133), *Night Watch* is primarily invested in the individual scales of history. Large-scale history looms a bit larger in *Land of Love and Drowning*, as mentioned above, with the events of the novel placed alongside the death of John Kennedy, Che Guevara, and Martin Luther King Jr. Nevertheless, the primary emphasis in this novel is on the individual scale as well—though with more attention to this layering of histories, such as Anette's observation that "when I make a turn by the bay, I see the restaurant that must have been a great house back in slavery days" (Yanique, *Land* 337).[48] The interrelations of the women of the Stemme, Bradshaw, and McKenzie families are brought to the fore, while slavery, Danish colonialism, and US neocolonialism are present but not centered.

What makes it into the official history books in the Virgin Islands speaks to the broader colonial power dynamics at work. Anette, the historian, is taught history from the victors' or colonizers' perspectives, as "There was no course where she could study Anegada history or Virgin Islands history at all. She taught American history and a general Caribbean history that focused mostly on the pirates of Jamaica. That is what there was for her to teach at the Anglican school" (Yanique, *Land* 290). The novel comments on the space given to Caribbean histories in the official accounts. Anette has only read about Anegada in the "'Pirates and Piracy' section of the world history textbook. It was also the only section where the Caribbean was mentioned at all" (388)—speaking to the peripheral nature of the Virgin Islands, which, like Iceland, is primarily of interest for its link to Denmark and later the US in global narratives of history.[49] Just as the characters in *Corregidora* attempt to create generations and pass down their experiences, Jones's novel itself serves to spotlight the histories erased, such as the endemic sexual abuse of enslaved women like Ursa's ancestors. Reading *Land of Love and Drowning* and *Night Watch* alongside *Corregidora* helps to emphasize the shared project of these novels, countering history's deletions and filling in the gaps by validating the cross-temporal, magical bonds between women and defying the constraints of reality. The novels record their own histories of these locations on the periphery of the former Danish empire, both writing back to the geopolitical marginality of the Virgin Islands and Iceland—locations often reduced to pithy symbols and stereotypes—and foregrounding the experiences of women. In this way, they can be considered palliative counterhistories to official accounts primarily recorded by and focusing on the experiences of men.[50]

Coda

PROCESSING THE PRESENT, LOOKING TO A DECOLONIAL FUTURE

In *Extreme North: A Cultural History*, Bernd Brunner writes that "while Alaska is the northernmost US state, it is almost never referred to as part of the North—politically speaking, it aligns with the American South (Alaska and the Gulf states Texas, Louisiana, Mississippi, and Alabama overwhelmingly depend on fossil-fuel exploitation), while Hawaii, the southernmost US state in terms of geography, is a reliable part of the political North" (6–7). Brunner's observation elucidates the fact that in terms of the geographies of the United States, the ideological and political associations of "north" and "south" would seem to be of equivalent importance to the spatial. Similarly, Diana Mulinari et al. assert that "'the Nordic' is understood partly as a specific set of politico-spatial locations, but also as a group of imagined spaces, and their attendant ideologies" (8), underscoring the regional fantasies associated with ideas of the Nordic, including progressive politics and desolate snowscapes. Discussing the Arctic more specifically, Kirsten Thisted and Ann-Sofie N. Gremaud argue that it is "now being politically, rather than geographically defined" (24). Whereas the original Arctic Council was composed of the "Arctic Five" or the states of the "Arctic Rim" bordering the Arctic Ocean, Iceland, Sweden, and Finland were added, as a result of "the successful branding of the Nordic countries as a unity" (24). As has been well-established across a number of disciplines, including the field of southern studies, our understandings of space have less to do with geographic location than with the political and ideological associations of nations and regions. While the US South is a region associated with political conservatism and Iceland with progressivism, *Intersecting Worlds* emphasizes

148

commonalities between them. For instance, neither space has effectively addressed its colonial histories, the ripples of which are felt in the present.

If the colonial ambiguity of the US South results from its dualistic position as the site of the colonization of enslaved Black Americans by White southerners and as a region depicted as colonized by the federal government during Reconstruction (1863–1877), then the post-emancipation period and the years following might have served as a decolonial moment to reckon with these histories. Reconstruction was a short-lived period of change in the US South, during which, for example, interracial marriages were briefly legal (Domínguez 57), and, according to historian Eric Foner, approximately 2,000 Black Americans held public office at the local, state, and federal levels (qtd. in Waxman 26). The numbers of Black office holders began to decline after 1877, and state legislators passed laws mandating poll taxes and literacy tests in the effort to prevent Black Americans from voting (Waxman 26). The lynching of Black Americans also increased in frequency, and in the 1890s "fell into a ritualistic pattern," with spectacle lynchings becoming more powerful and lynch mobs adapting "the rituals of public executions to the needs of vigilantism and racial control" (Hale 206). Patterns of racial exploitation and oppression inherited from the system of slavery, including sharecropping and convict leasing, became engrained in US southern society following Reconstruction, as there was a failure of any sustained efforts at decolonization.[1]

Comparably, countries in the Nordic region "never went through a clear period of critique of colonialism and its presence in everyday environments and encounters" in the way that other colonial centers did during the dismantling of empires (Mulinari et al. 2). For example, Gunlög Fur notes that what distinguishes Sweden from colonial centers like Britain and France is this lack of a decolonizing moment, which would have enabled Sweden to "rethink its position" ("Colonialism and Swedish History" 24). Swedish society has adopted postcolonial and decolonial theory without dealing with its own history of expansion, going from "no colonialism to post-colonialism without stopping at the in-between" and "without having to confront the challenges and ambiguities of decolonisation" (26, 27). While Sweden's position as a colonial power is unambiguous, I'd argue that this dynamic also applies to Iceland. To frame Iceland's failure to directly address its colonial histories and accompanying racial dynamics, I revisit a quotation from Guðbergur Bergsson's invented report by the Icelandic authorities, discussed in chapter 2, describing how by violently excluding Black and biracial people from the national imaginary, Iceland erases "*the tendency toward racial hatred and discrimination that would otherwise loom large within the nation, and which other countries must confront and seek a way past*" (221). Using the report writers as a sardonic mouthpiece, Bergsson makes the point that by attempting to avoid racial diversity—for instance, through the historical agreement that no Black US soldiers would be stationed in Iceland and the accompanying incidents of racism and discrimination—the nation was unable to confront these aspects or find a way beyond them.

The impacts of Iceland's complex coloniality are visible in recent history, such as Iceland's relationship to the European Union, the rise and fall of the *útrásarvíkingar* or "business Vikings," and the Icesave dispute. Eiríkur Bergmann argues that "Iceland's relationship with the EU only makes sense when taking into account its colonial history and postcolonial national identity, which emphasizes formal sovereignty" (49).[2] While remaining formally outside of the EU, Iceland entered the European Free Trade Association in 1970 and into the European Economic Area in 1994 (33), adopting the EU regulatory framework (34). Although not officially a member, Iceland is in some ways "more deeply involved in the European integration process than some of the EU's official member states," like Denmark, with its many formal opt-outs (34). However, what Bergmann terms Iceland's "Euro-scepticism" results from its colonial past: the "postcolonial emphasis on never again surrendering to foreign authority" is seen as underlying contemporary political discourse and becoming more explicit in times of crisis such as the Icesave dispute (35).[3] The issue is complex, however, with some Icelanders, including farmers and fishermen, skeptical of the EU for other valid political and economic reasons, including the impact of entry into the Union on their livelihoods or the power imbalance between the EU's core and periphery, revealed by the European Debt Crisis that began in 2008.[4] Thus, it is important to acknowledge how what Gremaud refers to as "the scar tissue left behind by past relations with other nations" has influenced Iceland's relationships in the recent past and present in multifaceted ways ("Iceland as Centre" 89).

In the early 2000s, Icelanders had success on the global finance scene buying up banks and creating companies around Europe with a focus on known landmarks in former colonial centers London and Copenhagen; this success was attributed to the unique qualities of the Icelandic people, as well as national myths grounded in the struggle for independence from Denmark (Bergmann 42).[5] In various speeches, Icelandic president Ólafur Ragnar Grímsson linked the contemporary *útrásarvíkingar* with the original Viking settlers through a shared spirit (43). Perhaps this connection rationalizing the fast success made it easier to dismiss the warnings predating Iceland's bank crash in 2008 as "malicious whining from envious foreigners" (43). Moreover, this rhetoric of the "Viking spirit" is embraced, yet the histories of Icelandic colonialism are disavowed—which is ironic, given the fact that the Viking spirit is one of violence and conquest. A parallel is thus created here between the Viking and the indomitable US southern cavalier figure of Lost Cause mythology, casting the Confederate cause as just and heroic. Although both figures are overtly colonial and terroristic, their violence is obscured and even absolved in the way they are repositioned as victims of colonialism by their respective mythologies.

While the short-lived triumphs were linked to aspects of the colonial past—both Viking settlers and Iceland's struggle for independence—shades of postcolonial imagery were also visible during and after the crash. For instance, the UK government invoked the Anti-Terrorist Act to freeze Icelandic assets, and Iceland was placed on the same list as "sanctioned regimes" of the Global South like Al-Qaeda, Burma, the Taliban, Zimbabwe, and North Korea (Bergmann 43), striking at the nation's "deepest insecurities" (Loftsdóttir, *Crisis and Coloniality* 116). Icelanders protested this positioning through a petition with 83,000 signatures and a campaign encouraging Icelanders to send in postcards of themselves "in their everyday clothing, smiling, with their children, toys or stuffed animals" with the phase "Do we look like terrorists, Mr. Brown?" (117). By assuming someone can *look* like a terrorist, this campaign relied on racist associations of Middle Easterners with terrorism, in addition to the assumptions of innocence projected by the participants' visible Whiteness. In this way, the campaign echoed a previous generation's protest of Iceland's inclusion, alongside Greenland and the Danish West Indies, in the Danish colonial exhibition of 1904, described in chapter 1. The postcolonial rhetoric was heightened during the Icesave dispute with the UK and Dutch governments: Iceland claimed to be forced into the hands of the International Monetary Fund and an unjust agreement after falling victim to an EU-led international conspiracy, resulting in President Grímsson's rejection of the agreement (Bergmann 44–45).

Although able to recognize themselves as victimized on a global stage, broadly speaking, Icelanders have failed to confront the ways their nation has benefited from colonialism. This failure, which Iceland shares with the US South, has resulted in the continued adherence to hierarchies of race, gender, and class in both societies, as demonstrated in the literature explored throughout this book. For example, the use of language to hierarchize bodies and protect the privileges granted to Whiteness and maleness discussed in chapter 1 and the depictions of socially sanctioned anti-Blackness, racial violence, and exclusion in chapter 2 illustrate the engrained nature of racism in both Icelandic and US southern societies in the twentieth century. A brief survey of the present moment of this writing reveals that these oppressive structures remain entrenched, establishing the continued relevance of this historically informed and cross-cultural work. In addition to the anti-Blackness explicit in the literature, which remains endemic across the globe in 2024, one could look to the rising levels of violence toward Asian Americans in the US during the COVID-19 pandemic, the record-high instances of antisemitism worldwide in 2021, or the suspicions toward immigrants in both Icelandic and US societies, which I'll consider in more depth, as contemporary examples of sustained adherence to racial hierarchies and the privileges granted to White bodies.[6]

Speaking of the Nordic nations more broadly, Steve Garner asserts that the ambivalent response to colonial histories impacts the Nordic versions of "postmulticultural" discourse that claim the integration of "non-Europeans into Europe" has failed due to cultural differences (414). According to Garner, this demonstrates "how discourses of domination linked to white supremacy in the colonial era can still re-emerge centuries later in the social relationships of countries that have themselves been colonised" (414). Iceland's immigrant population has grown in recent years: the number of Icelanders identified as foreign-born jumped from 5 percent in 2000 to 18 percent in 2020—a more than 240 percent increase—and the number of non-Icelandic citizens increased from 2 percent in 1990 to over 13 percent in 2020 (Valdimarsdóttir and Jónsdóttir 218). The number of asylum seekers in Iceland has also grown in the last few years, with the majority from Iran and Syria (Valdimarsdóttir and Jónsdóttir 218), linking the views of immigrants with those of refugees from Muslim-majority countries.[7] A survey by Margré Valdimarsdóttir and Gudbjorg Andrea Jónsdóttir revealed that while a large portion of Icelandic society supports the acceptance of more refugees, negative stereotypes of Muslims exist in Iceland, such as the stereotype of Muslims as a security threat (229). In a study of literature of the financial crash in Iceland (2008–2014), Alaric Hall relates the "unprecedented outburst of racist and Islamophobic politicking" in the 2014 municipal elections to anxieties in Icelandic culture (132), connecting back to its colonial past and questions about whether Iceland is really a "developed" nation (135).[8] Hall analyzes the need to "write Iceland in relation to the Islamic and/or developing world" around the time of the financial crash (136), as well as the ongoing reliance on stereotypes of the Islamic world (137). This modern example contains inflections of the dynamics discussed in chapter 1 when Icelanders in Laxness's novel rely on exotic stereotypes of Africans to position themselves as White and European. And the situation for immigrants in Iceland remains in flux. In March 2023, Iceland's Parliament passed a bill stripping asylum seekers of their rights, such as access to housing and healthcare, thirty days after the rejection of their applications, which has been criticized by human rights groups (Ćirić).

Additionally, the contemporary moment finds anti-immigrant, anti-refugee, and anti-Muslim sentiments widespread in the United States. As described early in this book, "national" and "southern" are not in competition, writing back to the concept of US southern exceptionalism or the South as existing apart from the nation's history and as the site of the nation's racism and backwardness. Leigh Anne Duck has called for "a clearer understanding of the ways in which U.S. nationalism has tended to code its investments in racial hierarchies as regional traits" (14), yet, while found in the South, such traits are representative of the nation as a whole. Following her lead, I acknowledge that the phenomena outlined in this coda are national in scope, but given the focus of the book on the US South, I zero in on that region as the data allow to continue sketching the parallel dynamics between Iceland and the US South. As some phenomena are conceptualized nationally rather than regionally, this emphasis is not without its tensions and involves some extrapolation. For instance, the polls gauging anti-refugee and anti-Muslim sentiments span the entire nation. However, as the South is composed largely of red or Republican-voting states, an analysis of the data accordingly may come close to revealing the majority views of southerners. For instance, a 2016 survey asking Americans if they held a favorable view of Islam revealed "a 40-point gap between Republicans and Democrats in general (24 percent of Republicans and 64 percent of Democrats). But the gap widens to 50 points between Clinton supporters (66 percent have a favorable view) and Trump supporters (16 percent), specifically" (McElvein and Newby).[9] Nevertheless, these views traverse the nation with a 2016 poll showing 62 percent of Americans reporting as having a favorable attitude toward Muslims but only 44 percent claiming to have a favorable attitude toward Islam (Telhami). Further, 46 percent of Americans who were against accepting refugees expressed concerns about links to terrorism (Telhami). The Southern Poverty Law Center lists seventeen anti-immigrant hate groups active throughout the US in 2023.[10]

With geopolitical instability around the globe, migration and the necessity of crossing borders are likely to be enduring aspects of society. Addressing anti-immigrant sentiments as a nation, region, or even local community would be an essential step toward neutralizing racialized hierarchies, a lingering effect of colonialism, which Andrew Stuhl notes "was, and continues to be, a tangle of intentional interference and its unintended consequences" (*Unfreezing the Arctic* 10). Concerning writing on race, Whiteness, and post-colonialism within a Nordic setting, Peter Hervik notes that there is a "striking absence of voices of non-Western people" and "little attention is being paid to racism towards aboriginal people, Islamophobia, anti-Semitism, and other forms of racist subordination" (19). A step forward in both localities might be an intentional focus on the publishing and reading of more texts by non-Western writers, immigrant writers, and writers of color, in addition to privileging writing by authors who identify as women, nonbinary, trans, or other marginalized genders.

Chapter 3 depicts the experiences of three gender nonconforming girls, including the sexualization and exploitation of young girls common to both Iceland and the US South, and chapter 4 depicts the interconnected experiences of women across the generations in two families. Both include a focus on the confining gendered and cisheteronormative expectations forced on women and girls. Sexual violence and gender-based harassment remain central issues in the contemporary moments of both Iceland and the US. While the roots of the #MeToo movement in the US can be traced back to Tarana Burke's coining of the phrase in 2006 to help survivors of sexual violence—and particularly girls and women of color—it was in 2017 that #MeToo went viral as the slogan of an anti-sexual harassment movement ("#MeToo"). The first instances, such as actress Ashley Judd's accusations against Harvey Weinstein, were primarily situated in the arenas of US politics and entertainment, but allegations soon spread across fields and industries with a global reach, also impacting the Nordic countries. In 2019, Iceland's then Prime Minister Katrín Jakobsdóttir hosted an international conference focusing on gender equality and violence against women. Jakobsdóttir noted that although Iceland had been "top for gender equality globally for five years" and considered "a gender equality paradise," many stories came to the fore as part of the movement; Icelanders were surprised by the volume of assaults reported and the experiences of double discrimination described by women with international backgrounds (Lindahl).[11] While perhaps not a "paradise," Iceland has been the nation ranked highest in terms of closing the gender gap for employment, education, health, and politics by the World Economic Forum for the last twelve years (Reid 11). Iceland has "the highest level of female participation in the workforce" and "little to no social stigma regarding single parents or young mothers," yet the Reykjavík women's shelter is often full, there were no female CEOs of companies trading on the Iceland Stock Exchange or Nasdaq Iceland as of 2021, and reports of domestic violence rose during the COVID-19 pandemic (Reid 12), demonstrating issues that remain in Icelandic society.

Like its reputation as "a gender equality paradise," Iceland is known as a queer-friendly tourist destination. The Icelandic word *hinsegin* ("the other way around") is an inclusive term that comprises all who identify as queer (Reid 81). Iceland was one of the first European nations to recognize same-sex partnerships in 1996 (and to recognize them as marriages in 2010), grant equal adoption and in vitro fertilization rights for same-sex couples in 2006, and formalize naming and identity changing processes for the trans and genderqueer communities through legislation in 2012 (Chapman).[12] In addition, the passage of a gender autonomy act in 2019 shortened the process for many trans people to get medical resources, added a third gender option to the National Registry, and enabled those under eighteen to change their registered gender with the confirmation of a parent or guardian (Fontaine, "Iceland Passes"). Laws removed from the 2019 bill protecting intersex children from unnecessary and nonconsensual surgeries and increasing the rights of trans children were then passed in December 2020, with updated and more gender inclusive language and the age for legally changing one's registered gender lowered to fifteen (Fontaine, "Passage of Bills"). Yet, as everywhere, there remains work to be done in Iceland. For instance, trans people have "a significantly higher risk of depression, anxiety, and suicide" (although Iceland-specific statistics are difficult to find) (Reid 88), and Icelandic law is vague when it comes to defining hate speech or hate crimes (Reid 130). There is always room for improvements in attitudes and vocabulary, as noted by Eva María Thórarinsdóttir Lange, cofounder of the travel agency Pink Iceland (Reid 81). In Iceland, as in other global spaces, recognizing the fluidity of language, as well as the importance of political rights and broader societal acceptance across identities, will foster more inclusive and equitable futures.

While the US saw a number of political victories for LGBTQIA+ rights in the 2010s—such as the end of the federal ban on marriage equality and the extension of the Military Equal Opportunity policy to include sexual orientation (Pellerin), both in 2015—these victories are increasingly under threat. President Joe Biden signed the Respect for Marriage Act, providing statutory authority for same-sex and interracial marriages ("United States, Congress, House"), and unspecified or other gender identity (X) became an option on US passports in 2022, but the same year also witnessed the "pronounced acceleration of anti-LGBTQ+ rhetoric and legislation" (Kane). This included laws regarding the teaching of sexuality in schools, banning trans student athletes, and preventing parents from helping gender-variant children obtain necessary care (Kane).[13] From 2020 to 2022, 306 bills targeting trans people were introduced in the US, with 86 percent of the legislation focusing on trans youth and more than half of the states seeking to restrict gender-affirming health care (Nakajima and Jin).[14] Many of these oppressive laws originate in red states, of which there are a high concentration in the US South; however, as with anti-immigrant sentiments, anti-LGBTQIA+ views span the nation as a whole. For example, the recent "Don't Say Gay" legislation, prohibiting instruction on gender identity and sexual orientation from kindergarten to the third grade, was devised in Florida, but conservative gubernatorial candidates in states like Michigan and New York also made promises to pass similar legislation in their more northern states in 2022 (Kane). Although, according to the Southern Poverty Law Center's Hate Map, there are a large number of anti-LGBTQIA+ hate groups based in the US South, it is important to recognize that these groups exist in all regions of the nation, with the highest number of organizations in a single state (nine) found in California; Florida is a close second with seven. In addition to anti-immigrant and anti-Muslim sentiments, common to Iceland and the US to varying degrees, limitations to LGBTQIA+ rights and inclusion exist in both nations, although more prevalently in the US.

Finally, a discussion of the stakes for exploring these spaces and their colonial inheritances in our present period would not be complete without a recognition of the importance of the climate crisis for every region of the globe. While the entire planet will feel the negative impact, the crisis will likely affect the nations of the Global South disproportionately: "having contributed a fraction of the historical GHG emissions, the Global South is currently experiencing the greatest harm (IPCC)" and compounding the problem, "the Global South is not able financially to adapt to the changing climate" (Beer 85). Additionally, women across the globe will feel a disproportionate impact.[15] At the same time, the melting of the Arctic directly impacts the Far North, thrusting northern nations like Iceland into a global spotlight: "A great deal of energy is devoted to being rediscovered by the next wave of globalization, that of tourism, following the emergence of the Arctic as a recently globalized region" (Moberg et al. 182). More specifically, Iceland's glaciers position it as a location for what's called last-chance tourism, "a niche tourism market where tourists explicitly seek vanishing landscapes or seascapes, and/or disappearing natural and/or social heritage" (Lemelin et al. 478); while last-chance tourism can raise awareness and promote conservation, the arrival of more tourists can also accelerate the negative effects.[16] With the shrinking ice revealing "previously inaccessible natural resources and transportation routes," the Arctic region has become "a hive of economic prospecting and governmental capacity building" (Stuhl, "The Disappearing Arctic?" 22). More specifically, 22 percent of "the world's undiscovered oil and gas" may exist in the Arctic (Beary 142), leading the US, Canada, Russia, Denmark, and Norway to assert their territorial holdings in the region; causing China to become a forceful player in the field (Rosenthal); and marginalizing Inuit participation in the circumpolar governance (Stuhl, "The Disappearing Arctic?" 22). Colonial and imperialist currents underlie the race for the resources in the

Arctic and the language surrounding it, a reiteration of historical dynamics explored in this book.[17]

Whether considering the treatment of immigrants, women, and members of the LGBTQIA+ communities in the US South and Iceland or the climate crisis's intensified impact on both the Global South and the Far North, these spaces will remain significant into the future. While the stakes of our current moment help produce timely scholarship in the fields of the environmental humanities, economics, sociology, and international relations, among others, I'd invite additional work in the field of comparative literature that investigates how these dynamics are represented in contemporary and forthcoming bodies of literature. Applying a comparative frame to literature, present or future, from spaces associated with the Global South and the Far North that explore the enduring legacies of colonialism, whether through the sustained reliance on colonial hierarchies or the effects of climate change on these regions, would benefit readers' understandings of texts, cultures, histories. Similar to the examination of twentieth-century literature in this project and the shared experiences of colonial liminality, racism, and cisheteropatriarchy across the US South and Iceland that are brought to the fore, a sustained exploration of these spaces alongside each other will reveal connections not otherwise centered. While scholarship in literary studies is not likely to solve the climate crisis, for instance, I believe it matters what we choose to pay attention to and where we focus our efforts as scholars.[18] Indeed, an eye to the contemporary illustrates that an understanding of colonial histories and their lingering impacts remains essential to both a consideration of the present and an anticipation of a more fully decolonial future.

NOTES

INTRODUCTION: LIMINAL COLONIAL WORLDS

1. Harilaos Stecopoulos notes that southern political moderate Faulkner's "longstanding problems with the federal state didn't so much vanish as intensify during a seven-year tenure as a Cold War literary diplomat" (144). Deborah Cohn asserts that Faulkner espouses positions in his imaginative work that were at odds with his public statements: "Cold warrior or not . . . the conflicting views of democracy offered by Faulkner as writer, Faulkner as public persona, and Faulkner as cultural diplomat speak to a figure who must be viewed from many lenses, and who resisted being reduced to the function that the State Department would have had him serve, let alone reconciled with himself" (419).

2. In an International Educational Exchange Service memo from March 15, 1956, entitled "Secret," William Gibson, counsellor of the US Embassy in Reykjavík, states that "the Icelanders clearly recognize that a cultural tug-of-war over Iceland is going on between the United States and Russia, and that one William Faulkner is worth in Iceland innumerable lesser lights," speaking to the respect for Faulkner's writing already widespread in Iceland in the 1950s (see figure 0.4) (Trent). Gibson's "Foreign Service Despatch" from October 25, 1955, describes Faulkner as having been "particularly successful in University circles, which have often been peculiarly subject to influences cool or even hostile to the United States, but the impact of his personality was not limited to intellectual groups" and notes that his press and his radio attention were more favorable than any other Americans brought under the program (see figure 0.3) (Gibson 1). One legation member wrote in the margins of the official report that Faulkner's visit was "just what the doctor ordered" (Blotner 612).

3. Wai Chee Dimock uses the concept of "weak reparation" to explore Faulkner as "an intensely local author with a surprising global reach, trying to atone for the past on just that basis, and, in not quite succeeding, also leaving room for input from others" (589); she also builds on sociologist Mark Granovetter's work on "the strength of weak ties" in the context of networking (590). Weak ties have the potential to deepen our understanding of singular entities through opening us up to less intuitive comparative connections.

4. Haukur Ingvarsson's groundbreaking study on Faulkner's reputation in Icelandic cultural life from 1930 to 1960, *Fulltrúi þess besta í bandarískri menningu: Orðspor Williams*

Faulkners í íslensku menningarlífi 1930–1960, has yet to be translated into English; however, see Brynjarr Perry Mendoza's review in *Scandinavian-Canadian Studies* for an English overview.

5. I extend recent work in Nordic Whiteness and postcolonial studies, such as *Denmark and the New North Atlantic: Narratives and Memories in a Former Empire* (2020), edited by Kirsten Thisted and Ann-Sofie N. Gremaud; *The Postcolonial North Atlantic: Iceland, Greenland and the Faroe Islands* (2020), edited by Lill-Ann Körber and Ebbe Volquardsen; *Racialization, Racism, and Anti-Racism in the Nordic Countries* (2019), edited by Peter Hervik; and *Whiteness and Postcolonialism in the Nordic Region: Exceptionalism, Migrant Others and National Identities* (2012), edited by Kristín Loftsdóttir and Lars Jensen.

6. Johan Höglund and Linda Andersson Burnett state that "Nordic and Scandinavian histories and cultures are, in fact, colonial and postcolonial histories and cultures" (2). Connecting to earlier models of global spatial relations, Erlend Eidsvik argues that "[t]he Nordic countries constitute a semi-peripheral region in a world conditioned by the imperial metropoles in their conquests of colonial territory" (15). I'd build on this by distinguishing the various positionings within and between Nordic nations—from Sweden's history as a colonial power to the Faroe Islands, a self-governing region under Danish control.

7. In challenge to geographic binaries, I'm interested in engaging with the US South, not solely as a region of the US, a nation of the Global North, but also as a space sharing commonalities with nations of the Global South, including, for instance, the warm climate, history of plantation slavery, and experience of occupation shared with many nations of the Caribbean (*Policing Intimacy* 7).

8. Exploring what he calls "the Postcolonial Turn" in Icelandic literature following the 2008 financial crash, Hall notes that "[e]xamining literature closely allows us to develop a richer sense of the cultural tensions and artistic potential of Iceland's post-colonial anxieties" (134). See also Vera Knútsdóttir's *Spectral Memories of Post-Crash Iceland: Memory, Identity and the Haunted Imagination in Contemporary Literature and Art* (2023) for a reading of the culture that followed the economic crash of 2008 and the relationship between memory, identity, and the "haunted imagination" in contemporary Icelandic literature and visual art (3).

9. Mai Palmberg catalogues different Nordic nations' overt involvement in colonization, including not only Denmark's actual colonies and the ways these nations profited economically from colonialism and the slave trade, but also participation in the spreading of Western and Christian superiority through missionary work and their role, especially Sweden's, in the history of eugenics (40, 45). Palmberg asks, "If we accept that Nordic exceptionalism is based on a myth, must we then see the Nordic colonial mind as a result of actual involvement?" (43–44).

10. Loftsdóttir asserts that "Whiteness is important in the Nordic context because 'Nordic' often assumes a white subject," as is the case in the discourses of equality around gender and immigration (*Crisis and Coloniality* 6).

11. Scholarship in southern studies has effectively addressed the complexities of considering the US South in colonial and postcolonial terms, including work by Hosam Aboul-Ela, Sara Gerend, Édouard Glissant, Taylor Hagood, George Handley, and John T. Matthews, as well as the anthologies *Look Away! The U.S. South in New World Studies* and *Global Faulkner: Faulkner and Yoknapatawpha, 2006*.

NOTES

12. Larry J. Griffin notes that "the white South" was "exceptional in its fierce commitment to slavery, in its failed experiment with secession and nationhood, in its military defeat and occupation by a conquering power, in its poverty, cultural backwardness, and religiosity, and in its pervasive, prolonged resistance to racial justice" (7). While poverty and racism span the nation, the experience of military occupation signals the region's unique position within the nation. Griffin asserts, based on polls conducted in the 1990s, that African Americans in the South are less likely to perceive the region as exceptional, and nonsoutherners are less likely to view exceptionalism as a positive (16).

13. Greeson notes that writers after the Civil War made these connections themselves and "explicitly envisioned their Reconstruction South as a 'new Africa,' an American analogue to the continent upon which the last great frenzy of Old World empire was being played out," and remaining to "some extent a domestic site within the nation, its occupation and administration provided an exceptional form for nascent U.S. empire overseas" (14–15).

14. As Gunlög Fur notes, by paying attention to each scholar's situatedness, "each historical account we produce should be truthful, built on respect for sources and their possibilities and limits, yet always aware of its limited and partial reach" ("Concurrences as a Methodology" 40). Indeed, what I see in the texts is affected by my own subject position, which I described as "a heterosexual, White-passing multiracial, cisgender woman from the northeastern United States" in my first book but have found to be more fluid (*Policing Intimacy* 8). This fluidity is inadvertently reflected in what I choose to examine in the second half of this book.

15. While scholars have noted that references to "White" and "non-White" have the effect of prioritizing Whiteness as the norm, others assert that the use of these terms elucidate the power relations involved (Loftsdóttir and Mörtudóttir 218). Conscious of both impacts, I intend to shed light on the power dynamics, leaving space for transnational, cross-cultural differences, as well as similarities.

16. Loftsdóttir and Jensen investigate the ways that "certain notions and structural inequalities that can be understood as being some sort of residue from the colonial period, become recreated or projected onto different groups in the contemporary Nordic countries and thus how borders of whiteness, and notions of Nordic-ness become reified" within North American and European contexts ("Introduction" 2).

17. Suvi Keskinen emphasizes that "colonial complicity" is useful "but needs to be complemented with the recognition of continued colonialism in the Arctic" (179); in other words, the ongoing nature of these dynamics also needs to be foregrounded.

18. Eirikur Bergmann notes that "postcolonial theories can contribute further to understanding Iceland's strained relationship with the EU" (34), demonstrating how these connections run from the twentieth century into the present period.

19. See Sciuto, "'[T]he critic must leave the Western hemisphere': Faulkner and World Literature" in *The New William Faulkner Studies* (2022), edited by Sarah Gleeson-White and Pardis Dabashi.

20. Kanafani directly referenced this influence in an interview, agreeing with critics that *All That's Left to You* is a "manifest expression of admiration" for Faulkner's *The Sound and the Fury*; however, he notes that his novella is "not an exact replica of Faulkner's devices" but an attempt at benefiting from them and from Faulkner's developments in Western Literature (qtd. in Azouqa 148n2).

CHAPTER 1: DELIMITING DIFFERENCE:
LANGUAGE, STEREOTYPES, AND REPETITION IN HALLDÓR LAXNESS,
WILLIAM FAULKNER, AND SVAVA JAKOBSDÓTTIR

1. Gavin Lucas and Angelos Parigoris note that Icelanders were exhibited alongside "primitive" Greenlanders in the "Northern Dwellers" exhibition at the World Fair of 1900 in Paris and then at the Danish colonial exhibition in 1904 (98, 97).

2. Each writer's positioning is complex and involves some liminality, defined by Ineke Jolink as located "on the threshold between two positions" ("The In-Between"). Writing from peripheralized spaces, but still from the perspectives of White, male writers of their times and places with all the privileges granted to them as a result, both Faulkner's and Laxness's obstructed views are evident through their representations, such as how they depict race, gender, and experiences of sexual violence.

3. In her study of representations of Africa in Icelandic elementary school textbooks, Loftsdóttir concludes that the overall description of Africa in the texts is "a relatively static one of dark people living in 'different' societies, which, although not necessarily characterized in negative terms, are nonetheless viewed as requiring modernisation and development," with an emphasis on skin color creating "a racialized landscape" ("Learning Differences?" 18).

4. Alix Johnson describes how "the growing data center industry in Iceland constitutes a new occasion for mobilizing these imaginaries" of Iceland's wilderness, but "like contested sites of place-making before it, these imaging efforts are often unstable, and raise the specter of their imperial roots" (5).

5. Pálsson places arcticality in conversation with David Arnold's use of tropicality, a manifestation of Orientalism aligning with the invention of the "tropics" in western discourse (276), through his consideration of the establishment and perhaps invention of "the Arctic Zone," a "fertile but somewhat slippery discursive space, as a relatively demarcated and monotonous site useful for the exploration of particular themes in contrast to the temperate Euroamerican world" (277).

6. Ísleifsson is careful to delineate between the different stereotypical associations of regions of the Far North, with Iceland and the Faroe Islands linked with the "Germanic North" (which played a role in the creation of nationalistic ideas in the nineteenth and twentieth centuries) and Greenland and Sámi territories with the "primitive North" in comparison (16), writing back to reductive conceptualizations of the Far North as a monolith.

7. The conceptualization of the North as superior to the South became more prevalent in the eighteenth and nineteenth centuries and would fuel the racism of the nineteenth and twentieth centuries, impacting societies spanning the globe (Ísleifsson 16).

8. See D'Amico, "The Whole World Is One Atom Station: Laxness, the Cold War, Postcolonialism, and the Economic Crisis in Iceland" for an in-depth consideration of the novel's postcolonial inflections.

9. Nicknames or pet names are very common in Iceland. Paul R. Peterson notes that "Nicknames in the sagas are important for providing motivation for actions and behavior" (91), and I see the Árland family's use of nicknames in the episode as revealing much about their characters as well. In the contemporary period, naming remains central to Icelandic society with regulations and an official naming committee that "judges, and then accepts or rejects new names in the Icelandic lexicon" (Fontaine, "Naming Committee").

NOTES 163

10. Unlike the continental Scandinavian languages, the Icelandic language has not changed much: "'Old' Icelandic remains—except for phonetic and lexicological differences—the mother tongue of twenty-first-century Iceland" (Peterson 90), and it is the "modern Scandinavian language closest to its Old Norse predecessor" (Sondrup and Sandberg 14). A continued interest in the saga tradition also retains connections to ancient times, while the Icelanders in this scene strive extra hard to disassociate themselves from anything taken as "uncivilized." There may be some irony here in the fact that "civilization" tends to be associated with modernity and earlier eras, such as the medieval period, with its lack; however, the reverse is seen in this case.

11. In addition to this opening scene, race appears overtly in two other places in the novel: the first is a racist toy that is mentioned twice (Laxness, *Atom Station* 52, 56). In another scene, the newspapers do not want to offend a murderer and his family by writing about the events, so "someone had the fine idea of blaming the murder on an unknown American negro, for it did not matter in the least if a black Yankee and his family were offended" (98). D'Amico refers to this moment as one in which Ugla "actually moderates the book's anti-American rhetoric and attacks the Icelanders for being localists and racists" (464). This last instance exposes a systemic racism that echoes the historical agreement between the Icelandic and the US governments that no Black soldiers would be stationed in Iceland, which I discuss at length in chapter 2.

12. With the emphasis on naming here, it is worth mentioning that Ugla in Icelandic means owl. Árland states, "A learned bird, and her time is the night" (2).

13. The entwinement of gender, race, and sexuality in this portrayal of Guðný and her Whiteness, lingering on her physical body—"fresh-coloured" skin, painted lips, and "supple fingers"—reflects efforts to control female sexuality and historic fears and obsessions surrounding the "protection" of White women from men of color. I discuss the cross-cultural fixation on controlling women's sexuality in chapter 2. Returning to the opening example, Icelanders' most significant problem with the Danish colonial exhibition involved the fact that Icelandic women were showcased alongside women from other dependent spaces. Sveinsson asks, "Must Iceland be known for its participation in such an exhibition, where Icelandic women in national costumes are posed next to Eskimo and Negro women?" (qtd. in Loftsdóttir, "Belonging" 63).

14. Gremaud notes the complex relationship between the two was characterized by "inequality as well as mutual identification: Icelandic cultural history was used as a reservoir of shared heritage that was often referred to in the 19th century national romantic discourse in Denmark" ("Iceland as Centre and Periphery" 85).

15. This category includes Stefán Hörður Grímsson (1919–2002), Einar Bragi (1921–2005), Jón Óskar (1921–1998), Hannes Sigfússon (1922–1997), and Sigfús Daðason (1928–1996) (Þorvaldsson 474–75). While this group was initially known as the atom poets, this phrase has "since been applied to all poets who wrote in a nontraditional manner, either entirely or in part" (Þorvaldsson 475).

16. The fictionalized attempt at returning the bones in *The Atom Station* was grounded in reality: "the industrialist Sigurjón Pétursson, an ex-wrestler and amateur scholar of Icelandic culture and psychic research, brought Jónas Hallgrímsson's bones back to Iceland, claiming that the poet himself had telepathically asked him to do so" (D'Amico 476). Pétursson intended to bury the bones in the north; however, the Icelandic government was opposed, and the police

returned them to Reykjavík to be buried at Thingvellir. According to Jón Karl Helgason, both Laxness and Czech novelist Milan Kundera, who fictionalized this event in *Ignorance* (1999), were unaware that Matthías Þórðarson, the director of the Icelandic National Museum, had written a "meticulous report of his excavation in Denmark in which he convincingly argued that it was indeed Hallgrímsson who was transported to Iceland in 1946" (60).

17. In the US, stereotypes of the southern region include rural (though of course there are major metropolises in the South), religious, and backwards (or not modern), which are qualities associated with the north in Iceland, reflecting inverse spatial hierarchies.

18. See Brannon Costello's *Plantation Airs: Racial Paternalism and the Transformations of Class in Southern Fiction, 1945–1971* for a more developed discussion of the intersection of race and class in the mid-twentieth-century South.

19. In her contribution to the collaborative exploration with Burgers, Parrish describes Shreve as an exemplar and even a parody of the Nordic type with his deep-breathing exercises in the zero-degree weather, vigor that she contrasts with Quentin's shaking. She argues that Faulkner signifies on "the kind of eugenicist claptrap published in the nineteen teens in the midst of fears of Nordic extinction brought on by a new influx of southern, and southern European, immigrants to northern US cities."

20. Using digital mapping, Parrish and Burgers provide a linguistic analysis of the use of racially charged language in *Absalom, Absalom!*, considering the character dynamics and specificities of time and place. For example, 87 percent of the instances where the n-word is used are connected to Sutpen.

21. The colonial hierarchies of race and class have had a violent effect on Sutpen's psyche, causing the embarrassment and shame he experiences in this moment; however, he later perpetuates this violence by working to achieve the status of a White enslaver himself within the same hierarchical system. Taylor Hagood emphasizes this liminality: Sutpen "is himself *both* poor white and aristocratic patriarch and colonizer," in addition to being both innocent and guilty (18). The hybridity or bivalence of his position mirrors that of the South when postcolonial concepts are applied, as well as Iceland's liminality as a formerly dependent nation on the periphery of Europe.

22. The more enlightened Quentin notes in *The Sound and the Fury* that "a n*** is not a person so much as a form of behavior; a sort of obverse reflection of the white people he lives among" (86), deconstructing the term even further.

23. The narrative structure of trauma can take different forms, including deferred revelation (the repression of the most accurate version of a memory until it later resurfaces) and traumatic repetition (the compulsive replaying of an event over and over until it seems to make sense or can be rendered less important).

24. This is another intertextual connection to Quentin in *The Sound and the Fury*, who describes a similar awareness of his perception by others in relation to northerners: "I used to think that a Southerner had to be always conscious of n***s. I thought that Northerners would expect him to be. . . . I'd have wasted a lot of time and trouble before I learned that the best way to take all people, black or white, is to take them for what they think they are, then leave them alone" (86). Quentin considers others to be always conscious of his southernness, and thus, that he should be.

25. This discrepancy is central to Ralph Ellison's *Invisible Man* (1952), which engages with what it means to be Black and American in a racist society.

NOTES   165

26. The power of the lodger over the couple—to infiltrate and stay in their home—is obscured in the story. However, at one point the woman asks herself more directly, "Where did these people get such terrifying power" (27), and later she notes that "the severity which she knew lay under the surface of his normal good manners was not far off" (62). Perhaps this can also be read as the US obscuring the power dynamics characteristic of its relationship to Iceland after World War II.

27. Sigurður A. Magnússon notes the reference to "the American military base in Iceland, which has become a part of the nation's daily life, an alien body around which the whole life of the nation revolves, on which it is constantly more dependent, and of which it will not be able to rid itself in the foreseeable future" ("The Icelandic Short Story" 211), emphasizing the alien and embodied nature of the intrusion.

28. There is also a focus on the couple presenting themselves as "civilized," with Peter telling the lodger, "We are civilized people, after all" (40), and the woman accepting a cigarette from the lodger "like a civilized person" (43). This emphasis resonates with the Árland family in Laxness's *The Atom Station*.

29. S. A. Magnússon observes that the "action is so naturalistic in every detail and the tone so matter-of-fact" that "the reader hardly notices the absurd touches" ("The Modern Icelandic Novel" 143). Vésteinn Ólason concurs that the "incredible story" is accepted because the "absurd and the irrational is not presented suddenly but in small portions, so that each step in its direction goes almost unnoticed" (96). I agree that it is easy to overlook the surreal aspects, such as the scene with the breast milk, due to the realist tone of the story. However, reading for these moments will reveal the gradual build.

30. And in the next paragraph, when both men put out their hands to her as she retreats— "At that same moment, Peter put out his hand. Or was it the lodger?" (41)—early shades of their enmeshment are discernable.

31. Although one of the men is her husband, the wife does not want to show a preference for either man. She finds only one set of slippers, "but there were four feet" (61). Since they had used their feet equally, she slips one slipper onto the left foot of her husband and one onto the right foot of the lodger.

32. In addition to her growing strength of self, the wife's domestic obligations seem to lessen through the lodger's stay. He doesn't want to be served as a guest: "She then sat down herself. Now there was no need to offer anything to anyone. They could help themselves whenever they wanted and to as much as they wanted" (22).

33. Guðni Thorlacius Jóhannesson asserts that "when national interests were at stake, pragmatism and real interests outdid sympathy and ideology," as demonstrated by the fact that "the Icelandic authorities did not support the independence struggle in Angola or Mozambique as convincingly as might have been expected" (132).

CHAPTER 2: AESTHETIC RADICALS:
WHITE VIOLENCE AS EXCLUSION IN GUÐBERGUR BERGSSON,
WILLIAM FAULKNER, AND JEAN TOOMER

1. Bergsson published these two works when he was only twenty-nine, leading Esbjörn Rosenblad and Rakel Sigurðardóttir-Rosenblad to position him as "the most productive innovator in Icelandic prose in the second half of this century" after Thor Vilhjálmsson (164).

2. Eysteinsson notes that "the absence of the modern urban experience so often associated with modernist literature and art" was perhaps the cause for modernism's late arrival in Iceland ("Icelandic Prose Literature" 410–11).

3. Bergsson deals more directly with the American army base in other works, such as the novels in his Tangi cycle (Eysteinsson, "Icelandic Prose Literature" 424). Eysteinsson notes that he does "not condemn the American presence in any simplistic way, instead inquiring relentlessly into its meaning for Icelandic culture" (425). For added context, he is also known for "the toppling of male images and patriarchal viewpoints" in his work more broadly (425).

4. More specifically, the US agreed to Icelandic Prime Minister Herman Jónasson's request for no Black soldiers to be stationed on the base in 1941 and then again in 1951 (Lacy 247). By 1964, as a result of human rights legislation, the US government could not accede; however, "some blacks sent to the base were still reassigned as late as 1972" (Lacy 247). Thus, while the racist policy ended by 1964, the effects were still felt up to 1972, demonstrating the lingering afterlife of such agreements. Since then, "blacks, Filipinos, and others have served with their units on the base without Icelandic protest, though some have felt the sting of prejudice," noted Lacy writing in 2000 (247).

5. According to a report by the Ministry of Justice, about 20 percent of women in Reykjavík had close contact with foreign soldiers, although, as Guðni Thorlacius Jóhannesson asserts, that figure was likely exaggerated and "the problem—the situation—was mainly in the minds of Icelandic men and the older generation" (108). While around 300 women married soldiers and moved abroad, this had no concrete impact on the future of the Icelandic population (108).

6. Young women who interacted with soldiers were moved to rural areas "for their own good and for the good of the nation," after having been subjected to "intimate medical examinations" to see if they'd been infected by diseases traced to the occupying armies (S. G. Magnússon 233). Oxfeldt et al. note that the officials' conduct towards the girls and women, the potential violation of their legal rights, and the more general repercussions for them were never investigated (49).

7. Neijmann continues with the observation that "even occupiers and occupied unite against a common greater enemy: woman," since the contempt and distrust of women creates a "bond between men that exceeds all politics and nationalisms it seems" ("Soldiers and Other Monsters" 111).

8. Þorsteinsson's son, Icelandic crime writer Arnaldur Indriðason, has a more recent novel, *The Shadow District* (2017; *Skuggasund*, 2015), that is also set in part during World War II and addresses the treatment of Icelandic women by foreign soldiers and Icelandic men alike during the period.

9. Seemingly intended as humor for the contemporary reader, the missing woman is indeed later found on a British cruiser where she had been for two weeks. However, this does not justify the newspaper's cavalier attitude for present-day feminist readers: "People like that will turn up, says the paper; no need to spend much money searching for them" (Þorsteinsson 100).

10. At one point, the platoon leader with whom Halla, Falkon's wife, will later have an affair "thrusts a large bag of oranges into her bosom so her big breasts undulate beneath the pink, form-fitting dress, which does nothing to hide her flat stomach and hips" (Þorsteinsson 37), representative of the sexualized attention to women's bodies in the novel. In another overt

NOTES   167

example, one Icelandic women's "breasts spill out of her red robe onto the window sill" when she attempts to watch men on motorcycles (49). The men "nickname the woman Lorelei and speak of her as nothing but a featureless, dumpy little brunette" (49), demonstrating the disrespect indicative of their characters, in addition to the portrayal of women in the novel more broadly.

11. Sexual policing across the color line in US and Caribbean literatures is the topic of my first book, *Policing Intimacy: Law, Sexuality, and the Color Line in Twentieth-Century Hemispheric American Literature* (2021).

12. The novel represents the writings and ramblings in Tómas's composition books, and thus, occasional passages and even entire vignettes are italicized, adding emphasis to those sections. This is an aesthetic connection to Faulkner's work. Joseph R. Urgo and Noel Polk observe that while in other novels, "Faulkner used italics to indicate varying levels of a character's conscious or unconscious thought," in *Absalom, Absalom!* the italics suggest "a narrator different from the relatively conventional narrator of chapters I and II, one somehow more distanced from the material," with these passages perhaps not spoken and heard but thought and imagined by someone different (26). In both cases, the typographical choices reflect aspects of how the stories are narrated—whether through Tómas's compositions or the layers of speaking, hearing, and imagining in Faulkner's novel.

13. In addition to exploding notions of identity—where, in Sigurdur A. Magnússon's terms, "all boundaries between inner and outer reality disappear, the personality is dissolved" ("The Modern Icelandic Novel" 140)—Vésteinn Ólason argues that the novel's inclusion of unoriginal texts and vignettes is "Guðbergur's device to parody all kinds of Icelandic prose-styles and reveal and make ridiculous the clichés of conventional Icelandic prose. He produces texts in order to reveal their emptiness" (98).

14. The use of milk specifically here also calls to mind the stealing of Sethe's breast milk in Morrison's novel *Beloved* (1987)—a form of gendered violence entwined also with her experience of sexual violence, highlighting themes of dehumanization and attempts to control women's bodies through a cross-cultural, transhistorical connection. Thanks to Laura Wilson for noting this link.

15. This passage is evocative of the conclusion of Faulkner's *Absalom, Absalom!*, referenced in chapter 1, when narrator Shreve McCaslin sardonically voices a fear that "in time the Jim Bonds are going to conquer the western hemisphere" and "as they spread toward the poles they will bleach out again like the rabbits and the birds do" until "in a few thousand years, I who regard you will also have sprung from the loins of African kings" (302). The Icelandic officials' report echoes Shreve's monologue in the voiced fear of "*the multiplication of blacks*" and a "*present and future chaos of racial tension*" (Bergsson 222).

16. Gunlög Fur argues that Swedish society adopted "postcolonial and decolonial theories of coloniality and modernity to contemporary Swedish society *without* having to deal with, either theoretically or empirically, a longer history of expansion and conflict" ("Colonialism and Swedish History" 26), which mirrors Bergsson's critique of Iceland here.

17. Icelanders failed to live up to the Nazi party's expectations of the isolated nation. As Helgi Hrafn Guðmundsson notes, "Nazi leadership had identified the Icelandic nation as a pure and brave 'Aryan nation'" but were soon disappointed. Gunnar Karlsson also asserts that Nazism never gained a foothold in Iceland as a political movement: the best outcome in local elections was in 1934 with 2.8 percent support (363). Sjón's recent novel *Red Milk*

(2022; *Korngult hár, grá augu*, 2019) is based on his research into a group of Icelandic neo-Nazis in the 1960s, demonstrating that Iceland is not free from these views, even though they may not achieve widespread support.

18. The "cultural and ethnic diversity of the Viking Age" is supported by silver hoards and furnished graves of the ninth and tenth centuries: analyzing skeletons with the "latest scientific techniques points to a mix of Scandinavian and non-Scandinavian peoples without clear ethnic distinctions in rank or gender" (Downham). For more on the associations between White supremacists and Viking history—for instance, the ways "the contemporary White supremacist revival of Odinism is deeply rooted in antisemitism and Nazism" (Weber)—see Weber, "White Supremacy's Old Gods: The Far Right and Neopaganism," Downham's "Vikings Were Never the Pure-Bred Master Race White Supremacists Like to Portray," and von Schnurbein, *Norse Revival: Transformations of Germanic Neopaganism*.

19. For more on the failure to make lynching a federal crime in the US in 2020, see Fandos, "Frustration and Fury as Rand Paul Holds Up Anti-Lynching Bill in Senate." In 2022, the Senate voted to pass anti-lynching legislation that would designate lynching as a federal hate crime, sending the bill to President Joe Biden—the first successful attempt out of two hundred since 1918 (Chen). In March 2022, President Biden signed the bill, named for Emmett Till, and ended over one hundred years of failed efforts by the federal government to outlaw lynching (Shear).

20. Chuck Jackson describes Gavin Stevens as spinning "a classically Gothic tale about the last moments of Christmas's life as a panicky, interior struggle of blood against blood, fetishizing and racializing his liquid interiors by repeating the terms 'black blood' and 'white blood' (448–49). Christmas's white blood, Stevens explains, provides him with moral reasoning, but his black blood rises against it . . ." (193). In contrast to Stevens's claim, Jackson asserts that it is "the whiteness of the force that ultimately destroys Christmas, not his 'blood', but the National Guard, embodied by Percy Grimm" (194).

21. See Sciuto, *Policing Intimacy: Law, Sexuality, and the Color Line in Twentieth-Century Hemispheric American Literature* and "Racial Ambiguity, Bootlegging, and the Subversion of Plantation Hierarchies in Faulkner's South."

22. Having grown up in New York, Frank was not a southerner either, complicating this claim.

23. For example, Joanna racializes Joe during their sexual encounters. She sometimes compels Joe to come to her through a window and at other times to seek her throughout the house or on the grounds "beneath certain shrubs . . . where he would find her naked, or with her clothing half torn to ribbons upon her, in the wild throws of nymphomania . . . and wild hands and her breathing: 'Negro! Negro! Negro!'" (Faulkner, *Light in August* 259–60). Joanna locates herself in the position of White plantation mistress/enslaver, leaving food for the Black laborer (she thinks, "*Set out for the n***. For the n****") played by Joe, forcing him to enter through the kitchen or even a window (238).

24. Arbour argues that the women are marginalized by the narrators who position them as metaphors and that Louisa is a metaphor for the "dying Southern folk culture" (318).

25. Borst discusses Bob's self-consciousness in relation to Du Bois's theories of double consciousness in the lives of Black Americans, discussed in chapter 1: if "double-consciousness is both a veil and a gift of second-sight for African-Americans, Stone's white

NOTES

double-consciousness creates nightmarish paranoia" (19). According to Borst, Stone attempts to fend off this White double-consciousness by "conjuring up the master-slave dialectic that offers him a clear subject position" (20), which is supported by his yearning for a stable identity and unchanging racial relations.

26. According to the one-drop rule, Louisa would have been positioned as Black; however, given her description in the text, I believe biracial or multiracial would be a more accurate positioning that incorporates more nuance beyond the binary system.

27. Notably, Faulkner's Joe Christmas can also be understood as a Christ figure. Not only is Joe "sacrificed" for his community, but Christ's name is contained within his own, and the two also share the initials "JC." For more on Joe Christmas as a Christ figure, see Spenko, "The Death of Joe Christmas and the Power of Words."

28. More radical interrogations have followed the writing analyzed in this chapter, such as Morrison's *Beloved* (1987), exploring the resonances of enslavement in the twentieth century through a magical realist mode; Mississippi writer Jesmyn Ward's *Salvage the Bones* (2011) and *Sing, Unburied, Sing* (2017), which examine similar themes to Faulkner's from the viewpoints of Black and biracial protagonists; Arnaldur Indriðason's *Arctic Chill* (2005) about the murder of a child of a Thai immigrant that enflames the tensions between preserving Icelandic history and culture and the shifts towards a more "multicultural society" (Indriðason 99); and Bergsveinn Birgisson's *The Black Viking* (2013), in which he recovers the story of his ancestor Geirmund Heljarskinn, a dark-skinned Viking with Asian features, and challenges myths about Vikings as a "pure Aryan" demographic.

CHAPTER 3: "I'M SICK OF BEING A GIRL!": NONCONFORMITY AND INTERSECTING HIERARCHIES OF IDENTITY IN HALLDÓR LAXNESS AND CARSON MCCULLERS

1. Salka is a literary icon, serving as "a role model for women in Iceland ever since the novel was published" because she is "strong, realistic, and resourceful" with a "great aspiration for freedom and independence, as well as her ability to look after herself" (Guðmundsdóttir 62).

2. For instance, I expand on Jaime Harker's locating "queerness as a resistance to and exposure of regimes of the normal" in McCullers's fiction by adding Laxness's novel to the discussion (102).

3. It is not possible to recover if the three protagonists would identify as masculine cisgender, nonbinary, genderqueer, transmasculine, or in another way in today's terms. Rachel Mesch's *Before Trans: Three Gender Stories from Nineteenth-Century France* considers "the ways in which the trans framework can be used to shine a light on earlier figures who resisted gender norms—to explore what 'trans before trans' might mean and the implications of casting back in history with a new set of critical tools" (Mesch 9). Greta LaFleur et al. describe their hope that *Trans Historical: Gender Plurality Before the Modern* "indexes the efflorescence of archaeologies of the past: a past that may hold a space for forms of transness that have not yet been fully articulated or imagined, a past that, in the future, may unfold forms of alterity unknown to us at present" (5).

170   NOTES

4. Andrea James, transgender activist and filmmaker, explains that "tomboy" is at present "a controversial word for masculine minors who were assigned female at birth" ("Tomboy Resources").

5. While I employ a more expansive view of queer, I agree with Heather Love that queerness has "indeterminacy" to offer "but not blank indeterminacy" (747).

6. Jennifer Ann Shapland observes that "the polar regions have long attracted the artistic attention of notable queer writers and artists in addition to the extreme adventurists, nature writers, and documentarians with whom we associate these landscapes" and that, as opposed to heteronormative capitalist society, "[t]he Arctic offers different kinds of openness to different kinds of longings" (131), at least in terms of the fantasies of Western writers and artists.

7. These literary examples span centuries and southern locales, with Henry and Bon interacting in 1860s Mississippi and John and Freddie in 1940s Louisiana.

8. See Bibler's *Cotton's Queer Relations: Same-Sex Intimacy and the Literature of the Southern Plantation, 1936–1968* for an illustration of how same-sex bonds depicted in US southern literature "produce an egalitarian social relation between individuals that ironically places them at odds with the hierarchical structures of the plantations they call home" (4).

9. Inga Dóra Björnsdóttir convincingly links this trope to former Icelandic president Vigdís Finnbogadóttir, the world's first democratically elected woman president (1980–1996). Moreover, Loftsdóttir notes the "strong association of Icelandic nationalism in the early 20th century with men and masculinities, with Icelandic men séen as responsible and credited for bringing about modernity while women were seen merely as representing the country's timeless nature" (*Crisis and Coloniality* 76).

10. Laxness wrote in support of modern women with bobbed hair in *Morgunblaðið* in 1925, stating that the style was "testimony of a new mentality, a new understanding of the status of women and their role in life" (qtd. in Rastrick, "Physical Appearance" 83).

11. Ellenberger notes that in the late 1800s and early 1900s, "members of Reykjavík's dominant class probably had more in common with Denmark's bourgeoisie, with whom they frequently socialized in Copenhagen, than [Iceland's] nobility" (1082).

12. Kress, Kristjánsdóttir, and Birgisdóttir are all groundbreaking scholars of feminist literary criticism in Iceland. For example, all three scholars presented on a panel at the University of Iceland in 2019 after which the discussion turned to the sexualized depictions of young girls in Laxness and the problematic interactions between men and girls. I thank Haukur Ingvarsson for translating essays by Birgisdóttir and Kristjánsdóttir on *Salka Valka*, which allowed me to cite them in this chapter.

13. Guðmundsdóttir recounts Magnus Magnusson's claim that as a social realist writer, Laxness was praised as Iceland's John Steinbeck, Sinclair Lewis, and Upton Sinclair, all combined into one (55).

14. The novel was originally written "as a screenplay for Metro-Goldwin-Mayer under the title 'Woman in Pants'" (Jóhannsson 381). Similarly, *The Member of the Wedding* was adapted by McCullers into a play produced on Broadway in 1950 and was made into a movie in 1952 and again in 1997. Although McCullers had nothing to do with the adaptation, *The Heart Is a Lonely Hunter* was made into a film in 1968.

15. This gendering of the North and South was typical of the postbellum era when southern women were positioned as "backbone of the Lost Cause doctrine," unlikely to

NOTES

look towards a reunited future (Keely 624). Thanks to Ryan Charlton for bringing these romances to my attention.

16. To avoid confusion, I will refer to her as Frankie, although her names for herself shift throughout the novel.

17. In addition to being compared to boys in their initial descriptions, both express an interest in dressing as boys to join the armed forces: Frankie envisions giving a false name and age to join the Marines (McCullers, *Member* 150), and Mick imagines cutting off her hair (*Heart* 245).

18. Salka's voice is defined in opposition multiple times—"her deep, almost masculine voice" (Laxness, *Salka Valka* 86)—as close to a man's voice but not one, echoing Homi Bhabha's concept of colonial mimicry or "the desire for a reformed, recognizable Other, *as a subject of difference that is almost the same, but not quite*" (122). Salka's voice is not a man's but also not typical of a girl's or woman's, diversifying expectations for women's voices.

19. Icelandic nicknames follow a pattern of abbreviations, ending in -i for men and -a for women (Neijmann, *Colloquial Icelandic* 23).

20. Iceland is named directly when the soldier disrupts Frankie's dreams of exotic places: "She could not see him any more in Burma, Africa, or Iceland, or even for that matter in Arkansas" (McCullers, *Member* 136).

21. Anna Young notes that Alaska is far away but a version of the restrictive, rustic town life that Frankie already knows, as opposed to "a bustling, sophisticated European metropolis" (88). This is also supported by scholarship connecting Alaska to the plantation South. Ryan Charlton's work, for example, explores the ways in which Elizabeth Robins's stories of the Alaska-Yukon gold rush imagine Alaska as a New South, enfolding the gold rush into plantation mythology designed to "conceal the racial violence and environmental exploitation at the heart of industrial modernity" with mineral extraction in the Far North following the "pattern established by plantation agriculture throughout the Global South" (46).

22. Adult Salka can be considered alongside Miss Amelia, McCullers's protagonist of *The Ballad of the Sad Café* (1951), who is read by critics like Gleeson-White and Constante González Groba as an adult tomboy.

23. In patriarchal societies where "masculinity is idealized and femininity devalued" (Elise 145), identifying with the masculine elements enables more agency; in other words, the limitations placed on young girls provide a base for masculine envy that exists "apart from any neurotic trends" (143).

24. In a later fantasy of wealth, Salka envisions herself as "a big girl in a fine house" and is confused about how she ended up there, "she who had always been a boy" (Laxness, *Salka Valka* 270). And later to Steinþór she states, "I'm no woman" (567), by which she might mean in a traditional sense. While this may be intended to lead him to stop sexualizing her, he seems drawn to her peculiarities and infamy in the community: the narrator describes her from his viewpoint as "this girl, about whom everyone spoke" (145).

25. This is another parallel. Mick works to ease the "great worry and tightness" of her family's financial situation after her brother Bubber/George accidentally shot Baby, resulting in her family needing to cover Baby's medical expenses (McCullers, *Heart* 317), and Salka provides for herself at the age of eleven but also her mother in at least one episode. Unbeknownst to Salka, her mother purchases an Easter dress for herself with the money

in her daughter's account, which leads to the Bogesen family bestowing on Salka one of Gústa's cast-off dresses.

26. As Abate details, "With their short bobs, androgynous Coco Chanel clothes and engagement in formerly male prerogatives like driving automobiles, smoking cigarettes and drinking now-illegal alcohol, flappers blurred the line between masculinity and femininity" (121).

27. A young Angantýr's comments to Salka and her mother underscore the link between the hierarchies of class, space, and coloniality: "I'm privileged. You're not. I'm supposed to go to Copenhagen again next summer. You're just from up north" (Laxness, *Salka Valka* 44). This connection is later amplified by a woman reflecting on his sister Gústa's seeming misery: "They can keep their Copenhagen, for all I care, those rich folks" (156).

28. This discussion occurs a page after Berenice's description of a boy, Lily Mae Jenkins, who "turned into a girl" after falling in love with a man. She says, "He changed his nature and his sex and turned into a girl" (McCullers, *Member* 81), which opens up the discussion of both gender identity and sexuality as fluid.

29. Abate reads the ending as the reinscription of the normative, with Frankie abruptly shifting to "behaviors that are stereotypically feminine, clearly heteronormative and unmistakably rooted in whiteness" (164). Rachel Adams asserts that a more negative understanding of the ending "ignores the lesbian implications of 'the wonder of her love' (*MW*, 151) for her new friend Mary Littlejohn at the close of the narrative" (573). Whereas Elizabeth Freeman focuses on Frankie's desire to "inhabit publicly a couple she is not a part of," which she distinguishes from "heterosexual or lesbian desire per se" (113), Melissa Free believes we should refer to Frankie as a lesbian, while not denying the "ambiguity of John Henry's gender identity or Honey Brown's sexual identity or the racial restrictions placed on Berenice" (437). Free argues that to refuse any classification is to universalize Frankie as a symbol, "interring her queerness in silence" (437), and that readings like Freeman's are guilty of "inadvertently desexualizing Frankie in attempting to queer her" (441).

30. Although I don't read the end as depicting Frankie's total conformity, I agree with Graham-Bertolini that the novel "depicts how rape culture is one outcome of racial and gender conformity, and how white women, within their conformity, often become perpetrators of racial violence against people of color" (17).

31. In an example that could be read as a shyness around the opposite gender, Salka suggests that she and the girls her age "just dance with each other," since she doesn't "feel like dancing with any boys, anyway," followed by a more problematic idea to dress up in disguise by painting their faces with lampblack (Laxness, *Salka Valka* 206). This is tempered by the fact that Salka also dreams "of dances at night; seeing the boys competing to ask her to dance, and then gliding with her through the air" (206), which could represent a fantasy of social acceptance, rather than her heterosexual desires.

32. After his return, Arnaldur describes a sleeping Salka merging again with the Icelandic countryside: "Her thick, bright locks flowed over the cropped grass. . . . She was berry-blue [covered in moss and hay]. . . . Her strong legs in their hole-ridden cotton stockings stuck out beneath the hem of her skirt, and her brawny, rounded hips complimented the landscape wonderfully" (Laxness, *Salka Valka* 616). Just as land can be conquered, he reflects on having "vanquished" her at their first kiss, only to learn she had "defeated" him, crushing his belief that he lived and breathed for the masses (587).

NOTES

33. Loftsdóttir describes how the article circulated via email in Icelandic companies in 2008 as "an introspective self-criticism" that establishes "how naïve Icelanders once were, not knowing what was appropriate to say," supporting the belief that racism existed apart from Iceland ("Imagining Blackness" 17).

34. McCullers also demonstrates an awareness of the constrictions of sexuality: Honey, a character coded as queer, is described by Berenice as feeling "like he just can't breathe no more. He feel like he got to break something or break himself" (120). Berenice's quote contains shades of James Baldwin's claim in *Notes of a Native Son* (1955) that "to smash something is the ghetto's chronic need," with the disenfranchised most often smashing "each other, and themselves" until the moment when these outlets don't work (120). Honey, like Frankie, puts up a futile struggle against the conformity and defies sexual and racial categories (González Groba 73).

35. Wright also notes that McCullers's "quality of despair is unique and individual; and it seems to me more natural and authentic than that of Faulkner" ("Inner Landscape" 17). I emphasize this to refute scholars like Leslie Fiedler, who have read McCullers, along with Eudora Welty and Flannery O'Connor, as derivative of Faulkner or "merely 'distaff Faulknerians' who corrupted a vigorous masculine impulse" (Westling 64).

36. An example from US southern literature of a White character associated with criminality and coded as Black is Popeye in Faulkner's *Sanctuary* (1931).

37. An issue of the conservative newspaper *Morgunblaðið* from January 20, 1920, contains an advertisement for a screening of Griffith's film in Iceland, an article about the film, and references to Thomas Dixon's book *The Clansman*, on which the film was based (figure 3.1). As Ingvarsson has mentioned to me, Griffith's name seems to have been well-known by that time, with his other films having been shown previously.

38. In addition to the priest interested in "sacrific[ing] himself for the salvation of the heathens in Asia" (Laxness, *Salka Valka* 324), attendees fighting at a meeting are described "as if they believed that whoever made the most racket would win, as it is said that the Chinese do when they battle one another" (410). A woman donates a large sum to "the China mission, which means that every year, she actually converts a three-hundred-and-sixtieth part of the Chinese population" (422).

39. I credit Ingvarsson with the observation that terms that describe something burned are often associated with dark skin in Icelandic, the point about Herborg's removal of her national costume, and also for encouraging me to consider Laxness's obstructed views.

40. In contrast, Arnaldur is frequently depicted as "pale" (Laxness, *Salka Valka* 154), as are the wealthy Bogesen siblings.

41. In one instance, he tricks her into believing he suffered for eighteen months to earn her a worthless ring (Laxness, *Salka Valka* 268). In another he offers to go to prison for her, and she believes she is "witness[ing] a man earnestly and humbly lay[ing] his existence at her feet" (250).

42. Steinþór describes exploits such as fighting "bare-fisted against armed foreigners in three continents" and sailing to Africa (Laxness, *Salka Valka* 63). It is later revealed that his "actual knowledge of 'foreign lands,' however, was limited to the immoral wharf areas of port towns," as he had been "too much of a loner among the exotic peoples of foreign seas to assimilate different customs and mentalities" (122), held back by his biases.

43. For more on the genesis of minstrelsy in US culture, see Lott, *Love and Theft: Blackface Minstrelsy and the American Working Class* (1993).

44. Abate notes that many tomboy figures, such as the title character of Kate Douglas Wiggin's *Rebecca of Sunnybrook Farm* (1903) and Caroline Snedeker's heroine in *Downright Dencey* (1927), are associated with dark White skin tones and connected with stereotypes of racial otherness, specifically Blackness (xxvii).

45. Dr. Copeland's notes on Lancy describe his "[u]nsuccessful attempt at self-emasculation," as well as the way he "[w]ept boisterously during two visits" and was "[v]oluble—very glad to talk through the paranoiac" (McCullers, *Heart* 184).

46. While Mick has a negative sexual experience with Harry Minowitz, given that he is only two years older than she is and more consent appears to be involved, it does not follow the same pattern as the other two instances.

47. Westling notes that as Mick "loses her physical freedom through wearing a dress," similar clothing leads Frankie "unwittingly close to rape," and "she does not understand that her feminine looks make her sexual prey" (177). While I don't disagree with Westling that the dress makes her more vulnerable (178), I can't imagine a change of clothing making Frankie look significantly older than her twelve years, which is why I read the soldier as a sexual predator.

48. Steinþór attempts to rape Sigurlína when he first brings them to stay with his parents (Laxness, *Salka Valka* 75), until he is "repulsed by mother and daughter" and described as "the enemy" (76). Salka views Steinþór's abuse of her mother for what it is: "She was all that I had, and you took her from me and destroyed her and made her into a creature like yourself, and then you thought you could do the same thing to me, when I was just a child of eleven" (225). Sigurlína also views his actions towards Salka as abuse when it suits her or when she can use it to demonstrate power over him: "All winter, you've been pawing at the girl, trying to get her to do your will by every conceivable means" (140). Later, she says, "You have treated me disgracefully in every respect, yes, including nearly committing a crime against my little girl—so I can have you sent to jail whenever I want" (241).

49. Although just a child, Salka senses that by accepting coins from Steinþór, she "was creating a rivalry between herself and her mother" (Laxness, *Salka Valka* 135). Birgisdóttir notes that Steinþór drives a wedge between the mother and daughter, dividing them into "two girls," and that this marks a turning point in their relationship (14). Building on Birgisdóttir, Kristjánsdóttir adds that by looking at Salka as a competitor, Sigurlína makes her into a sexual object in the same way that Steinþór does (9). Kristjánsdóttir also argues that it doesn't matter if Steinþór succeeded in raping Salka or not, since both mother and daughter believe he has, and, thus, Salka's life is marked by the encounter (10).

50. Édouard Glissant describes Faulkner's use of deferred revelation as working "to point out and to hide a secret or a bit of knowledge (that is to postpone its discovery)" in a way that builds the significance through this postponement (6). Although divorced from the original context of the plantation Americas central to Glissant's theorization, analyzing this narrative technique in these terms in Laxness's works evokes Glissant's readings of White male southerner Faulkner's deeper unaccountability, which can be read with a difference back into Laxness, his relationship to Icelandic society, and Icelandic society's relationship to globally southern spaces, as itself a crypto-colonial society, simultaneously oppressor and oppressed.

51. The fighting is vividly described: "Their bodies pressed savagely against each other in wild, lustful exertions, as if striving to pulverize each other, like two beasts intent on

NOTES 175

devouring each other . . . just as life struggles against itself because it hates and loves itself in equal measure at the same time" (Laxness, *Salka Valka* 499).

52. According to Cleanth Brooks, for example, "the pervading sense of community" is a key element of life in the South that is clearly reflected in southern literature (240). For a more complex examination of community in southern literature, see Romine, *The Narrative Forms of Southern Community*, which argues that "insofar as it is cohesive, a community tends to be coercive" (2).

53. As an additional example, Arnaldur cheats on Salka by seducing Guja, a sick orphan who is only fifteen (582).

CHAPTER 4: "A WOMAN'S WILDNESS": POWER, MAGIC, AND INTERGENERATIONAL TIES IN TIPHANIE YANIQUE AND FRÍÐA ÁSLAUG SIGURÐARDÓTTIR

1. Kirsten Thisted and Ann-Sofie N. Gremaud observe that "While the relationship between Iceland and Denmark in particular may not have been one of classical colonization, the many centuries under Danish rule have had consequences for the development of Icelandic society and for the developments of perceptions of national identity in both nations" (47).

2. The intergenerational structure common to other Caribbean diasporic novels—including Edwidge Danticat's *Breath, Eyes, Memory* (1994), Junot Díaz's *The Brief Wondrous Life of Oscar Wao* (2007), Shani Mootoo's *Cereus Blooms at Night* (1996), and Nelly Rosario's *Song of the Water Saints* (2002)—also serves as a connection to Iceland and the US South.

3. According to Yanique, the novel is narrated by the "old wives" of the island, who "are the ones who receive and pass on the stories" ("The Wisdom"). She notes that the label of "old wives' tale" is often thought to derive from myth or superstition, or worse, "often considered false in part *because* it is told by old women." In her family, older women are the historians, and she writes back to this trope, making the Old Wives "the authoritative narrators."

4. Regarding a scene where Anette, dressed in red, appears to will an actress's wig to catch fire, Rebecca Romdhani writes, "The association of a red dress and fire may recall Antoinette, here not Anette's mother, but the character in Jean Rhys's *Wide Sargasso Sea* (1966), a rewriting of Charlotte Brontë's *Jane Eyre* (1847), before she burns Thornfield Hall" (92). The link between fire and feminine power thus has a literary predecessor in the Caribbean canon.

5. I thank Martyn Bone for pointing out this linguistic connection, as well as leading me to Yanique's novel and Wright's short story.

6. Nina's material wealth also impacts her mother's life: "'She was very pleased with both the tumble-drier and the microwave oven,' I retort quickly, defending my gifts with a stern look" (Sigurðardóttir 132). However, this gap in lifestyle leads others in the family, such as Nina's sister Martha, to view her as "the glamour girl Nina, the privileged bitch" (124)—though importantly this is according to Nina.

7. Although a term like "vicar" has European connotations, religion could have also been imposed alongside government in the "distant parts" of the Danish empire, or the governor could be imposing his own terminology onto the culture he observes.

8. One constant is the exploitation of women, as demonstrated by recent advertising campaigns that position "Icelandic women as a sexual resource for the tourist industry" drawing on the stereotypes and colonial associations of Icelandic women not only as sexually available but also "closely connected to Icelandic nature" (Loftsdóttir, "The Exotic North" 255). Jennifer Donahue asserts that Yanique writes back to the "hypersexualized image of the Caribbean" that relies on stereotypical understandings of Caribbean sexuality as "excessive, pathological, and unruly" (108).

9. Bone describes the contrasting histories of slavery and colonialism in the US versus Denmark: "whereas the U.S. South introduced thousands of Africans to its own soil and developed slave plantations within its own borders, Denmark confined its own form of racial slavery" to the Danish West Indies, with few "black Danes" traveling to Denmark itself after emancipation in 1846 (64). These variant histories resulted in differing racial ideologies.

10. The treatment of the Virgin Islanders here is not just due to questions of citizenship, but also its intersection with race, class, and color. Parallels can be made to the abandonment of Black US southerners during Hurricane Katrina, a focus of Mississippi writer Jesmyn Ward's *Salvage the Bones*, which is amplified by the way the South is seen as the nation's "abjected regional Other" (Baker and Nelson 236).

11. Louisiana "offered the potential for a different racial paradigm" with its proximity to the Caribbean and Latin and South America, as well as its "racial and linguistic mixtures" and its colonial connections to France and Spain (T. Davis, *Southscapes* 8). However, by the Jim Crow period (1877 to the 1950s), the binary system had won out (Hirsch and Logsdon 189).

12. Allusions to a pillar of salt are made throughout the novel, beginning with the unattributed epigraph.

13. A classic example of this structure is Zora Neale Hurston's *Their Eyes Were Watching God* (1937), in which the life of protagonist Janie Crawford can be broken up according to her three relationships. However, the development of Janie's voice and her decisions regarding when and how to use it form the heart of the novel, in addition to her friendship with Pheoby, to whom she returns by the novel's end.

14. While not as overt, Ursa's relationships follow a similar pattern in *Corregidora*. Ursa was taught to focus on her family's history and Corregidora's role in that trauma, and she falls for and marries Mutt, whom she leaves for Tadpole after Mutt pushes her down the stairs. Here, the dynamics are more complicated, with Corregidora acting as more of a shadowy presence than physical man and Ursa returning to Mutt in the end of the novel—reminiscent of Anette and Jacob's ongoing affair that survives their later marriages.

15. Ursa Corregidora's sexuality after her fall is also detached from reproduction, despite her own and her family's shared desires for descendants.

16. Sarah strokes Nina's cheek after Thordis's death "as though [Nina] were the child, not she, and says, 'I shouldn't have let you be so very alone.' Her voice is full of contrition" (Sigurðardóttir 161).

17. While the slave trade connected the North, South, and Central Americas together, there were important social and cultural differences between these spaces. For instance, the prostitution of enslaved women was commonly practiced in Brazil, as we see in Jones's novel (see Bellamy), whereas in the US South sexual violence was institutionalized but not commercialized in the same way. *Corregidora* links these disparate spaces, shedding light

on the ubiquity of violence towards women running across distinct national practices, cultural differences, and generations.

18. Ursa's mother describes her body as wanting Ursa even though she didn't want a man, speaking to the complications of motherhood when the goal is to raise daughters as witnesses to the previous generations' trauma. This tension leads Ursa's father to feel used and to the toxic relationship that forms between her parents.

19. Additionally, Sunneva's "very young" age is highlighted when she is introduced: Stefan, who is in his fifties at the time, returns to town with her as his fiancée (Sigurðardóttir 12), adding to her exoticization.

20. Responding to Yolanda Martínez-San Miguel's claim that the novel's incestuous relationships between Anette and Jacob as well as Eeona and Owen are not associated with rape but positioned as love relationships, Romdhani argues that such readings neglect to "name alleged paedophilia as alleged paedophilia" and in turn fail to recognize the "strategies of highlighting the practice of ignoring and excusing violence" (81).

21. Rather than sanctioning these dynamics, Romdhani argues that through this disgust, the reader is led to question the "veracity of what she is reading, but also the way in which scenes are being described" (85)—in other words, the motivations of the narrators like the family's former caretaker Hippolyte, who according to Romdhani may be one of the Old Wives. Hippolyte connects intertextually to a character in Herman Wouk's *Don't Stop the Carnival* (1965) and is a more developed sinister force in that text. This leads Romdhani to argue that the development of disgust in response to the sexualization of young girls is intended as social critique grounded in Hippolyte's problematic narration.

22. That is, at least in the novel's present; the abuse of young girls was coupled with incest in terms of Ursa's forebearers' experiences on Corregidora's plantation in Brazil.

23. Although outside of the immediate scope of this chapter, I acknowledge the distinctions between the Portuguese and the Danish colonial systems. The opening scene of *The Land of Love and Drowning* emphasizes the connection between Danish colonial histories and the abuse of young girls when Owen Bradshaw watches a demonstration of electricity at the home of Danish businessman Mr. Lovernkrandt involving a little girl tied up with lace and silk and hooked from the ceiling. The active role of "the American scientist" underscores a connection to US neocolonialism (Yanique, *Land* 4).

24. At one point Ursa imagines a conversation with Mutt in which he insinuates that she may have inherited insanity from them as well: "*Tell me, Ursa, do insanity run in your family?*" (Jones 99). She replies that Corregidora went mad, to which Mutt ambiguously responds, "*They all do*" (99). The unclear pronoun "they" could refer to White men, enslavers, and/or abusers.

25. Katherine recalls others who claim to have seen Solveig at Witch's Cliff—"a white spectre rising from the snow to dance under the stars and the northern lights" (Sigurðardóttir 59)—with the landmark underscoring the magical associations of Sunneva and her descendants. This moment connects the shawl directly to the other worldly aspects of the novel—here Solveig's dancing ghost.

26. Martha's resentments echo those of Jason Compson in Faulkner's *The Sound and the Fury*, who begrudges his dead brother, Quentin, for dying by suicide after the family sold Benjy's pasture to fund Quentin's year at Harvard University.

178 NOTES

27. A similar dynamic is seen in Toni Morrison's *Tar Baby* (1981), which primarily takes place in the US and the Caribbean. Protagonist Jadine rejects the traditional role her aunt has taken on—centered on family and the domestic sphere—for a more modern, international existence as a fashion model. Coincidentally, both Jadine and Nina possess sealskin coats, which align with their lifestyle choices, class positions, and taste for the contemporary.

28. Regarding magical realism in literature, Einar Már Guðmundsson inquires, "What exactly is this term supposed to imply? That there is a realism without magic? The sagas, outstanding for their 'realism,' are full of magic. That there is a magic without realism? As if there were no realism in the stories of Borges or H.C. Andersen!" (qtd. in Neijmann, "'Girl Interrupting'" 58).

29. Neijmann believes that the focus on fusion and connection in magical realist literature enables "women to write in a female storytelling tradition that has survived in Iceland across the centuries," creating "a variety of ways to re-tell, and re-affirm, Icelandic life, history and tradition from a shared, community perspective, to repossess historical experience through storytelling and art" ("'Girl Interrupting'" 65).

30. She recalls someone telling her that "Art is the human being's effort to encapsulate reality," which she revises to "Not encapsulate reality, nor to lash it down: to break open the chasm" (Sigurðardóttir 47). Words are spacious, "break[ing] open the chasm of reality" and extending it beyond the physical body and its limited lifespan.

31. Associated with Anglo-Creole Caribbean histories, obeah is a complex term that describes "practices involving ritual attempts to manipulate a world of spiritual power," animated by use of the law, and not the term people would use to describe their own practices (Paton 2). Benjamin McKenzie was supposed to have disappeared in the rainforest but returns as a myth, not as a man. To stay alive as "the Anancy, he needed to hear stories about himself," which he steals "from any lady of the sea" (Yanique, *Land* 197), such as his lover Eeona, who eventually breaks his hold and returns to her life after giving birth to his stillborn son.

32. Nina's use of "alien" in relation to Sunneva underscores her imagined connection to her ancestor, thinking Martha sees her as "an alien Nina" (Sigurðardóttir 124).

33. The Duene, with whom Eeona identifies, are said to "protect the wild places" (Yanique, *Land* 295). The term "wild" is also applied to nature throughout the novel, such as the description of the hurricane as "a wild-woman storm" (309). The problematic connection between women and wild nature connects to Icelandic women and the linking of women's bodies with land in colonial literature. Loftsdóttir affirms that feminist scholars have long understood the significance of women's bodies in constructions of nation, while women are mostly excluded from full citizenship and power (*Crisis and Coloniality* 37). For a reading of how Yanique's novel centers "the space of the beach and the movement to reclaim that space to highlight the consequences of trespass on land and women's bodies" (108), see Donahue.

34. Anette associates her sister with witches in both her figurative language—"She jump on me like a witch on a broom" (Yanique, *Land* 208)—and her direct statements, such as telling Franky, "I waiting the witch out" (375). Yet Anette is also connected to this family power.

35. In their work on witches, midwives, and nurses, Barbara Ehrenreich and Deirdre English argue that the "suppression of women health workers and the rise to dominance of male professionals" was "a political struggle, first, in that it is part of the history of sex struggle in general" (xx, xxi). In addition, Federici argues that "witch-hunting in Europe

NOTES   179

was an attack on women's resistance to the spread of capitalist relations and the power that women had gained by virtue of their sexuality, their control over reproduction, and their ability to heal," as well as being essential to the construction of "a new patriarchal order where women's bodies, their labor, their sexual and reproductive powers were placed under the control of the state and transformed into economic resources" (170).

36. Youme has inherited the supposed signs of her predecessors' infidelity and incest on her own body. Although her father has not touched her, her pubic hair is silver, which Eeona misreads as a shared sign of abuse (Yanique, *Land* 321–22).

37. Nina also suspects Eric of reading her thoughts in *Night Watch* when she first arrives to visit Thordis (Sigurðardóttir 7).

38. Here the diagnosis of "wildness" attempts to limit the power and magic associated with the Bradshaw women, which relates to the efforts to contain women through the medical diagnosis of hysteria in the US in the late nineteenth century, illustrated, for instance, in Charlotte Perkins Gilman's "The Yellow Wallpaper."

39. The episodes are also related to the folklore she shares. After she disappears, her housekeeper states, "Some stories come back to haunt she. She get real funny. Funny like in the head. Episodes, she calling it" (Yanique, *Land* 347). These episodes are another link between Eeona and Youme, who removes her shoes and shirt during her solo swim-in at the lime-in: she "had not meant to expose herself. Perhaps she was coming into her gift. Perhaps she was out of her mind, having her own episode" (356).

40. The association of women with danger also connects back to *Corregidora* when Mutt's brother Jim asks Ursa, "You trying to get dangerous?" and she responds, "Naw, I'm not trying to get dangerous" (Jones 58). However, the phrases "getting evil" or "looking evil" are used more frequently (9)—particularly for women in the novel.

41. Ironically, Eeona considers Jacob, or the risk of incest he embodies, as the danger: she worries about her sister when "faced with the danger that was Esau" (Yanique, *Land* 203).

42. The Far North is also depicted in Sigurðardóttir's novel as a lawless land: people are "used to all sorts of things here in the north. They generally have to settle their own affairs, which in any case is preferable to relying on orders from erratic officials" (16). The North infiltrates Yanique's text as well through Antoinette's and Eeona's dreams of New York, "the classy capital of this new world," to quote Mrs. Lovernkrandt (29), or in Antoinette's mind "the milk-and-honey streets of New York City" (35). A waiter from Connecticut also appears towards the end of the novel and doesn't know the history of Villa by the Sea (338).

43. Stefan loves Jacob "more than his own son, more than was good for him" (Sigurðardóttir 29)—the ambiguity of the phrasing leaving open the possibility of a queer reading.

44. This trope runs across genres from Benedikt Gröndal's poetry in the 1840s to contemporary crime fiction like Arnaldur Indriðason's *Strange Shores* (2010) and Baltasar Kormákur's science fiction series *Katla* (2021). The trope likewise appears in a US southern literary classic, Kate Chopin's *The Awakening* (1899), in which a young, overwhelmed mother indulges the embrace of the sea, walking into the Gulf of Mexico.

45. Associating the Bradshaw women too closely with the land and wild places harkens back to the problematic colonial trope linking the bodies of colonized women to the land, as well as to the exoticization of colonized women. This connects also to the recent advertisement campaigns for Iceland that draw on the supposed sexual availability of Icelandic women.

180   NOTES

46. Thordis's sentiments here connect her to fellow fatalists Judith Sutpen and Charles Bon in Faulkner's *Absalom, Absalom!* The latter is described frequently as a fatalist by narrator Jason Compson and reveals as much in his letter, writing, "*I now believe that you and I are, strangely enough, included among those who are doomed to live*" (Faulkner 105). Judith reveals similar sentiments about the letter itself: "Read it if you like or dont read it if you like. Because it makes so little impression, you see" (100). Relatedly, Nina does not know who actually made the comment or whether or not it matters.

47. Nina emphasizes the passing of time in her narration, thinking, "Something to kill time: a time-killer. What strange expressions we use—kill time—our enemy—kill—" (Sigurðardóttir 9), as well as its implication that time is our enemy. Nina channels Faulkner's Quentin Compson, who begins his section of *The Sound and the Fury* by obsessing over time and its passing: "When the shadow of the sash appeared on the curtains it was between seven and eight oclock and then I was in time again, hearing the watch" (76). Echoing Quentin, Nina describes setting her watch: "in spite of an insistent notion about an eternal moment, a point at which all things converge, spinning—a whirlpool—as in Arnar's painting, with total calm at its centre. I do it anyway; set my watch, as though time matters. As though a watch or a clock could convey time. Five to three" (Sigurðardóttir 118). Time and its passing matter to Quentin, who wishes to stop time and feel how he feels forever, whereas nihilist Nina doesn't believe that time matters or that it is anything that a watch or clock would be able to convey.

48. Comparable to *Land of Love and Drowning*, large-scale historic events are positioned as the background to those on an individual scale in Faulkner's *Absalom, Absalom!*, such as the use of the Civil War as the backdrop to more personal, familial dramas, like that between Charles Bon, Henry, and Judith Sutpen. A self-reflexive interest in storytelling is common to both *Night Watch* and *Absalom, Absalom!*, where the ability to know or record any "truths" about the past is called into question.

49. This erasure of particular experiences is made more overt by returning to *Corregidora*: "Anyway, they ain't nothing you can do when they tear the pages out of the book and they ain't no record of it. They probably burned the pages" (Jones 78). The experiences of Ursa and the other women in her family are central to the novel, alongside the larger-scale events that linger in the background through references to Queen Isabella and emancipation history, as well as Mutt's reference to slave auctions and wanting to sell off Ursa: "I got me a piece a ass for sale" (159).

50. While references to Faulkner are relegated to the footnotes of this chapter, I can't help wondering about how the stories layered into Faulkner's *Absalom, Absalom!* would change if women's perspectives were more central. I'm interested in the details of Rosa's, Judith's, and Clytie's experiences when the men were off fighting in the Civil War, as well as the experiences of the many unnamed women of color positioned as tangential to the primary narratives.

CODA: PROCESSING THE PRESENT, LOOKING TO A DECOLONIAL FUTURE

1. Under the sharecropping system, those formerly enslaved were free in name and compensated with a share of the crop, which limited mobility, since laborers needed to remain on the plantation until the conclusion of the crop year to receive payment (Mandle 22).

NOTES 181

Under the convict lease system, southern states leased out convicts to labor on plantations, in mines, or on railroads, but without capital invested in the workers, employers did not have incentive to treat them well (Wagner).

2. For more on the intricacies of these dynamics that I briefly outline, see Bergmann, "Iceland: A Postimperial Sovereignty Project."

3. Iceland's relationship with the US and its multigenerational military presence is also controversial. The impacts of this relationship are still present, as the US is obliged to defend Iceland from attack, according to both the obligations of NATO and a defense treaty between the US and Iceland (Karlsson 397).

4. Thanks to Kári Páll Óskarsson for this insight.

5. President Grímsson related the success of the so-called business Vikings to the Cod Wars that occurred between Iceland and the UK in the 1950s–1970s in a speech in London, "reminding his audience that Iceland was the 'only nation on earth to defeat the British Navy, not once but three times' (Grímsson, 2005)" (Bergmann 43).

6. During the editing of this manuscript in 2024, there has been a rise in both antisemitism and anti-Muslim hate in the US, resulting from the Israel-Hamas conflict (DeRose), in addition to anti-Palestinianism, as specified by Hani Sabra, as not all Palestinians are Muslim.

7. A 2009 report by the Icelandic Human Rights Centre notes that the Icelandic population shifted from "a largely homogeneous and mono-cultural one to a multicultural one in little more than a decade," with the influx precipitated in large part by the economic boom resulting from the banking expansion. However, when the crash led to soaring unemployment, foreign nationals comprised a disproportionate 15 percent of the unemployed amidst concern over the rise of anti-immigrant and nationalist sentiments.

8. Terry G. Lacy notes that Iceland has welcomed refugees since World War II, including Hungarians and Poles in the 1950s: "The Red Cross helped 34 Vietnamese refugees in 1979 and a further 60 in 1990–1991 to find jobs and housing and to learn the language" (247).

9. Republicans and Trump supporters span the nation, of course; however, all the states south of the Mason–Dixon line went to Trump in the 2016 election, aside from Maryland and Virginia ("2016 Presidential Election Results"), with Georgia joining these two blue states in 2020 (Vestal).

10. Although anti-immigrant hate groups span the nation, aside from organizations in Colorado, Maryland, New Jersey, Oregon, and Washington, the majority are located in the US South or the southwestern states that border Mexico.

11. Iceland saw a resurgence of the movement in 2021 when the entire Icelandic Football Association's executive committee resigned after accusations that allegations of sexual assault by an international team player were covered up (Holroyd).

12. In 2009 Iceland's Jóhanna Sigurdardóttir became "the world's first openly gay head of government and the country's first female prime minister" (Reid 82).

13. Similarly, threatened by critical race theory's acknowledgement that racism is built into US systems and institutions, politicians in several states have proposed legislation banning the teaching and discussion of race in classrooms. As of 2024, forty-four states have considered legislation or other regulations restricting education on race and gender, and eighteen states have enacted policy (Sawchuk).

14. Only about fifteen percent of these bills have become law, but regardless, the proposition of the bills has a harmful effect: 85 percent of trans and nonbinary youth report a negative impact on their mental health, and more than half state that they had "seriously considered" suicide in the past year (Nakajima and Jin).

15. For more on the climate crisis's global impact on women, see *Climate Justice: Hope, Resilience, and the Fight for a Sustainable Future* (2019) by Mary Robinson, Ireland's former president and UN Special Envoy on Climate Change.

16. Z. Abrahams et al. propose that if the impact of climate change is emphasized, for instance, on tours to Sólheimajökull Glacier in Iceland, then this has "the potential to drive more sustainable tourism and investment towards high-impact climate change mitigation which protects the glaciers" (11).

17. For example, Alaskan Senator Lisa Murkowski stated that "the Arctic is one of the last spaces on Earth whose borders are not set" and that the "U.S. needs to be a player, not an outsider. We have an opportunity that is unparalleled around the world" (Beary 125).

18. I credit Michael Bibler's comments following his keynote at the 2023 Faulkner and Yoknapatawpha Conference, "Queer Faulkner," for this sentiment in response to the sustained interest in the character of White supremacist Percy Grimm: which characters we decide to devote our attention to matters ("Slapstick").

WORKS CITED

PRIMARY SOURCES

Baldwin, James. *Notes of a Native Son*. 1955. Beacon Press, 2012.

Bergsson, Guðbergur. *Tómas Jónsson, Bestseller*. Translated by Lytton Smith, Open Letter, 2017.

Birgisson, Bergsveinn. *Den svarte vikingen [The Black Viking]*. Spartacus, 2013.

Birth of a Nation. Directed by David W. Griffith. 1915. Image Entertainment, 1998.

Chopin, Kate. *The Awakening*. Herbert S. Stone, 1899.

Conrad, Joseph. *Heart of Darkness*. 1899. Coyote Canyon Press, 2007.

Jones, Gayl. *Corregidora*. Beacon Press, 1987.

Dixon, Thomas, Jr. *The Clansman: An Historical Romance of the Ku Klux Klan*. 1905. Kessinger Publishing, 2005.

Douglass, Frederick. *Narrative of the Life of Frederick Douglass, an American Slave*. Anti-Slavery Office, 1845. *Documenting the American South*. 1999. University Library, University of North Carolina at Chapel Hill.

Du Bois, W. E. B. *The Souls of Black Folk*. 1903. Oxford, 2007.

Ellison, Ralph. *Invisible Man*. 1952. Vintage, 1995.

Faulkner, William. *Absalom, Absalom!* 1936. Vintage International, 1990.

Faulkner, William. *Go Down, Moses*. 1942. Vintage International, 1990.

Faulkner, William. *Light in August*. 1932. Vintage International, 1990.

Faulkner, William. *The Sound and the Fury*. 1929. Vintage International, 1984.

Gaines, Ernest J. *Of Love and Dust*. 1967. Vintage Books, 1994.

García Márquez, Gabriel. *One Hundred Years of Solitude*. 1967. Harper Perennial, 2006.

Gibson, William. "Foreign Services Despatch." 25 Oct. 1955, Hal Howland-William Faulkner Papers, 1954–1976, Accession #11615, Albert H. Small Special Collections Library, University of Virginia, Charlottesville, VA.

Gilman, Charlotte P. *The Yellow Wallpaper*. 1892. Virago, 2012.

Guðmundsson, Einar Már. *Angels of the Universe*. Translated by Bernard Scudder, St. Martin's Press, 1997.

Hurston, Zora Neale. *Their Eyes Were Watching God*. 1937. Harper Perennial, 1998.

Indriðason, Arnaldur. *Arctic Chill*. Translated by Bernard Scudder and Victoria Cribb, Picador, 2010.

WORKS CITED

Jakobsdóttir, Svava. *The Lodger and Other Stories*. Translated by Julian Meldon D'Arcy, et al., U of Iceland P, 2000.

Kanafani, Ghassan. *All That's Left to You*. 1966. Translated by May Jayyusi and Jeremy Reed, Interlink Books, 2005.

Larsen, Nella. *Quicksand and Passing*. 1928/1929. Edited by Deborah E. McDowell, Rutgers UP, 2005.

Laxness, Halldór. *The Atom Station*. 1948. Translated by Magnus Magnusson, Vintage, 2014.

Laxness, Halldór. *The Great Weaver From Kashmir*. 1927. Translated by Philip Roughton, Archipelago, 2008.

Laxness, Halldór. *Salka Valka*. 1931. Translated by Philip Roughton, Archipelago, 2022.

McCullers, Carson. *The Heart Is a Lonely Hunter*. 1940. Mariner Books, 2004.

McCullers, Carson. *The Member of the Wedding*. 1946. Mariner Books, 2004.

Morrison, Toni. *Beloved*. 1987. Vintage, 2004.

Morrison, Toni. *Playing in the Dark: Whiteness and the Literary Imagination*. Vintage, 1992.

Morrison, Toni. *Tar Baby*. 1981. Vintage, 2004.

Ólafsdóttir, Auður Ava. *Miss Iceland*. Translated by Brian FitzGibbon, Grove Press, 2020.

Rhys, Jean. *Wide Sargasso Sea*. 1966. W. W. Norton, 1999.

Sigurðardóttir, Fríða Áslaug. *Night Watch*. Translated by Katjana Edwardsen, Greyhound, 1995.

Sjón. *Moonstone: The Boy Who Never Was: A Novel*. Translated by Victoria Cribb, Farrar, Straus and Giroux, 2016.

Sjón. *Red Milk*. Translated by Victoria Cribb, MCD Books, 2022.

Toomer, Jean. *Cane*. 1923. Liveright Publishing, 1975.

Trent, Mary Vance. "Secret." 15 Mar. 1956, Hal Howland-William Faulkner Papers, 1954–1976, Accession #11615, Albert H. Small Special Collections Library, University of Virginia, Charlottesville, VA.

Þorsteinsson, Indriði. *North of War*. 1971. Translated by May and Hallberg Hallmundsson, Iceland Review Library, 1981.

United States, Executive Office of the President [Harry S. Truman]. Executive order 9981: Desegregation of the Armed Forces. 26 July 1948. *Federal Register*, vol. 13, no. 146, 28 July 1948, pp. 4313, archives.federalregister.gov/issue_slice/1948/7/28/4311-4313.pdf.

Wouk, Herman. *Don't Stop the Carnival*. 1965. Back Bay Books, 1992.

Wright, Richard. "Big Black Good Man." 1957. *Eight Men*, Harper Perennial 1996, pp. 93–109.

Yanique, Tiphanie. *Land of Love and Drowning*. Riverhead Books, 2015.

SECONDARY SOURCES

"2016 Presidential Election Results." *New York Times*, 9 Aug. 2017, www.nytimes.com/elections/2016/results/president.

Abate, Michelle Ann. *Tomboys: A Literary and Cultural History*. Temple UP, 2008.

Abdur-Rahman, Aliyyah I. "'What Moves at the Margin': William Faulkner and Race." *The New Cambridge Companion to William Faulkner*, edited by John T. Matthews, Cambridge UP, 2015, pp. 44–58.

WORKS CITED

Abdur-Rahman, Aliyyah I. "White Disavowal, Black Enfranchisement, and the Homoerotic in William Faulkner's *Light in August*." *The Faulkner Journal*, vol. 22, no. 1–2, 2006/2007, pp. 176–92.

Aboul-Ela, Hosam M. *Other South: Faulkner, Coloniality, and the Mariátegui Tradition*. U of Pittsburgh P, 2007.

Aboul-Ela, Hosam M. "William Faulkner and the World Literature Debate: Is the Radical in Radical Form the Radical in Radical Politics?" *A Companion to World Literature*, edited by B. Venkat Mani and Ken Seigneurie, vol. 6, John Wiley and Sons, 2019, pp. 1–10. *Wiley Online Library*, doi.org/10.1002/9781118635193.ctwl0246.

Abrahams, Z., et al. "Glacier Tourism and Tourist Reviews: An Experiential Engagement with the Concept of 'Last Chance Tourism.'" *Scandinavian Journal of Hospitality and Tourism*, vol. 22, no. 1, 2022, pp. 1–14.

Adams, Jessica. *Wounds of Returning: Race, Memory, and Property on the Postslavery Plantation*. U of North Carolina P, 2007.

Adams, Rachel. "'A Mixture of Delicious and Freak': The Queer Fiction of Carson McCullers." *American Literature*, vol. 71, no. 3, 1999, pp. 551–83.

Agnarsdóttir, Anna. "Iceland in the Eighteenth Century: An Island Outpost of Europe?" *Sjuttonhundratal*, vol. 10, no. 11, 2013, pp. 11–38.

Alexander, Michelle. *The New Jim Crow: Mass Incarceration in the Age of Colorblindness*. The New Press, 2011.

"Anti-Immigrant Hate Map." *Southern Poverty Law Center*, 2023, www.splcenter.org/hate-map?ideology=anti-immigrant.

"Anti-LGBTQ Hate Map." *Southern Poverty Law Center*, 2023, www.splcenter.org/hate-map?ideology=anti-lgbt.

Arbour, Robert. "Figuring and Reconfiguring the Folk: Women and Metaphor in Part 1 of Jean Toomer's *Cane*." *Texas Studies in Literature and Language*, vol. 55, no. 3, 2013, pp. 307–27.

Arnarsdóttir, Eygló Svala. "A Tragic Comedy: Angels of the Universe." *Iceland Review*, 26 May 2009, www.icelandreview.com/reviews/tragic-comedyangels-universe.

Avery, Tamlyn. "The Métis and the Multiple 'Me' in Carson McCullers's *The Member of the Wedding*." *Mississippi Quarterly*, vol. 72, no. 1, 2019, pp. 69–93.

Azouqa, Aida. "Ghassan Kanafani and William Faulkner: Kanafani's Achievement in 'All That's Left to You.'" *Journal of Arabic Literature*, vol. 31, no. 2, 2000, pp. 147–70.

Baker, Houston A., and Dana D. Nelson. "Preface: Violence, the Body and 'The South.'" *American Literature*, vol. 73, no. 2, 2001, pp. 231–44.

Baldwin, David S. "The Reading Room: Salka Valka." *Blog: Medical Humanities*, 27 May 2016, blogs.bmj.com/medical-humanities/2016/05/27/the-reading-room-salka-valka/.

Banks, William M. *Black Intellectuals: Race and Responsibility in American Life*. W. W. Norton, 1996.

Bhabha, Homi K. *The Location of Culture*. Taylor and Francis, 2012.

Blaagaard, Bolette, and Rikke Andreassen. "Disappearing Act: The Forgotten History of Colonialism, Eugenics and Gendered Othering in Denmark." *Teaching "Race" with a Gendered Edge*, edited by Brigitte Hipfl and Kristín Loftsdóttir, ATGENDER/Central European UP, 2012, pp. 81–95.

Blake, Susan L. "The Spectatorial Artist and the Structure of *Cane*." *CLA Journal*, vol. 17, no. 4, 1974, pp. 516–34.

Beary, Brian. "Race for the Arctic: Who Owns the Region's Undiscovered Oil and Gas?" *Issues for Debate in Environmental Management: Selections from CQ Researcher*, Sage, 2010, pp. 123–52.

Beer, Christopher Todd. "Climate Justice, the Global South, and Policy Preferences of Kenyan Environmental NGOs." *The Global South*, vol. 8, no. 2, 2014, pp. 84–100.

Bell, Madison Smartt. "'Land of Love and Drowning' by Tiphanie Yanique." *The Boston Globe*, 26 July 2014, www.bostonglobe.com/arts/books/2014/07/26/review-land-love -and-drowning-tiphanie-yanique/KrddOMRzJ3KtE4EIaa4L9O/story.html.

Bellamy, Maria Rice. *Bridges to Memory: Postmemory in Contemporary Ethnic American Women's Fiction*. U of Virginia P, 2015.

Benediktsdóttir, Ásta Kristín. "'Rise, thou youthful flag of Iceland!' *Moonstone* and Sjón's Queer Anti-Patriotism." *Iceland–Ireland: Memory, Literature, Culture on the Atlantic Periphery*, edited by Fionnuala Dillane and Gunnthórun Gudmundsdóttir, Brill, 2022, pp. 135–54.

Benediktsdóttir, Ásta Kristín. "The Spirit of Contemporary Life: Icelandic Queer Modernism." *Re-Reading the Age of Innovation: Victorians, Moderns, and Literary Newness, 1830–1950*, edited by Louise Kane, Routledge, 2022, pp. 217–32.

Bergmann, Eirikur. "Iceland: A Postimperial Sovereignty Project." *Cooperation and Conflict*, vol. 49, no. 1, 2014, pp. 33–54.

Bibler, Michael P. *Cotton's Queer Relations: Same-Sex Intimacy and the Literature of the Southern Plantation, 1936–1968*. U of Virginia P, 2009.

Bibler, Michael. "Slapstick, S&M, and Civil Rights: Faulkner's Queer Violence in *Light in August* and *Intruder in the Dust*." Faulkner and Yoknapatawpha Conference, 24 July 2023, Jackson, MS. Keynote address and discussion.

Birgisdóttir, Soffía Auður. "'Hvað er kona af konu fædd? Getur hún aldrei orðið frjáls?': Um samband móður og dóttur í *Sölku Völku*." *Tímarit Máls og menningar*, vol. 92, no. 3, 1992, pp. 9–19.

Bjarnadóttir, Birna. *Recesses of the Mind: Aesthetics in the Work of Guðbergur Bergsson*. McGill-Queen's UP, 2012.

Björnsdóttir, Inga Dóra. "The Mountain Woman and the Presidency." *Images of Contemporary Iceland: Everyday Lives and Global Contexts*, edited by Gísli Pálsson and E. Paul Durrenberger, U of Iowa P, 1996, pp. 106–25.

Blotner, Joseph. *Faulkner: A Biography*. Vintage International, 1991.

Bone, Martyn. *Where the New World Is: Literature about the U.S. South at Global Scales*. The U of Georgia P, 2018.

Borst, Allan G. "Gothic Economic: Violence and Miscegenation in Jean Toomer's 'Blood-Burning Moon.'" *Gothic Studies*, vol. 10, no. 1, May 2008, pp. 14–28.

Brooks, Cleanth. "Southern Literature: The Wellsprings of Its Vitality." *The Georgia Review*, vol. 16, no. 3, 1962, pp. 238–53.

Brown, Kimberly Juanita. *The Repeating Body: Slavery's Visual Resonance in the Contemporary*. Duke UP, 2015.

Brunner, Bernd. *Extreme North: A Cultural History.* Translated by Jefferson Chase, W. W. Norton, 2022.

Butler, Judith. "Performative Acts and Gender Constitution: An Essay in Phenomenology and Feminist Theory." *Theatre Journal*, vol. 40, no. 4, December 1988, pp. 519–31.

Carrigan, Anthony. *Postcolonial Tourism: Literature, Culture, and Environment.* Routledge, 2011.

Chapman, Richard. "The Ultimate Guide to Gay Iceland: LGBT+ History, Rights and Culture." *Guide to Iceland*, guidetoiceland.is/history-culture/a-bit-about-gay-iceland.

Charlton, Ryan. "Elizabeth Robins's Alaskan Fiction and the Global New South." *The Global South*, vol. 16, no. 2, 2023, pp. 31–48.

Chen, Shawna. "Senate Sends Anti-Lynching Bill to Biden's Desk in Historic First." *Axios*, 7 Mar. 2020, www.axios.com/2022/03/08/senate-antilynching-bill.

Ćirić, Jelena. "Highly-Criticised Immigration Bill Passed in Iceland." *Iceland Review*, 16 Mar. 2023, www.icelandreview.com/politics/highly-criticised-immigration-bill-passed -in-iceland.

Cohen, Hannah Jane. "The Queer Canon of Iceland: Ásta Kristín Benediktsdóttir Explores an Oft-Ignored Topic." *The Reykjavík Grapevine*, 26 July 2018, grapevine.is/ icelandic-culture/literature-and-poetry/2018/07/26/the-queer-canon-of-iceland -asta-kristin-benediktsdottir-explores-an-oft-ignored-topic.

Cohn, Deborah. "'In between propaganda and escapism': William Faulkner as Cold War Cultural Ambassador." *Diplomatic History*, vol. 40, no. 3, 2016, pp. 392–420.

Costello, Brannon. *Plantation Airs: Racial Paternalism and the Transformations of Class in Southern Fiction, 1945–1971.* Louisiana State UP, 2007.

D'Amico, Giuliano. "The Whole World Is One *Atom Station*: Laxness, the Cold War, Postcolonialism, and the Economic Crisis in Iceland." *Scandinavian Studies*, vol. 87, no. 4, Winter 2015, pp. 457–88.

Danbolt, Mathias, and Lene Myong. "Racial Turn and Returns: Recalibrations of Racial Exceptionalism in Danish Public Debates on Racism." *Racialization, Racism, and Anti-Racism in the Nordic Countries*, edited by Peter Hervik, Palgrave, 2019, pp. 39–62.

Davis, Adrienne. "'Don't Let Nobody Bother Yo' Principle': The Sexual Economy of American Slavery." *Sister Circle: Black Women and Work*, edited by Sharon Harley and the Black Women and Work Collective, Rutgers UP, 2002, pp. 103–27.

Davis, Angela Y. *Women, Culture, and Politics.* Vintage, 1984.

Davis, Angela Y. *Women, Race, and Class.* Vintage, 1981.

Davis, Lisa Selin. "The Racist History of Celebrating the American Tomboy." *Literary Hub*, 11 Aug. 2020, lithub.com/the-racist-history-of-celebrating-the-american-tomboy.

Davis, Thadious. *Southscapes: Geographies of Race, Religion, and Literature.* U of North Carolina P, 2011.

Deans, Philip W. *The Uninvited Guests: Britain's Military Forces in Iceland, 1940–1942.* 2012. University of Chester, MA thesis.

Denard, Carolyn C. *Toni Morrison: Conversations.* UP of Mississippi, 2008.

Demurtas, Alice. "Racist Party in Iceland Breaks Historic Electoral Record." *The Reykjavík Grapevine*, 28 May 2018, grapevine.is/news/2018/05/28/racist-party-in-iceland-breaks -historic-electoral-record.

DeRose, Jason. "Concerns over Antisemitism Rise as Jews Begin Observing Passover." *NPR.org*, 23 April 2024, www.npr.org/2024/04/23/1246380646/concerns-over-antisemitism-rise-as-jews-begin-observing-passover.

De Souza, Pascale. "Creolizing Anancy: Signifyin(g) Processes in New World Spider Tales." *A Pepper-Pot of Cultures: Aspects of Creolization in the Caribbean*, edited by Gordon Collier and Ulrich Fleischmann, Rodopi, 2004, pp. 339–63.

Dimock, Wai Chee. "Weak Network: Faulkner's Transpacific Reparations." *Modernism/modernity*, vol. 25, no. 3, 2018, pp. 587–602.

Domínguez, Virginia R. *White by Definition: Social Classification in Creole Louisiana*. Rutgers UP, 1986.

Donahue, Jennifer. *Taking Flight: Caribbean Women Writing from Abroad*. UP of Mississippi, 2020.

Downham, Clare. "Vikings Were Never the Pure-Bred Master Race White Supremacists Like to Portray." *The Conversation*, 28 Sept. 2017, theconversation.com/vikings-were-never-the-pure-bred-master-race-white-supremacists-like-to-portray-84455.

Duck, Leigh Anne. *The Nation's Region: Southern Modernism, Segregation, and U.S. Nationalism*. U of Georgia P, 2006.

Durrenberger, E. Paul, and Gísli Pálsson. Introduction. *Images of Contemporary Iceland: Everyday Lives and Global Contexts*, edited by Gísli Pálsson and E. Paul Durrenberger, U of Iowa P, 1996.

Duvall, John N. "Faulkner's Crying Game: Male Homosexual Panic." *Faulkner and Gender: Faulkner and Yoknapatawpha, 1994*, edited by Donald M. Kartiganer and Ann J. Abadie, UP of Mississippi, 1996, pp. 48–72.

Edwards, Laura F. "Southern History as U.S. History." *Journal of Southern History*, vol. 75, no. 3, 2009, pp. 533–64.

Ehrenreich, Barbara, and Deirdre English. *Witches, Midwives & Nurses: A History of Women Healers*. 2nd ed., Feminist Press, 2010.

Eidsvik, Erlend. "Colonial Discourse and Ambivalence: Norwegian Participants on the Colonial Arena in South Africa." *Whiteness and Postcolonialism in the Nordic Region: Exceptionalism, Migrant Others and National Identities*, edited by Kristín Loftsdóttir and Lars Jensen, Ashgate, 2012, pp. 13–28.

Elise, Dianne. "Tomboys and Cowgirls: The Girl's Disidentification from the Mother." *Sissies and Tomboys: Gender Nonconformity and Homosexual Childhood*, edited by Matthew Rottnek, New York UP, 1999, pp. 140–52.

Ellenberger, Íris. "Transculturation, Contact Zones and Gender on the Periphery: An Example from Iceland 1890–1920." *Women's History Review*, vol. 28, no. 7, 2019, pp. 1078–95.

"Embassy of Iceland in Copenhagen." *Government of Iceland*, www.government.is/diplomatic-missions/embassy-of-iceland-in-copenhagen.

Eysteinsson, Ástráður. "Icelandic Prose Literature, 1940–1980." *A History of Icelandic Literature*, edited by Daisy Neijmann, U of Nebraska P, 2007, pp. 404–38.

Eysteinsson, Ástráður. "Icelandic Resettlements." *Symplokē*, vol. 5, no. 1/2, 1997, pp. 153–66.

Fandos, Nicholas. "Frustration and Fury as Rand Paul Holds Up Anti-Lynching Bill in Senate." *The New York Times*, 5 June 2020, www.nytimes.com/2020/06/05/us/politics/rand-paul-anti-lynching-bill-senate.html.

WORKS CITED

Fontaine, Andie Sophia. "Foreign Nationals Now 14.5% of Iceland's Population." *The Reykjavík Grapevine*, 15 Dec. 2021, grapevine.is/news/2021/12/15/foreign-nationals-now-14-5-of-icelands-population.

Fontaine, Andie Sophia. "Iceland Passes Major Gender Identity Law: 'The Fight Is Far From Over.'" *The Reykjavík Grapevine*, 19 June 2019, grapevine.is/news/2019/06/19/iceland-passes-major-gender-identity-law-the-fight-is-far-from-over.

Fontaine, Andie Sophia. "Naming Committee Approves New Batch of Names, No Gender Restrictions Applied." *The Reykjavík Grapevine*, 15 Jan. 2021, grapevine.is/news/2021/01/15/naming-committee-approves-new-batch-of-names-no-gender-restrictions-applied.

Fontaine, Andie Sophia. "Passage of Bills Protecting Intersex Children and Others All But Certain." *The Reykjavík Grapevine*, 16 Dec. 2020, grapevine.is/news/2020/12/16/passage-of-bills-protecting-intersex-children-and-others-all-but-certain.

Foster, Frances Smith. *'Til Death or Distance Do Us Part: Love and Marriage in African America*. Oxford UP, 2010.

Frank, Waldo. "Foreword." *Cane* (1923). By Jean Toomer. Norton Critical Edition, 1988, pp. 138–140.

Federici, Silvia. *Caliban and the Witch: Women, the Body and Primitive Accumulation*. Autonomedia, 2004.

Free, Melissa. "Relegation and Rebellion: The Queer, the Grotesque, and the Silent in the Fiction of Carson McCullers." *Studies in the Novel*, vol. 40, no. 4, 2008, pp. 426–46.

Freeman, Elizabeth. "'The We of Me': *The Member of the Wedding*'s Novel Alliances." *Women and Performance: A Journal of Feminist Theory*, vol. 8, no. 2, 1995, pp. 111–35.

Friedman, Susan Stanford. *Planetary Modernisms: Provocations on Modernity Across Time*. Columbia UP, 2015.

Fur, Gunlög. "Colonialism and Swedish History: Unthinkable Connections?" *Scandinavian Colonialism and the Rise of Modernity: Small Time Agents in a Global Arena*, edited by Magdalena Naum and Jonas M. Nordin, Springer, 2013, pp. 17–36.

Fur, Gunlög. "Concurrences as a Methodology for Discerning Concurrent Histories." *Concurrent Imaginaries, Postcolonial Worlds: Towards Revised Histories*, edited by Diana Brydon, et al., Brill, 2017, pp. 33–57.

Garner, Steve. "Injured Nations, Racialising States and Repressed Histories: Making Whiteness Visible in the Nordic Countries." *Social Identities*, vol. 20, no. 6, 2014, pp. 407–22.

Gleeson-White, Sarah. *Strange Bodies: Gender and Identity in the Novels of Carson McCullers*. U of Alabama P, 2003.

Glissant, Édouard. *Faulkner, Mississippi*. Translated by Barbara Lewis and Thomas C. Spear, Farrar, Straus and Giroux, 1999.

González Groba, Constante. "'So Far as I and My People Are Concerned the South Is Fascist Now and Always Has Been': Carson McCullers and the Racial Problem." *Atlantis*, vol. 37, no. 2, 2015, pp. 63–80.

Greeson, Jennifer Rae. *Our South: Geographic Fantasy and the Rise of National Literature*. Harvard UP, 2010.

Graham-Bertolini, Alison. "Understanding Sexual Politics and the #MeToo Movement through the Fiction of Carson McCullers." *South Atlantic Review*, vol. 86, no. 3, 2021, pp. 1–20.

Gremaud, Ann-Sofie Nielsen. "Iceland as Centre and Periphery: Postcolonial and Crypto-Colonial Perspectives." *The Postcolonial North Atlantic: Iceland, Greenland and the Faroe Islands*, edited by Lill-Ann Körber and Ebbe Volquardsen, Nordeuropa-Institut, 2020, pp. 83–104.

Gremaud, Ann-Sofie Nielsen. "Iceland-Denmark—A Crypto-Colonial Relation?" *Ann-Sofie Gremaud*, 21 Feb. 2013, annsofiegremaud.wordpress.com/2013/02/21/iceland-denmark-a-crypto-colonial-relation.

Gremaud, Ann-Sofie N. "Power and Purity: Nature as Resource in a Troubled Society." *Environmental Humanities*, vol. 5, no. 1, 2014, pp. 77–100.

Griffin, Larry J. "The American South and the Self." *Southern Cultures*, vol. 12, no. 3, 2006, pp. 6–28.

Grosfoguel, Ramon, et al. "'Racism,' Intersectionality and Migration Studies: Framing Some Theoretical Reflections." *Identities: Global Studies in Culture and Power*, vol. 22, no. 6, 2014, pp. 635–52.

Grossmann, Kurt R. "The Final Solution." *The Antioch Review*, vol. 15, no. 1, 1955, pp. 55–72.

Guðmundsdóttir, Kristín. *The Construction of Femininity in Halldór Laxness' Salka Valka*. 2006. University of York, MA thesis.

Guðmundsson, Halldór. *The Islander: A Biography of Halldór Laxness*. Translated by Philip Roughton. MacLehose P, 2008.

Guðmundsson, Helgi Hrafn. "A Nazi's Disappointment with Iceland." *The Reykjavík Grapevine*, 6 Mar. 2014, grapevine.is/mag/articles/2014/03/06/a-nazis-disappointment-with-iceland.

Gurdin, Julie E. "Motherhood, Patriarchy, and the Nation: Domestic Violence in Iceland." *Images of Contemporary Iceland: Everyday Lives and Global Contexts*, edited by Gísli Pálsson and E. Paul Durrenberger, U of Iowa P, 1996, pp. 126–45.

Hagood, Taylor. *Faulkner's Imperialism: Space, Place, and the Materiality of Myth*. Louisiana State UP, 2008.

Halberstam, Jack. "Oh Bondage Up Yours! Female Masculinity and the Tomboy." *Sissies and Tomboys: Gender Nonconformity and Homosexual Childhood*, edited by Matthew Rottnek, NYU P, 1999, pp. 153–79.

Hálfdanarson, Guðmundur. "Iceland: A Peaceful Secession." *Scandinavian Journal of History*, vol. 25, no. 1–2, 2000, pp. 87–100.

Hálfdanarson, Guðmundur. "Iceland Perceived: Nordic, European or Colonial Other?" *The Postcolonial North Atlantic: Iceland, Greenland and the Faroe Islands*, 2nd ed, edited by Lill-Ann and Ebbe Volquardsen, Nordeuropa-Institut, 2020, pp. 39–66.

Hálfdanarson, Guðmundur. "Severing the Ties—Iceland's Journey from a Union with Denmark to a Nation-State." *Scandinavian Journal of History*, vol. 31, no. 3–4, 2006, pp. 237–54.

Hale, Grace Elizabeth. *Making Whiteness: The Culture of Segregation in the South, 1890–1940*. Vintage International, 1999.

Hall, Alaric. *Útrásarvíkingar! The Literature of the Icelandic Financial Crisis (2008–2014)*. Punctum Books, 2020.

Hallmundsson, Hallberg. "Halldór Laxness and the Sagas of Modern Iceland." *The Georgia Review*, vol. 49, no. 1, 1995, pp. 39–45.

Handley, George B. *Postslavery Literatures in the Americas: Family Portraits in Black and White*. U of Virginia P, 2000.

Haring, Lee. "Against Untranslatability." *Narrative Culture*, vol. 1, no. 2, 2014, pp. 145–74.

Harker, Jaime. *The Lesbian South: Southern Feminists, the Women in Print Movement, and the Queer Literary Canon*. U of North Carolina P, 2018.

Harmon, Charles. "*Cane*, Race, and 'Neither/Norism.'" *The Southern Literary Journal*, vol. 32, no. 2, 2000, pp. 90–101.

Heith, Anne. "Aesthetics and Ethnicity: The Role of Boundaries in Sámi and Tornedalian Art." *Whiteness and Postcolonialism in the Nordic Region: Exceptionalism, Migrant Others and National Identities*, edited by Kristín Loftsdóttir and Lars Jensen, Ashgate, 2012, pp. 159–73.

Haney López, Ian F. "The Social Construction of Race." *Critical Race Theory: The Cutting Edge*, 2nd ed, edited by Richard Delgado and Jean Stefancic, Temple UP, 2000, pp. 163–75.

Helgason, Jón Karl. "A Poet's Great Return: Jónas Hallgrímsson's reburial and Milan Kundera's *Ignorance*." *Scandinavian-Canadian Studies/Études scandinaves au Canada*, vol. 20, 2011, pp. 52–61.

Hervik, Peter. "Racialization in the Nordic Countries: An Introduction." *Racialization, Racism, and Anti-Racism in the Nordic Countries*, edited by Peter Hervik, Palgrave, 2019, pp. 3–37.

Herzfeld, Michael. "The Absent Presence: Discourses of Crypto-Colonialism." *The South Atlantic Quarterly*, vol. 101, no. 4, 2002, pp. 899–926.

Hirsch, Arnold R., and Joseph Logsdon. *Creole New Orleans: Race and Americanization*. Louisiana State UP, 1992.

Hoerning, Johanna. "Dividing the 'World': Spatial Binaries in Global Perspective." *Considering Space: A Critical Concept for the Social Sciences*, edited by Dominik Bartmanski et al., Routledge, 2024, pp. 113–35.

Höglund, Johan. "Christina Larsdotter and the Swedish Postcolonial Novel." *Scandinavian Studies*, vol. 91, no. 1–2, 2019, pp. 238–58.

Höglund, Johan, and Linda Andersson Burnett. "Introduction: Nordic Colonialisms and Scandinavian Studies." *Scandinavian Studies*, vol. 91, no. 1–2, 2019, pp. 1–12.

Holland, Samantha, and Julie Harpin. "Who is the 'Girly Girl'? Tomboys, Hyper-Femininity and Gender." *Journal of Gender Studies*, vol. 24, no. 3, 2015, pp. 293–309.

Holroyd, Matthew. "Iceland's Entire Football Association Resigns after Sexual Assault Scandal." *Euronews*, 3 Sep. 2021, www.euronews.com/2021/08/31/iceland-s-entire -football-association-resigns-after-sexual-assault-scandal.

Howard, John. *Men Like That: A Southern Queer History*. U of Chicago P, 1999.

Ingvarsson, Haukur. *Fulltrúi þess besta í bandarískri menningu: Orðspor Williams Faulkners í íslensku menningarlífi 1930–1960*. Sögufélag, 2021.

"Introduction to African Languages." *The African Language Program at Harvard*, alp.fas .harvard.edu/introduction-african-languages.

Ísleifsson, Sumarliði R. "Introduction: Imaginations of National Identity and the North." *Iceland and Images of the North*, edited by Sumarliði R. Ísleifsson with Daniel Chartier, Presses de l'Université du Québec/ReykjavíkurAkademían, 2011, pp. 3–22.

Jackson, Chuck. "American Emergencies: Whiteness, the National Guard, and *Light in August*." *Faulkner and Whiteness*, edited by Jay Watson, UP of Mississippi, 2011, pp. 194–208.

James, Andrea. "Tomboy Resources." *Transgender Map*, 3 May 2022, www.transgendermap .com/welcome/for-trans-people/gender-diverse/tomboy.

Jóhannesson, Guðni Thorlacius. *The History of Modern Iceland*. Greenwood, 2013.

Jóhannsson, Jón Yngvi. "Realism and Revolt: Between the World Wars." *A History of Icelandic Literature*, edited by Daisy Neijmann, U of Nebraska P, 2007, pp. 357–403.

Johnson, Alix. "Emplacing Data within Imperial Histories: Making Iceland Information's 'Natural' Home," *Culture Machine*, vol. 17, 2019, pp. 1–12.

Jolink, Ineke [*published as* Ineke Bockting]. "The In-Between of Jazz and the Blues: Beyond Marginality in Esi Edugyan's *Half-Blood Blues*." *Babel*, vol. 40, 2019, pp. 275–90.

Jordan, Winthrop D. *White over Black: American Attitudes Towards the Negro, 1550–1812*. The Kingsport Press, 1968.

Kane, Peter-Astrid. "After Years of Progress on Gay Rights, How Did the US Become So Anti-LGBTQ+?" *The Guardian*, 28 Apr. 2022, www.theguardian.com/us-news/2022/ apr/28/lgbtq-rights-us-dont-say-gay.

Karlsson, Gunnar. *Iceland's 1100 Years: The History of a Marginal Society*. C. Hurst, 2000.

Keely, Karen A. "Marriage Plots and National Reunion: The Trope of Romantic Reconciliation in Postbellum Literature." *The Mississippi Quarterly*, vol. 51, no. 4, 1998, pp. 621–48.

Keskinen, Suvi. "Intra-Nordic Differences, Colonial/Racial Histories, and National Narratives: Rewriting Finnish History." *Complying With Colonialism: Gender, Race and Ethnicity in the Nordic Region*, edited by Suvi Keskinen et al., Routledge, 2009, pp. 257–72.

Kim, Dorothy. "White Supremacists Have Weaponized an Imaginary Viking Past. It's Time to Reclaim the Real History." *Time.com*, 12 Apr. 2019, time.com/5569399/viking -history-white-nationalists.

Kjartansdóttir, Katla, and Schram, Kristinn. "'Something in the Air': Performing the North within Norden." *Performing Nordic Heritage: Everyday Practices and Institutional Culture*, edited by Peter Aronsson and Lizette Gradén, Ashgate, 2013, pp. 53–71.

Knútsdóttir, Vera. *Spectral Memories of Post-Crash Iceland: Memory, Identity and the Haunted Imagination in Contemporary Literature and Art*. Brill, 2023.

Körber, Lill-Ann. "Mapping Greenland: The Greenlandic Flag and Critical Cartography in Literature, Art and Fashion." *The Postcolonial North Atlantic: Iceland, Greenland and the Faroe Islands*, edited by Lill-Ann Körber and Ebbe Volquardsen, Nordeuropa-Institut, 2020, pp. 361–90.

Körber, Lill-Ann, et al. "Introduction: Arctic Modernities, Environmental Politics, and the Era of the Anthropocene." *Arctic Environmental Modernities: From the Age of Polar Exploration to the Era of the Anthropocene*, edited by Lill-Ann Körber et al., Palgrave, 2017, pp. 1–20.

Kristjánsdóttir, Dagný. "*Litlar stelpur*." *Tímarit Máls og menningar*, vol. 84, no. 1, 2023, pp. 5–13.

WORKS CITED

Lacy, Terry G. *Ring of Seasons: Iceland—Its Culture and History.* U of Michigan P, 2000.

LaFleur, Greta, et al. "Introduction: The Benefits of Being Trans Historical." *Trans Historical: Gender Plurality Before the Modern*, edited by Greta LaFleur et al., Cornell UP, 2021, pp. 1-23.

Lassiter, Matthew D., and Joseph Crespino. "Introduction: The End of Southern History." *The Myth of Southern Exceptionalism*, edited by Matthew D. Lassiter and Joseph Crespino, Oxford UP, 2010, pp. 3-24.

Lemelin, Harvey, et al. "Last-Chance Tourism: The Boom, Doom, and Gloom of Visiting Vanishing Destinations." *Current Issues in Tourism*, vol. 13, no. 5, 2010, pp. 477–93.

Levine, Caroline. *Forms: Whole, Rhythm, Hierarchy, Network.* Princeton UP, 2015.

Lightweis-Goff, Jennie. *Blood at the Root: Lynching as American Cultural Nucleus.* State U of New York P, 2011.

Lindahl, Björn. "Why Did #MeToo Hit the Nordics Differently?" *Nordic Labor Journal*, 16 Sep. 2019, www.nordiclabourjournal.org/nyheter/news-2019/article.2019-09-04.2946493042.

Loftsdóttir, Kristín. "Belonging and the Icelandic Others: Situating Icelandic Identity in a Postcolonial Context." *Whiteness and Postcolonialism in the Nordic Region: Exceptionalism, Migrant Others and National Identities*, edited by Kristín Loftsdóttir and Lars Jensen, Ashgate, 2012, pp. 57–71.

Loftsdóttir, Kristín. *Crisis and Coloniality at Europe's Margins: Creating Exotic Iceland.* Routledge, 2018.

Loftsdóttir, Kristín. "Dualistic Colonial Experiences and the Ruins of Coloniality." *Scandinavian Studies*, vol. 91, no. 1–2, 2019, pp. 31–52.

Loftsdóttir, Kristín. "The Exotic North: Gender, Nation Branding and Post-colonialism in Iceland." *NORA Nordic Journal of Feminist and Gender Research*, vol. 23, 2015, pp. 246–60.

Loftsdóttir, Kristín. "Imagining Blackness at the Margins: Race and Difference in Iceland." *Afro-Nordic Landscapes: Equality and Race in Northern Europe*, edited by Michael McEachrane, Routledge, 2014, pp. 17–38.

Loftsdóttir, Kristín. "Learning about Africa: The Imagination of Africa in Icelandic Schoolbooks." *Afroeurope@n Configurations: Readings and Projects*, edited by Sabrina Brancato, Cambridge Scholars Publishing, 2011. pp. 81–97.

Loftsdóttir, Kristín. "Learning Differences? Nationalism, Identity and Africa in Icelandic School Textbooks." *Identitätskonstruktionen und -präskriptionen in Schulbüchern/Identity Constructions and Prescriptions in School Textbooks*, vol. 29, no. 1, 2007, pp. 5–22.

Loftsdóttir, Kristín. "Republishing 'The Ten Little Negros': Exploring Nationalism and Whiteness in Iceland." *Ethnicities*, vol. 13, no. 3, 2013, pp. 295–315.

Loftsdóttir, Kristín, and Lars Jensen. *Exceptionalism.* Routledge, 2021.

Loftsdóttir, Kristín, and Lars Jensen. "Introduction: Nordic Exceptionalism and the Nordic 'Others.'" *Whiteness and Postcolonialism in the Nordic Region: Exceptionalism, Migrant Others and National Identities*, edited by Kristín Loftsdóttir and Lars Jensen, Ashgate, 2012, pp. 1–11.

Loftsdóttir, Kristín, and Gísli Pálsson. "Black on White: Danish Colonialism, Iceland, and the Caribbean." *Scandinavian Colonialism and the Rise of Modernity: Small Time Agents in a Global Arena*, edited by Magdalena Naum and Jonas Nordin, Springer, 2013, pp. 37–52.

Loftsdóttir, Kristín, and Sanna Magdalena Mörtudóttir. "'Where Are You From?': Racism and the Normalization of Whiteness in Iceland." *Journal of Critical Mixed Race Studies*, vol. 1, no. 2, 2022, pp. 215–32.

Lorentsen, Kristin, and Jakob Stougaard-Nielsen. "North Atlantic Drift: Contemporary Greenlandic and Sami Literatures." *Introduction to Nordic Cultures*, edited by Annika Lindskog and Jakob Stougaard-Nielsen, UCL Press, 2020, pp. 130–45.

Lott, Eric. *Love and Theft: Blackface Minstrelsy and the American Working Class*. Oxford UP, 1993.

Love, Heather. "Introduction: Modernism at Night." *PMLA*, vol. 124, no. 3, 2009, pp. 744–48.

Lucas, Gavin, and Angelos Parigoris. "Icelandic Archaeology and the Ambiguities of Colonialism." *Scandinavian Colonialism and the Rise of Modernity: Small Time Agents in a Global Arena*, edited by Magdalena Naum and Jonas M. Nordin, Springer, 2013, pp. 89–104.

Lunde, Arne, and Anna Westerstahl Stenport. "Helga Crane's Copenhagen: Denmark, Colonialism, and Transnational Identity in Nella Larsen's *Quicksand*." *Comparative Literature*, vol. 60, no. 3, 2008, pp. 228–43.

Lundström, Catrin, and Benjamin R. Teitelbaum. "Nordic Whiteness: An Introduction." *Scandinavian Studies*, vol. 89, no. 2, 2017, pp. 151–58.

Lynching in America: Confronting the Legacy of Racial Terror. 3rd ed., Equal Justice Initiative. 2017, lynchinginamerica.eji.org/report/.

Magnússon, Sigurður A. "The Icelandic Short Story: Svava Jakobsdóttir." *Scandinavian Studies*, vol. 49, no. 2, 1977, pp. 208–16.

Magnússon, Sigurður A. "The Modern Icelandic Novel: 'From Isolation to Political Awareness.'" *Mosaic: A Journal for the Interdisciplinary Study of Literature*, vol. 4, no. 2, 1970, pp. 133–43.

Magnússon, Sigurður A. "The World of Halldór Laxness." *World Literature Today*, vol. 66, no. 3, 1992, pp. 457–463.

Magnússon, Sigurður Gylfi. *Wasteland with Words: A Social History of Iceland*. Reaktion Books, 2010.

Mandle, Jay R. *Not Slave, Not Free: The African American Economic Experience Since the Civil War*. Duke UP, 1992.

Martínez-San Miguel, Yolanda. "De Macondo a Anegada: El icesto como dispositivo narrativo en el Caribe." *80 grados: Prensa sin prisa*, 18 Apr. 18 2016, www.80grados.net/demacondo-a-anegada-el-incesto-como-dispositivo-narrativo-en-el-caribe.

Mass, Noah. "'Caught and Loose': Southern Cosmopolitanism in Carson McCullers's *The Ballad of the Sad Café* and *The Member of the Wedding*." *Studies in American Fiction*, vol. 37, no. 2, 2010, pp. 225–46.

Matthews, John T. "Many Mansions: Faulkner's Cold War Conflicts." *Global Faulkner: Faulkner and Yoknapatawpha, 2006*, edited by Annette Trefzer and Ann J. Abadie, UP of Mississippi, 2009, pp. 3–23.

WORKS CITED 195

McElvein, Elizabeth, and Anna Newby. "Poll Shows American Views on Muslims and the Middle East Are Deeply Polarized." *Brookings*, 27 July 2016, www.brookings.edu/blog/markaz/2016/07/27/poll-shows-american-views-on-muslims-and-the-middle-east-are-deeply-polarized.

"#MeToo: A Timeline of Events." *Chicago Tribune*, 4 Feb. 2021, www.chicagotribune.com/2021/02/04/metoo-a-timeline-of-events.

Menakem, Resmaa. *My Grandmother's Hands: Racialized Trauma and the Pathway to Mending Our Hearts and Bodies*. Central Recovery Press, 2017.

Mendoza, Brynjarr Perry. "Haukur Ingvarsson. 2021. *Fulltrúi þess besta í bandarískri menningu. Orðspor Williams Faulkners í íslensku menningarlífi 1930–1960*." *Scandinavian-Canadian Studies*, vol. 30, Apr. 2023, pp. 1-3, doi:10.29173/scancan245.

Mesch, Rachel. *Before Trans: Three Gender Stories from Nineteenth-Century France*. Stanford UP, 2020.

Michaels, Walter Benn. *Our America: Nativism, Modernism, and Pluralism*. Duke UP, 1995.

Moberg, Bergur Rønne. "Place and Translation: Perspectives on Geomodernism and Periphery in William Heinesen's *Laterna Magica*." *Scandinavian Studies*, vol. 84, no. 2, 2012, pp. 191–206.

Moberg, Bergur Rønne. "The Faroese Rest in the West: Danish-Faroese World Literature between Postcolonialism and Western Modernism." *The Postcolonial North Atlantic: Iceland, Greenland and the Faroe Islands*, edited by Lill-Ann Körber and Ebbe Volquardsen, Nordeuropa-Institut, 2020, pp.165–94.

Moberg, Bergur Rønne, et al. "The Blue Atlantic: North Atlantic Imagined Geographies." *Denmark and the New North Atlantic: Narratives and Memories in a Former Empire*, vol. 2, edited by Kirsten Thisted and Ann-Sofie N. Gremaud, Aarhus UP, 2020, pp. 181–268.

Morgan, Jennifer. *Laboring Women: Reproduction and Gender in New World Slavery*. U of Pennsylvania P, 2004.

Mulinari, Diana, et al. "Introduction: Postcolonialism and the Nordic Models of Welfare and Gender." *Complying With Colonialism: Gender, Race and Ethnicity in the Nordic Region*, edited by Suvi Keskinen et al., Routledge, 2009, pp. 1–18.

Muñoz, José Esteban. *Disidentifications: Queers of Color and the Performance of Politics*. U of Minnesota P, 1999.

Nakajima, Koko, and Connie Hanzhang Jin. "Bills Targeting Trans Youth Are Growing More Common—and Radically Reshaping Lives." *NPR*, 28 Nov. 2022, www.npr.org/2022/11/28/1138396067/transgender-youth-bills-trans-sports

Naum, Magdalena, and Jonas M. Nordin "Introduction: Situating Scandinavian Colonialism." *Scandinavian Colonialism and the Rise of Modernity: Small Time Agents in a Global Arena*, edited by Magdalena Naum and Jonas M. Nordin, Springer, 2013, pp. 3–16.

Neijmann, Daisy L. *Colloquial Icelandic: The Complete Course for Beginners*. Routledge, 2014.

Neijmann, Daisy. "Foreign Fictions of Iceland." *Iceland and Images of the North*, edited by Sumarliði R. Ísleifsson with Daniel Chartier, Presses de l'Université du Québec/ReykjavíkurAkademían, 2011, pp. 481–512.

Neijmann, Daisy L. "Girl Interrupting: History and Art as Clairvoyance in the Fiction of Vigdís Grímsdóttir." *Scandinavian-Canadian Studies Journal / Études scandinaves au Canada*, vol. 17, 2007, pp. 54–68.

Neijmann, Daisy L. "Soldiers and Other Monsters: The Allied Occupation in Icelandic Fiction." *Scandinavian Canadian Studies Journal / Études scandinaves au Canada*, vol. 23, 2016, pp. 96–120.

Nelson, Alondra. *Body and Soul: The Black Panther Party and the Fight against Medical Discrimination.* U of Minnesota P, 2013.

Nisetich, Rebecca. "When Difference Becomes Dangerous: Intersectional Identity Formation and the Protective Cover of Whiteness in Faulkner's *Light in August*." *The Faulkner Journal*, vol. 31, no. 1, 2017, pp. 43–66.

Nuechterlein, Donald E. *A Cold War Odyssey.* UP of Kentucky, 1997.

Ólason, Vésteinn. "Modernism in the Post-War Icelandic Novel up to 1990." *Scandinavian-Canadian Studies Journal / Études scandinaves au Canada*, vol. 18, 2009, pp. 86–104.

Olney, James. "'I Was Born': Slave Narratives, Their Status as Autobiography and as Literature." *Callaloo*, no. 20, Winter 1984, pp. 46–73.

"Omar 1." *Nordic Names*, https://www.nordicnames.de/wiki/Omar_1.

Oxfeldt, Elisabeth, et al. "National (Gender) Trouble: Race, Bodies and Sexualities." *Denmark and the New North Atlantic: Narratives and Memories in a Former Empire*, vol. 2, edited by Kirsten Thisted and Ann-Sofie N. Gremaud, Aarhus UP, 2020, pp. 11–96.

Pálsson, Gísli. "Arcticality: Gender, Race, and Geography in the Writings of Vilhjalmur Stefansson." *Narrating the Arctic: A Cultural History of Nordic Scientific Practice*, edited by Michael Bravo and Sverker Sörlin, Science History Publications, 2002, pp. 275–309.

Palmberg, Mai. "The Nordic Colonial Mind." *Complying With Colonialism: Gender, Race and Ethnicity in the Nordic Region*, edited by Suvi Keskinen, Salla Tuori, Sara Irni, Diana Mulinari, Routledge, 2009, pp. 35–50.

Parrish, Susan Scott. "The Bitter Sum: Accounting for Racist Speech in *Absalom, Absalom!*" Faulkner's Fetishized Words Conference, 20 May 2021, Zoom. Partial conference presentation transcript.

Parrish, Susan Scott, and Johannes Burgers. "The Bitter Sum: Accounting for Racist Speech in *Absalom, Absalom!*" *joostburgers.github.io*, 24 May 2023, joostburgers.github.io/absalom_sentiment_analysis.

Paton, Diana. *The Cultural Politics of Obeah: Religion, Colonialism and Modernity in the Caribbean World.* Cambridge UP, 2015.

Pellerin, Cheryl. "DoD Updates Equal Opportunity Policy to Include Sexual Orientation." *U.S. Department of Defense*, 9 June 2015, www.defense.gov/News/News-Stories/Article/Article/604797.

Perry, Constance M. "Carson McCullers and the Female Wunderkind." *The Southern Literary Journal*, vol. 19, no. 1, 1986, pp. 36–45.

Peterson, Paul R. "Old Norse Nicknames: Origins and Terminology." *Names: A Journal of Onomastics*, vol. 67, no. 2, 2019, pp. 89–99.

Portwood, Jerry. "The Surrealist Storyteller of the North." *Out*, 30 Oct. 2014, www.out.com/entertainment/art-books/2014/10/28/sj%C3%B3n-moonstone-author-gay-book-iceland.

WORKS CITED

Quimby, Karin. "The Story of Jo: Literary Tomboys, Little Women, and the Sexual-Textual Politics of Narrative Desire." *GLQ*, vol. 10, no. 1, 2003, pp. 1–22.

Ramsey, William M. "Jean Toomer's Eternal South." *The Southern Literary Journal*, vol. 36, no. 1, Fall, 2003, pp. 74–89.

Rastrick, Ólafur. "'Not Music but Sonic Porn': Identity Politics, Social Reform, and the Negative Reception of Jazz." *Cultural History*, vol. 10, no.1, 2021, pp. 91–110.

Rastrick, Ólafur. "Physical Appearance and the Moral Conduct of the Female Subject in Inter-War Iceland." *Constructing Cultural Identity, Representing Social Power*, edited by Kim Esmark et al., U of Pisa P, 2010, pp. 77–88.

Reconstruction in America: Racial Violence after the Civil War, 1865–1876. Equal Justice Initiative, 2020, eji.org/report/reconstruction-in-america.

Reid, Eliza. *Secrets of the Sprakkar: Iceland's Extraordinary Women and How They Are Changing the World*. Sourcebooks, 2022.

"Resmaa Menakem on Why Healing Racism Begins with the Body." *Conversations on Compassion* from the Center for Compassion Studies, University of Arizona, 26 Aug. 2019, compassioncenter.arizona.edu/podcast/resmaa-menakem.

Romdhani, Rebecca. "Violating Virgins: Symbolic Violence in Tiphanie Yanique's *Land of Love and Drowning*." *Narrating Violence in the Postcolonial World*, edited by Rebecca Romdhani and Daria Tunca, Routledge, 2022, pp. 79–98.

Romine, Scott. *The Narrative Forms of Southern Community*. Louisiana State UP, 1999.

Rosenblad, Esbjörn, and Rakel Sigurðardóttir-Rosenblad. *Iceland from Past to Present*. Translated by Alan Crozier, Mál og menning, 1993.

Rosenthal, Elisabeth. "Race Is On as Ice Melt Reveals Arctic Treasures." *New York Times*, 18 Sep. 2012, www.nytimes.com/2012/09/19/science/earth/arctic-resources-exposed -by-warming-set-off-competition.html.

Rúnarsdóttir, Anna Lísa. "Making of an Exhibition: Iceland in the World, the World in Iceland." *Nordic Museology*, vol. 29, no. 2, 2020, pp. 82–95.

Sabra, Hani. "Let's Name It: Not Just Islamophobia, but Anti-Palestinianism." *The Intercept*, 18 Mar. 2024, https://theintercept.com/2024/03/18/muslim-islamophobia-palestinians/.

Saldívar, Ramón, and Sylvan Goldberg. "The Faulknerian Anthropocene: Scales of Time and History in *The Wild Palms* and *Go Down, Moses*." *The New Cambridge Companion to William Faulkner*, edited by John T. Matthews, Cambridge UP, 2015, pp. 185–203.

Sawchuk, Stephen. "Anti-Critical-Race-Theory Laws Are Slowing Down. Here Are 3 Things to Know." *Education Week*, 26 March 2024, https://www.edweek.org/teaching -learning/anti-critical-race-theory-laws-are-slowing-down-here-are-3-things-to -know/2024/03.

Schram, Kristinn. "Banking on Borealism: Eating, Smelling, and Performing the North." *Iceland and Images of the North*, edited by Sumarliði R. Ísleifsson with Daniel Chartier, Presses de l'Université du Québec/Reykjavík Academy 2011, pp. 305–27.

Sciuto, Jenna Grace. "'[T]he critic must leave the Western hemisphere': Faulkner and World Literature." *The New William Faulkner Studies*, edited by Sarah Gleeson-White and Pardis Dabashi, Cambridge UP, 2022, pp. 51–66.

Sciuto, Jenna Grace. "Introduction: Engaging with the Poetics of Peripheralization." *The Global South*, vol. 11, no. 1, 2017, pp. 1–9.

Sciuto, Jenna Grace. *Policing Intimacy: Law, Sexuality, and the Color Line in Twentieth-Century Hemispheric American Literature*. UP of Mississippi, 2021.

Sciuto, Jenna Grace. "Racial Ambiguity, Bootlegging, and the Subversion of Plantation Hierarchies in Faulkner's South." *Southern Comforts: Drinking and the U.S. South*, edited by Conor Picken and Matthew Dischinger, Baton Rouge: Louisiana State UP, 2020, pp. 193–206.

Shapland, Jennifer Ann. *Narrative Salvage*. 2016. U of Texas at Austin, PhD dissertation.

Sharpe, Christina E. "The Costs of Re-Membering: What's at Stake in Gayl Jones's *Corregidora*." *African American Performance and Theater History: A Critical Reader*, edited by Harry J. Elam Jr. and David Krasner, Oxford UP, 2001, pp. 306–28.

Shear, Michael D. "Biden Signs Bill to Make Lynching a Federal Crime." *New York Times*, 29 Mar. 2022, www.nytimes.com/2022/03/29/us/politics/biden-signs-anti-lynching-bill.html.

Sherrard-Johnson, Cherene. "'Perfection with a hole in the middle': Archipelagic Assemblage in Tiphanie Yanique's *Land of Love and Drowning*." *Journal of Transnational American Studies*, vol. 10, no.1, 2019, pp. 93–123.

Silber, Nina. *The Romance of Reunion: Northerners and the South, 1865–1900*. U of North Carolina P, 1997.

Skaptadóttir, Unnur Dís. "Housework and Wage Work: Gender in Icelandic Fishing Communities." *Images of Contemporary Iceland: Everyday Lives and Global Contexts*, edited by Gísli Pálsson and E. Paul Durrenberger, U of Iowa P, 1996, pp. 87–105.

Smith, Jon, and Deborah Cohn. "Introduction: Uncanny Hybridities." *Look Away! The U.S. South in New World Studies*, edited by Jon Smith and Deborah Cohn, Duke UP, 2004, pp. 1-19.

Solard, Alain. "Myth and Narrative Fiction in Cane: 'Blood-Burning Moon.'" *Callaloo*, no. 25, Autumn, 1985, pp. 551–62.

Sondrup, Steven P., and Mark B. Sandberg. "General Project Introduction." *Nordic Literature: A Comparative History*, vol. 1, edited by Steven P. Sondrup et al., John Benjamins Publishing Company, 2017, pp. 1–18.

Spenko, James Leo. "The Death of Joe Christmas and the Power of Words." *Twentieth Century Literature*, vol. 28, no. 3, 1982, pp. 252–68.

Spillers, Hortense J. "Mama's Baby, Papa's Maybe: An American Grammar Book." *Diacritics*, vol. 17, no. 2, 1987, pp. 64–81.

Spoth, Daniel. "Totalitarian Faulkner: The Nazi Interpretation of *Light in August* and *Absalom, Absalom!*" *ELH*, vol. 78, no. 1, 2011, pp. 239–57.

Stahuljak, Zrinka. "Translation." *Transnational Modern Languages: A Handbook*, edited by Jennifer Burns and Derek Duncan, Liverpool UP, 2022, pp. 313–22.

Stecopoulos, Harilaos. "William Faulkner and the Problem of Cold War Modernism." *Faulkner's Geographies*, edited by Jay Watson and Ann J. Abadie, UP of Mississippi, 2015, pp. 143–62.

Stuhl, Andrew. "The Disappearing Arctic? Scientific Narrative, Environmental Crisis, and the Ghosts of Colonial History." *Arctic Environmental Modernities From the Age of Polar Exploration to the Era of the Anthropocene*, edited by Lill-Ann Körber et al., Palgrave, 2017, pp. 21–42.

WORKS CITED

Stuhl, Andrew. *Unfreezing the Arctic: Science, Colonialism, and the Transformation of Inuit Lands.* U of Chicago P, 2016.

Telhami, Shibley. "American Attitudes toward Muslims and Islam." *Brookings,* 27 July 2016, www.brookings.edu/research/american-attitudes-toward-muslims-and-islam.

Thisted, Kirsten. "Politics, Oil and Rock 'n' Roll: Fictionalising the International Power Game about Indigenous People's Rights and the Fight over Natural Resources and Financial Gain in the Arctic." *The Postcolonial North Atlantic: Iceland, Greenland and the Faroe Islands,* edited by Lill-Ann Körber and Ebbe Volquardsen, Nordeuropa-Institut, 2020, pp. 329–60.

Thisted, Kirsten, and Ann-Sofie N. Gremaud. "Envisioning the North Atlantic: Current Narratives and Official Discourses." *Denmark and the New North Atlantic: Narratives and Memories in a Former Empire Volume I,* edited by Kirsten Thisted and Ann-Sofie N. Gremaud, Aarhus UP, 2020, pp. 17–90.

Þorvaldsson, Eysteinn. "Icelandic Poetry since 1940." Translated by Gunnþórunn Guðmundsdóttir. *A History of Icelandic Literature,* edited by Daisy Neijmann, U of Nebraska P, 2007, pp. 471–502.

United States, Congress, House. Respect for Marriage Act. *Congress.gov,* www.congress .gov/bill/117th-congress/house-bill/8404. 117th Congress, 2nd session, House Resolution 8404, passed 13 Dec. 2022.

Urgo, Joseph R., and Noel Polk. *Reading Faulkner: Absalom, Absalom!* UP of Mississippi, 2010.

Valdimarsdóttir, Margré, and Gudbjorg Andrea Jónsdóttir. "Attitudes towards Refugees and Muslim Immigrants in Iceland: The Perceived Link to Terrorism." *Veftímaritið Stjórnmál og stjórnsýsla,* vol. 16, no. 2, 2020, pp. 217–41.

Van Baar, Annika, and Wim Huisman. "The Oven Builders of the Holocaust: A Case Study of Corporate Complicity in International Crimes." *The British Journal of Criminology,* vol. 52, no. 6, 2012, pp. 1033–50.

van der Liet, Henk. "Iceland: A Postcolonial Literary Landscape?" *Amsterdamer Beiträge zur älteren Germanistik,* vol. 67, 2011, pp. 447–71.

Van Deusen, Natalie M. "Colours, Colour Symbolism, and Social Critique in Halldór Laxness's *Salka Valka." Scandinavian-Canadian Studies,* vol. 18, 2009, pp. 56–70.

Vegh, Beatriz. "Introduction: A Latin American Faulkner." *The Faulkner Journal,* vol. 11, no. 1–2, 1995–1996, pp. 5–10.

Vestal, Allan James, et al. "Presidential Election Results." *Politico,* 8 Nov. 2022, www.politico .com/2020-election/results/president.

Volquardsen, Ebbe, and Lill-Anne Körber. "The Postcolonial North Atlantic: An Introduction." *The Postcolonial North Atlantic Iceland, Greenland and the Faroe Islands,* edited by Lill-Ann Körber and Ebbe Volquardsen, Nordeuropa-Institut, 2020, pp. 7-29.

von Schnurbein, Stefanie. *Norse Revival: Transformations of Germanic Neopaganism.* Brill Publishers, 2016.

Wagner, Nancy O'Brien. "Convict Leasing." *Slavery by Another Name,* PBS, 2021, www.pbs .org/tpt/slavery-by-another-name/themes/convict-leasing.

Watson, Jay. "Overdoing Masculinity in Light in August: Or, Joe Christmas and the Gender Guard." *The Faulkner Journal,* vol. 9, no. 1–2, 1993, pp. 149–77.

Waxman, Olivia B. "Reconstruction's Black Politicians." *TIME Magazine*, vol. 199, no. 7/8, Feb. 2022, p. 26.

Weber, Shannon. "White Supremacy's Old Gods: The Far Right and Neopaganism." *Political Research Associates*, 1 Feb. 2018, www.politicalresearch.org/2018/02/01/white-supremacys-old-gods-the-far-right-and-neopaganism.

Westling, Louise. *Sacred Groves and Ravaged Gardens: The Fiction of Eudora Welty, Carson McCullers, and Flannery O'Connor.* U of Georgia P, 1985.

Williams, Jennifer D. "Jean Toomer's 'Cane' and the Erotics of Mourning." *The Southern Literary Journal*, vol. 40, no. 2, 2008, pp. 87–101.

Worley, Paul M., and Melissa Birkhofer. "Latinxs in the Attic: (Erasing Latinx Presence and the) Policing (of) Racial Borders in Faulkner's *Light in August.*" *The Comparatist*, vol. 43, 2019, pp. 324–40.

Wright, Richard. "Inner Landscape." *Critical Essays on Carson McCullers*. Eds. Beverley Lyon Clark and Melvin J. Friedman. MacMillan, 1996, pp. 17–18.

Yanique, Tiphanie. "The Wisdom of Old Wives' Tales." *Bookpage*, 10 July 2014, www.bookpage.com/behind-the-book/16811-wisdom-old-wives-tales-fiction.

Young, Anna. "North to the Future: Captivity and Escape in *The Member of the Wedding.*" *The Southern Literary Journal*, vol. 47, no. 1, 2014, pp. 81–97.

Zevy, Lee. "Sexing the Tomboy." *Sissies and Tomboys: Gender Nonconformity and Homosexual Childhood*, edited by Matthew Rottnek, New York UP, 1999, pp. 180–98.

INDEX

Italicized page numbers indicate illustrations.

Abate, Michelle Ann, 89, 90, 172n29

Abdur-Rahman, Aliyyah I., 41, 67, 69–70

Aboul-Ela, Hosam, 4–6, 16–17, 24, 36, 52, 108, 115

Abrahams, Z., 182n16

Absalom, Absalom! (Faulkner), 16, 19, 35–44, 68, 180n46; gendered issues, 85; "The Lodger," parallels with, 48; racism, depictions of, 50; toxic Whiteness, 54

Adams, Jessica, 14

Africa: African nicknames, 19, 30–31; colonization of, 11, 23, 24, 55, 113; languages, 31; mythology and folklore, 136; presence in US literature, 104; stereotypes of, 25, 35, 43, 152, 162n3; as "uncivilized," 31–32, 64

Al-Amin, Jamil, 22

Alaska, 92, 148, 171n21

Alcott, Louisa May, 90

alienation as theme, 82, 93

All That's Left to You (Kanafani), 17

Amin, Samir, 6

Andersen, Hans Christian, 125

Angels of the Universe (Guðmundsson), 104–5

animal imagery, 27, 32, 38, 42, 66, 74, 77, 106–7

anti-immigrant movements, 153, 155–56, 181n7, 181n10

Arbour, Robert, 74

Arctic Chill (Indriðason), 169n28

Arctic Council, 148

Arctic Environmental Modernities (Körber), 15

Arctic regions, 148; "arcticality," 26, 162n5; "Arctic Five," 148; "Arctic Orientalism," 26; and climate change, 156–57; landscapes, 92

Árnadóttir, Nína Björk, 83

Arnold, David, 162n5

Ástandið ("the Situation"), 56, 58, 86, 103

atom poets, 33–34, 163n15

Atom Station, The (Laxness), 19, 30–35, 124; racism portrayed in, 163n11

Auden, W. H., 27

author's methodology, 3–8, 11–12, 18–22, 153–57

Avery, Tamlyn, 87

Awakening, The (Chopin), 179n44

Baldwin, David S., 100

Baldwin, James, 173n34

"barbarian names," 19, 30–31, 32

Before Trans (Mesch), 169n3

Bell, Madison Smartt, 116

Beloved (Morrison), 167n14, 169n28

Benediktsdóttir, Ásta Kristín, 12, 82, 83, 84

Bergmann, Eiríkur, 150, 161n18

Bergsson, Guðbergur, 4, 52–54, 83, 149–50; anti-Blackness, depictions of, 50; and Faulkner, comparisons, 67–72; *Tómas Jónsson, metsölubók*, 19, 52, 53–54, 58–67

Bhabha, Homi, 13, 82

Bibler, Michael P., 84–85, 170n8, 182n18

Biden, Joe, 155, 168n19
"Big Black Good Man" (Wright), 59–60
binary frameworks, 8–9; and gender, 90, 92–93
biography as genre, 53
biracial characters, 4, 13, 30–31, 68, 72–74, 76, 169n26. *See also* interracial relationships; mixed-race children
Birgisdóttir, Soffía Auður, 88, 100
Birgisson, Bergsveinn, 169n28
Birkhofer, Melissa, 70
Birth of a Nation, The (film), 105, *106*, 173n37
Bjarnadóttir, Birna, 53
Björnsdóttir, Inga Dóra, 170n9
"black blood," concept of, 62–63, 68–69, 72, 168n20
Blackness: Black rapist, myth of, 69, 70–71, 76, 79, 107, 109; Black soldiers, 56–57; coded, 105, 107–8; commodification of, 31, 32–33, 44; erasure of, 54; as "Other," 107–8; stereotypes of, 105. *See also* racism
Black Viking, The (Birgisson), 169n28
Blake, Susan L., 73, 74
"Blood-Burning Moon" (Toomer), 16, 19, 54, 72–79
Bone, Martyn, 175n5, 176n9
"borealism," 26–27
Borges, Jorge Luis, 27
Borst, Allan G., 73, 168n25
Bragi, Einar, 163n15
breast milk, 46, 165n29, 167n14
Breath, Eyes, Memory (Danticat), 175n2
Brennunjáls Saga (Laxness), 5
Brief Wondrous Life of Oscar Wao, The (Díaz), 175n2
Brooks, Cleanth, 175n52
Brown, H. Rap (Jamil Al-Amin), 22
Brown, Kimberly Juanita, 76
Brunner, Bernd, 148
Burgers, Johannes, 36
Burke, Tarana, 154
Burnett, Linda Andersson, 160n6
Butler, Judith, 70, 80

Caliban and the Witch (Federici), 138
Cane (Toomer), 19, 54, 72–79
castration, 62, 66, 67, 70
Cereus Blooms at Night (Mootoo), 175n2
Chastellux, Marquis de, 28
Chopin, Kate, 179n44
Clansman, The (Dixon), 173n37
climate change, 156–57, 182n16
coded language, 20, 104–8
Cohn, Deborah, 159n1
Cold War. See *Atom Station, The* (Laxness)
colonialism: of Black population in US, 10; and "civilization," 31–32; "colonial complicity," 161n17; commodification of women, 102; and Eurocentrism, 16; and exploitation, 11; frameworks of, 7; and global linkages, 21, 113; Iceland as "White" colony, 55; neocolonialism, 10, 18, 21, 50, 114, 118, 122; Nordic region, 149–50; postcolonial concepts, 4, 9, 11, 13, 17, 24, 25–26, 52, 55, 149–51, 160n8; stereotypes of colonized people, 25
colonial liminality: concepts and definitions, 4–7; Iceland vs. US South, 10–13, 83
Condé, Maryse, 16
Conrad, Joseph, 31
convict lease system, 149, 180n1
Copenhagen, Denmark, 120–21
core-periphery frameworks, 7, 11, 52, 55, 150
Corregidora (Jones), 17, 21, 114, 128–29, 131–32, 134, 147
Cotton's Queer Relations (Bibler), 170n8
COVID-19 pandemic: domestic violence, 154; racism, 152
Cowley, Malcolm, 70
Crespino, Joseph, 14

Daðason, Sigfús, 163n15
D'Amico, Giuliano, 30, 33, 56
Danbolt, Mathias, 15
Dano-Icelandic Act of Union (1918), 10, 28, 85, 118
Danticat, Edwidge, 175n2

INDEX

Davis, Adrienne, 76
Davis, Angela Y., 54, 76
Davis, Lisa Selin, 90, 108
Denmark: Atlantic slavery, history of, 136, 176n9; colonial exhibition (1904), 23–24, 151; colonial history, 9, 10, 21, 86, 113, 175n1; colonialism portrayed in literature, 114–24; Copenhagen as center, 120–21; cultural links to Iceland, 122
Díaz, Junot, 175n2
Dimock, Wai Chee, 159n3
disidentification, 13, 82, 94–95, 97, 111
Dixon, Thomas, 173n37
domestic ideologies, 86–87, 93. *See also* gendered roles
Donahue, Jennifer, 122, 176n8
Don't Stop the Carnival (Wouk), 177n21
double consciousness, 42–43, 48, 168n25
Douglass, Frederick, 4
Du Bois, W. E. B., 42
Duck, Leigh Anne, 14, 153
Durrenberger, E. Paul, 84
Duvall, John N., 70

Edda, 33
Egill's Saga, 33
Ehrenreich, Barbara, 178n35
Eidsvik, Erlend, 160n6
Elise, Dianne, 90
Ellenberger, Iris, 170n11
Ellison, Ralph, 67
English, Deirdre, 178n35
enslaved persons/enslavement. *See* slavery
Equal Justice Initiative, 66–67
Eurocentrism, 104, 116, 120, 125
European Debt Crisis, 150
European Economic Area, 150
European Free Trade Association, 150
exceptionalism: concept of, 13–15; Icelandic, 49; Nordic, 10–11, 14–15, 25; US, 13; US South, 12, 13–14, 27–28
exclusion: and racial violence, 66, 67–72, 73; and racism, 56, 63, 76

exile as theme, 48, 82, 84
"exoticism": exoticization of Blackness, 31, 152; exoticization of Iceland, 26–27, 55, 122; Far North vs. US South, 27–28; of Global South, 122
Extreme North (Brunner), 148
Eysteinsson, Ástráður, 12, 28, 31, 45, 53, 59, 166n2

Fable, A (Faulkner), *51*
Far North, 6–7, 27–28, 162n6. *See also* "exoticism"; North
Faroe Islands, 113, 160n6, 162n6
Faroe Islanders, 25
Faulkner, William: *Absalom, Absalom!*, 35–44; and Bergsson's work, comparisons, 52–53, 67–72; *Brennunjáls Saga*, gifted copy, 5; *A Fable*, gifted copy, *51*; Iceland visit (1955), 3, 6, 7, 159–60nn1–4; impact on world literature, 16; and Latin American writers, comparisons, 53; Whiteness, language of, 24
Faulkner Journal, 53
Federici, Silvia, 138, 178n35
femininity. *See* gendered roles
"Final Solution," 65–66, 67
Finland, 148
Finnish people, 25
Finnbogadóttir, Vigdís, 170n9
"First World" nations, 55. *See also* South contrasted with North
Fivush, Robyn, 38
Fjallkonan (Lady of the Mountain), 58, 86
Foner, Eric, 149
Frank, Waldo, 72
Freeman, Elizabeth, 92
Friedman, Susan Stanford, 17
Fuentes, Carlos, 53
Fur, Gunlög, 149, 161n14, 167n16

Gaines, Ernest, 85
García Canclini, Néstor, 6
García Márquez, Gabriel, 16, 52–53

Garner, Steve, 25, 152

gendered issues: gender as binary framework, 90, 92–93; misogyny, 57, 66, 72–73, 166n7; and national identity, 58; tourism and exploitation of women, 176n8; US soldiers and Icelandic women, 56–57, 166nn5–6; women defined in relation to men, 125–26

gendered roles: clothing choices and femininity, 94–97, 174n47; domestic ideologies, 86–87; identity and behavior, 47–48; limitations on women, 87–88; masculinity, 18, 20, 27, 74, 92–93, 171n23; matriarchal frameworks, 116, 135; nonconformity in Laxness's and McCullers's novels, 20, 81–85; patriarchal frameworks, 53–54, 171n23; performative aspects, 80–81; rejection of femininity, 90–91; in *Salka Valka* (Laxness), 100–101; subversive female characters, 143–47; US South contrasted with Iceland, 85–89; women linked with wild places, 179n45; women's "wildness" and "madness," 139–40. *See also* "tomboyishness"

Gibson, William, 159n2

Gleeson-White, Sarah, 87, 95

Glissant, Édouard, 174n50

Global South, 8–9. *See also* "exoticism"; South contrasted with North

Go Down, Moses (Faulkner), 43, 61, 72

Graham-Bertolini, Alison, 87–88, 97, 98–99, 109, 172n30

Granovetter, Mark, 159n3

Great Weaver from Kashmir, The (Laxness), 83

Greenland: as autonomous territory, 14, 55; as colony, 25, 113, 151; and Denmark, 26; and White supremacy, 25

Greenlanders, 25, 162n1

Greeson, Jennifer Rae, 11

Gremaud, Ann-Sofie Nielsen, 9, 12, 26, 55, 148, 150, 175n1

Grettir's Saga, 33

Griffin, Larry J., 28, 161n12

Griffiths, D. W., 105, 173n37

Grímsdóttir, Vigdís, 83

Grímsson, Ólafur Ragnar, 49, 150, 151

Grímsson, Stefán Hörður, 163n15

Gröndal, Benedikt, 179n44

Guðmundsson, Einar Már, 4, 104–5, 178n28

Guðmundsson, Helgi Hrafn, 167n17

Hagood, Taylor, 164n21

Halberstam, Jack, 90

Hálfdanarson, Guðmundur, 55

Hall, Alaric, 9, 12, 152, 160n8

Hallgrímsson, Jónas, 30, 34, 163n16

Hallmundsson, Hallberg, 107

Hamsun, Knut, 53

Harker, Jaime, 84, 169n2

Harlem Renaissance, 31

Harmon, Charles, 75, 78

Harpin, Julie, 91

Hawaii, 148

Heart Is a Lonely Hunter, The (McCullers), 16, 20, 80, 87, 88, 90–91, 103–4; film version, 170n14; and sexual violence, 108–9

Heart of Darkness (Conrad), 31

Heith, Anne, 15

Hervik, Peter, 153

Herzfeld, Michael, 9

heteronormativity, 18, 97–98, 99, 101, 140, 154

hierarchical frameworks, 36, 37–38, 44; embodied, 63

Hitler, Adolf, 65–66

Hoerning, Johanna, 9

Höglund, Johan, 160n6

Holland, Samantha, 91

homosexuality, 70; and national identities, 84; regarded as threat, 84, 86. *See also* LGBTQIA+ issues; queerness; same-sex partnerships

Horning, Audrey, 22

Howard, John, 84

Hurston, Zora Neale, 176n13

INDEX 205

hybridity, cultural, 13, 83, 164n21

Iceland: *Ástandið* ("the Situation"), 56, 58, 86, 103; colonial history, 9, 24, 25–26, 86, 118; contemporary issues and Global South, 151; cultural links to Denmark, 122, 175n1; Danish colonial exhibition (1904), student protests, 23–24; ethnicity, 122; European Union, 150; "Euro-scepticism," 150; exceptionalism, self-perceived, 23; family intergenerational connections, 124–34; *Fjallkonan* (Lady of the Mountain), 58; gender roles, 85–89; ghosts and realism, 134–35; and global finance, 150–51; history, 10; immigrant populations, 152; isolation of, 103; landscape portrayed in literature, 17; language, 163n10; multiracial presence, 122, 181n7; naming and nicknames, 134; national identity, 46; NATO membership, 28; northern vs. southern, cultural distinctions, 33–35; peripheral position, 25; queer-friendliness, 154–55; and settler colonialism, 25; sexuality and gender identity, 83–84; social hierarchies, 49, 87; stereotypes of, 27; suicide, 142; and tourism industry, 26; US military presence, 28–30, 45–46, 54–58, 103, 118, 124, 166n4; "Viking spirit," 150–51; Whiteness and identity formation, 26, 36, 55

Icelandic culture, racial identity, 62–64

Icelandic literature: modern poets, 33–34; sagas, 10, 33, 135; translation of, 13

identity formation: binary reinforcement, 44–45; disidentification, 13, 82, 94–95, 97, 111; gender and nationalism, 86; Icelandic, 59, 62–64; intersectional, 70; during occupation, 45–46; in US South, 42–43; women's, 47–48. *See also* national identities

"inbetween" spaces, 4, 13, 26, 82–83

incest, 130–31

Indriðason, Arnaldur, 166n8, 169n28, 179n44

Ingimundarson, Valur, 56

Ingvarsson, Haukur, 159n4, 173n39

International Monetary Fund, 151

interracial relationships, 54, 68–69, 73–74, 103; Icelandic women/US servicemen, 56–57, 59–61. *See also* biracial characters; mixed-race children

Invisible Man (Ellison), 67

Ísleifsson, Sumarliði R., 27, 30, 162n20

Jackson, Chuck, 168n20

Jakobsdóttir, Katrín, 154

Jakobsdóttir, Svava, 4, 24, 135; "The Lodger," 44–49; *The Lodger and Other Stories*, 13

James, Andrea, 170n4

Jefferson, Thomas, 28

Jensen, Lars, 14

Jóhannesson, Guðni Thorlacius, 165n33, 166n5

Jóhannsson, Jón Yngvi, 100

Johnson, Alix, 162n4

Jolink, Ineke, 162n2

Jónasson, Herman, 166n4

Jónatan, Hans, 113

Jones, Gayl, 4, 114, 128–29

Jónsdóttir, Gudbjorg Andrea, 152

Jónsson, Ragnar, *A Fable* (Faulkner), gifted copy, 51

Judd, Ashley, 154

Kanafani, Ghassan, 16, 17, 161n20

Karlsson, Gunnar, 167n17

Katla (Kormákur), 179n44

Keflavík, Iceland, US military base, 3, 118

Keflavík Agreement (1946), 28, 30

Keskinen, Suvi, 161n17

Kjartansdóttir, Katla, 55

Körber, Lill-Ann, 15

Kormákur, Baltasar, 179n44

Kress, Helga, 88

Kristjánsdóttir, Dagný, 88, 110

Kristjánsson, Kristinn, 56–57

Lacy, Terry G., 181n8

Lady of the Mountain (*Fjallkonan*), 58, 86

LaFleur, Greta, 169n3

Land of Love and Drowning (Yanique), 16–17, 21, 114–18, 119, 123–24; alternative histories, 144–45, 146–47; family histories, 125–26, 127–28, 130–31, 132, 134; realism in, 136, 137–41, 142–43

Lange, Eva María Thórarinsdóttir, 155

language: African, 31; coded, 20, 104–8; dehumanizing, 35–36, 42, 59–60, 61, 64–65; derogatory and racist, 38–39, 164n20; French, 32; and hierarchy, 151; Icelandic, 163n10; and identity formation, 36; Old Norse, 23

Larsen, Nella, 30, 114

Lassiter, Matthew D., 14

Laxness, Halldór, 4; *The Atom Station*, 30–35; on female sexuality, 112; nuclear weapons, statement on, 29; racial issues, treatment of, 103–8; *Salka Valka*, 12, 80–81; as social realist, 170n13; Whiteness, language of, 24

Levine, Caroline, 18, 24, 44

LGBTQIA+ issues: heteronormativity, 18, 97–98, 99, 101, 140, 154; homosexuality, 70, 84, 86; LGBTQIA+ rights, 155–56. *See also* queerness

Light in August (Faulkner), 19, 54, 67, 68

Lightweis-Goff, Jennie, 70

liminality, 22; colonial, 4–7, 10–13, 83; of foreignness, 26–27; liminal spaces and queerness, 97–103

Little Mermaid, The (Andersen), 125

Little Women (Alcott), 90

"Lodger, The" (Jakobsdóttir), 17–18, 19, 44–49

Loftsdóttir, Kristín, 10, 12, 14, 23, 26, 56, 103, 105, 113, 162n3, 173n33, 178n33

Lorentsen, Kristin, 26

Love, Heather, 82, 170n5

Lucas, Gavin, 9, 162n1

Lunde, Arne, 114

lynching/lynch mobs, 19, 54, 63, 66–68, 73, 77–78, 79, 149, 168n19. *See also* terrorism; violence

MacNeice, Louis, 27

magical realism, 135, 178nn28–29. *See also* realism in Icelandic literature

Magnússon, Sigurður A., 46, 164n29, 165n27, 165n29, 167n13

Magnússon, Sigurður Gylfi, 28

Mar, Elías, 83

Mariátegui, José Carlos, 6

Martínez-San Miguel, Yolanda, 177n20

masculinity. *See* gendered roles

matriarchal frameworks. *See* gendered roles

McCullers, Carson, 4, 12–13; gender nonconforming heroines, 80–81; *The Heart Is a Lonely Hunter*, 80; racial issues, treatment of, 103–8; women's roles, 87–88

McKenzie, Jacob, 122–123

Member of the Wedding, The (McCullers), 20, 81, 87, 90, 103; on Broadway, 170n14; queerness portrayed in, 97–98

Menakem, Resmaa, 39

Mesch, Rachel, 169n3

#MeToo movement, 154

Michaels, Walter Benn, 57–58

misogyny, 57, 66, 72–73, 166n7. *See also* gendered issues

Miss Iceland (Ólafsdóttir), 84

mixed-race children, 56–57, 61. *See also* biracial characters

Moberg, Bergur Rønne, 17

mob mentality, 71, 76–78. *See also* lynching/lynch mobs

modernism, 17–18; Bergsson, 59; "nativist modernism," 57–58; and queerness, 82

Monénembo, Tierno, 16

Moonstone (Sjón), 83–84

Mootoo, Shani, 175n2

Morgan, Jennifer, 76

Morrison, Toni, 4, 50, 104, 167n14, 169n28, 178n27

Mörtudóttir, Sanna Magdalena, 105

INDEX
207

Mouse That Skulks, The (Bergsson), 52
Mulinari, Diana, 148
Muñoz, José Esteban, 12–13, 82
Murkowski, Lisa, 182n17
Myong, Lene, 15

Nakagami, Kenji, 16
naming practices: "barbarian names,"
19, 30–31, 32; and generational family
relationships, 134; nicknames, use of,
19, 30–31, 104–5, 162n9, 171n19
narrative: nonlinear structures, 16, 120, 138;
perspectives, 35–36, 59–60; slave narratives, 37, 40, 42; structure of trauma,
164n23; as tool for insight, 35–36
Narrative of the Life of Frederick Douglass
(Douglass), 40
national identities: and mixed-race children,
57; nationalism and gender identity, 86;
and nativism, 57–58; US nationalism,
153. *See also* identity formation
nativism, 57–58
nature: as brand in Iceland, 25, 26; women
linked with wild places, 141–42, 178n33,
179n45
Naum, Magdalena, 55
Nazism, 65–66, 67, 70, 167n17
Neijmann, Daisy L., 12, 56–57, 134–35, 166n7,
178n29
neocolonialism, 10, 18, 21, 50, 114, 118, 122
nicknames, use of, 19, 30–31, 104–5
Night Watch (Sigurðardóttir), 17, 21, 114,
118–23, 124; alternative histories, 143–44,
145–47; family histories, 124–25, 126–27,
130, 132–34; realism in, 135, 136–37, 141–42
Nisetich, Rebecca, 70
Njáll's Saga, 33
Nordic exceptionalism, 10–11, 14–15, 25
Nordic literary studies, 11–12
Nordic region, 148; colonialism in, 149–50
Nordin, Jonas M., 55
North: Far North as lawless, 179n42; nature
and setting of, 141–42; northern land-
scapes and imagery, 92; US, political

vs. geographic North, 148. *See also* Far
North; South contrasted with North
Northern Lights, 92
North of War (Þorsteinsson), 57, 60
Norway, 10, 113
Notes of a Native Son (Baldwin), 173n34
nuclear weapons, 29

obeah women, 128, 136, 139, 179n31
O'Connor, Flannery, 98
Of Love and Dust (Gaines), 85
Ólafsdóttir, Auður Ava, 4, 84
Ólason, Vésteinn, 59, 165n29, 167n12
Old Norse language, 23, 163n10
Ómarsdóttir, Kristín, 83
One Hundred Years of Solitude (García
Márquez), 16, 52–53
Orientalism, 26, 162n5
Óskar, Jón, 163n15
Outsider perspectives, 12, 84, 91, 93–94,
122–23, 136
Oxfeldt, Elisabeth, 57

Palmberg, Mai, 160n9
Pálsson, Gísli, 26, 84, 113, 162n5
Pan (Hamsun), 53
Parigoris, Angelos, 9, 162n1
Parrish, Susan Scott, 36, 164nn19–20
patriarchal frameworks. *See* gendered roles
Pedro Páramo (Rulfo), 53
peripheralization: concept of, 4–7, 16–18;
historiography of, 115–16; peripheral
spaces, 82; periphery and core, 55; poetics of, 4–5, 16–18, 24, 33, 36, 45, 52, 59,
73, 115–16, 129; and queerness, 12–13
Perry, Constance M., 98–99, 109
Peterson, Paul R., 162n9
Planetary Modernisms (Friedman), 17
plantation system, 87. *See also* slavery
Playing in the Dark (Morrison), 104
"poetics of peripheralization," 4–5, 16–18, 24,
33, 36, 45, 52, 59, 73, 115–16, 129
Polk, Noel, 167n12
postbellum reunion romances, 88–89

postcolonial theories, 4, 9, 11, 13, 17, 24, 25–26, 52, 55, 149–51, 160n8

Professor's House, The (Cather), 57

"purity," glorification of, 34, 56, 72–73

queerness: *hinsegin* and queer-friendliness, 154–55; in Laxness's and McCullers's novels, 81–85; in liminal spaces, 97–103; and peripheral spaces, 12–13; resistance to heteronormativity, 101–2. *See also* LGBTQIA+ issues

Quicksand (Larsen), 30–31, 114

Quimby, Karin, 82, 102

racial issues: interracial relationships, 54, 56–57, 59–61, 68–69, 73–74, 103; "racial purity," glorification of, 72–73

racism: anti-Black, US and Iceland, 31; anti-immigrant movements, 153, 155–56, 181n7, 181n10; anti-Muslim movements, 152–53; "black blood," concept of, 50, 62–63, 68–69, 72, 168n20; Blackness as "Other," 107–8; Black rapist, myth of, 69, 70–71, 76, 79, 107, 109; Black soldiers, 56–57; Black/White binary, 72–73; contemporary US, 181n13; COVID-19 pandemic, 152; derogatory language, 38–39; and double consciousness, 42–43; multiracial futures, fear of, 43–44; pathological racism, 70–71; postracial societies, 14–15; Reconstruction period, 149; slavery in US, 64–67; stereotypes in textbooks, 25; systemic, 15; violence as exclusion, 67–72. *See also* Blackness; Whiteness; White supremacy

rape, 69, 70–71; Black rapist, myth of, 69, 70–71, 76, 79, 107, 109; and White male exploitation, 20, 54; White perpetrators, 109

Rastrick, Ólafur, 64

realism in Icelandic literature, 134–43

Repeated Words (Bergsson), 52

Rhys, Jean, 116, 175n4

Romdhani, Rebecca, 175n4, 177nn20–21

Rosario, Nelly, 175n2

Rosenblad, Esbjörn, 165n1

Rulfo, Juan, 53

Saer, Juan José, 53

saga culture, 23; Icelandic sagas, 10, 33, 135

Said, Edward, 26

Salka Valka (Laxness), 20, 80–81; domestic ideologies/women's roles, 87–89; and gender identities, 86; queerness portrayed in, 97–98; and racialized stereotypes, 105–7; tomboy figures, 89, 91

Salvage the Bones (Ward), 169n28, 176n10

same-sex partnerships, 154–55, 170n8. *See also* homosexuality; LGBTQIA+ issues

Sámi people, 25; Sámi territories, 162n6

Schram, Kristinn, 26, 55

Scudder, Bernard, 52

Sedgwick, Eve, 73

Seeling, Beth, 38

sexual harassment, 154

sexuality: autoeroticism, 101–2; control of women, 88; exploitation of enslaved women, 75–76, 108, 147, 176n17; exploitative sex and White male privilege, 74–76; of Icelandic women, 56–57; nonconformity, 84–85, 98–100; sexualization of young girls, 128–31, 154; sexualized racism, 73; sexual violence, 108–12, 121–22, 154; of White women, 19, 54, 163n13

Shapland, Jennifer Ann, 92, 170n6

sharecropping systems, 149, 180n1

Sherrard-Johnson, Cherene, 125, 136, 139

Sigfússon, Hannes, 163n15

Sigurðardóttir, Fríða Áslaug, 4, 114. See also *Night Watch* (Sigurðardóttir)

Sigurdardóttir, Jóhanna, 181n12

Sigurðardóttir, Lilja, 83

Sigurðardóttir-Rosenblad, Rakel, 165n1

Sigurjónsson, Árni, 100

Sing, Unburied, Sing (Ward), 169n28

Sjón, 4, 83–84

Skaptadóttir, Unnur Dís, 86

slavery: and colonialism, 149; girls and tomboyism, 108; hierarchical distinctions, 37–38; impact and legacy, 78, 169n28; and sexual exploitation, 75–76, 108, 147, 176n17; slave narratives, 37, 40, 42; slave trade, 176n17; social hierarchies, 36–38, 39–40, 42–43; in US South, 66–67, 72–73, 161n12; and violence, 40–41

social stratification: Iceland, 32, 34–35, 49, 85, 88, 94, 119–22; US South, 19, 36–37, 38, 39–40, 44, 49, 108

Solard, Alain, 78

Song of the Water Saints (Rosario), 175n2

Souls of Black Folk, The (Du Bois), 42

Sound and the Fury, The (Faulkner), 17, 57, 85, 164n24, 177n26, 180n47

South contrasted with North, 8, 124; and climate crisis, 156–57; global binaries, 8–9, 26, 55. *See also* North

Southern Poverty Law Center, 153, 156

"spawn," use of term, 42, 43

Spiller, Hortense J., 108

Spoth, Daniel, 70

St. Croix (Virgin Islands), 113, 118

Stecopoulos, Harilaos, 159n1

Stenport, Anna Westerstahl, 114

stereotypes: of Africans, 152; of Icelanders, 27; racialized, in Iceland, 104–5; US South, 27–28

Stevens, Gavin, 168n20

St. John (Virgin Islands), 113, 118

Stougaard-Nielsen, Jakob, 26

Strange Shores (Indriðason), 179n44

stream-of-consciousness, 16, 52

St. Thomas (Virgin Islands), 113, 114, 115, 118, 122–23

Stuckart, Franz, 65

Stuhl, Andrew, 22, 153

suicide, 142

Svanurinn (Bergsson), 52

Sveinsson, Gísli, 23

Swan, The (Bergsson), 52

Sweden, 149, 160n7, 160n9

Tar Baby (Morrison), 178n27

Ten Little Negros, The (Thorsteinsson, ill.), 25

terrorism, 151, 152–53. *See also* lynching/lynch mobs

Their Eyes Were Watching God (Hurston), 176n13

Third Space, 13, 82–83

Thisted, Kirsten, 15, 26, 148, 175n1

Thorsteinsson, Guðmundur, 25

Þorsteinsson, Indriði G., 4, 57, 60, 166n8

tolerance, Icelandic myth of, 56, 64

Tómas Jónsson, metsölubók (*Tómas Jónsson, Bestseller*) (Bergsson), 19, 52, 53–54, 58–67, 167n12

"tomboyishness," 81–82, 87–89, 169n3, 170n4; racist roots of, 108; tomboy figures in literature, 89–97, 174n44. *See also* gendered issues

Toomer, Jean, 4; "Blood-Burning Moon," 72–79

tourism, 123, 154–55; and climate change, 156–57; and exploitation of women, 176n8; tourism industry, 26

Transfer Day (Danish West Indies), 115, 116–18, *117*, 123

Trans Historical (LaFleur et al.), 169n3

trauma responses, 39; intergenerational, 17, 128–29, 131; and narrative structure, 164n23

Truman, Harry S., 56

United States: anti-immigrant movements, 153; army occupation, 54; colonialism in South, 11; and Iceland during World War II, 54–58; LGBTQIA+ rights, 155–56; military presence in Iceland, 3, 10, 28–30, 103, 124, 166n4; nationalism, 153; neocolonialism, 122; Reconstruction period, 149; Respect for Marriage Act, 155; slavery, 64–67; Transfer Day (Danish West Indies), 115, 116–18, *117*

United States South: colonial ambiguity, 148–49; exceptionalism, 13–14, 27–28; gender roles, 85–89; Lost Cause mythology, 151; plantation system, 87; postbellum reunion romances, 88–89; and sexual deviance, 84–85; social stratification, 19, 36–37, 38, 39–40, 44, 49, 108; stereotypes of, 27–28

Urgo, Joseph R., 167n12

útrásarvíkingar "business Vikings," 150

Valdimarsdóttir, Margré, 152

van der Liet, Henk, 17, 25, 26

Van Deusen, Natalie, 95

Vegh, Beatriz, 53

Vikings: "Viking spirit," 150–51; and White supremacy, 168n18

Vilhjálmsson, Thor, 165n1

violence: and Black bodies, 76–78, 79; and mob mentality, 71; racially motivated, 62–64; racial violence as exclusion, 67–72; sexual violence, 108–12, 121–22, 154; sexual violence toward young girls, 109–12; White violence, 54, 67. *See also* lynching/lynch mobs

Virgin Islands, 25, 115, 122–23, 136, 147, 176n10

Virgin Islands Open Shorelines Act, 123

Ward, Jesmyn, 169n28, 176n10

Watson, Jay, 70

Weinstein, Harvey, 154

West Indies, 4, 21, 115, 118, 122, 151

Westling, Louise, 174n47

Whiteness: base of power, 122; complexity of, 8; as default in US South, 43–44; and double consciousness, 42–43; expressed in *The Atom Station* (Laxness), 32–33; Nordic concepts of, 10–11, 160n5; as privilege, 18, 19, 24; and racist stereotypes, 10; social stratification, 39–41; toxic Whiteness, 19–20, 54; in US southern literature, 12; and "White" colonies, 55; "White innocence," 40; White male privilege and exploitative sex, 74–76; White racial violence, 67. *See also* racism

White supremacy, 25, 36, 39, 79; in *Light in August* (Faulkner), 69–70; and Viking history, 168n18

Wide Sargasso Sea (Rhys), 116, 175n4

wildness and madness, 139–40, 178n33, 179n38

Williams, Jennifer, 76, 78

witch hunts, 138–39, 178n35

women. *See* gendered issues; gendered roles

World Economic Forum, 154

World War II, 54–58

Worley, Paul M., 70

Wouk, Herman, 177n21

Wright, Richard, 4, 59–60, 104, 173n35

Yanique, Tiphanie, 4, 122–23. See also *Land of Love and Drowning* (Yanique)

Young, Anna, 92, 171n21

ABOUT THE AUTHOR

Photo courtesy of the author

JENNA GRACE SCIUTO is a professor of English at the Massachusetts College of Liberal Arts. She received her BA from Brown University, MA from Boston University, and PhD from Northeastern University. Her first book, *Policing Intimacy: Law, Sexuality, and the Color Line in Twentieth-Century Hemispheric American Literature*, was published by the University Press of Mississippi in 2021. Her work has also appeared in *ARIEL*, the *Faulkner Journal*, the *Global South*, and the *Journal of Commonwealth and Postcolonial Studies*, as well as the collections *Faulkner and the Black Literatures of the Americas* (University Press of Mississippi, 2016), *Southern Comforts: Drinking and the U.S. South* (Louisiana State University Press, 2020), and *The New William Faulkner Studies* (Cambridge University Press, 2022).